Call Me Charlie

Call Me Charlie

THE AUTOBIOGRAPHY
OF
LORD BROCKET

POCKET
BOOKS

LONDON • SYDNEY • NEW YORK • TORONTO

First published in Great Britain by Simon & Schuster UK Ltd, 2004
First published in paperback by Pocket Books, 2005
An imprint of Simon & Schuster UK Ltd
A Viacom company

1 3 5 7 9 10 8 6 4 2

Simon & Schuster UK Ltd
Africa House
64–78 Kingsway
London WC2B 6AH

www.simonsays.co.uk

Simon & Schuster Australia
Sydney

A CIP catalogue record for this book is
available from the British Library.

ISBN 0 7434 9585 3
EAN 9780743495851

Typeset by M Rules
Printed and bound in Great Britain by
Cox & Wyman Ltd, Reading, Berks

PICTURE CREDITS
All photographs copyright the author except:

Bramshill courtesy Centrex
Cast of *I'm A Celebrity, Get Me Out of Here!* courtesy ITV
Portrait of Charles Brocket courtesy Les Wilson

To my family, who have borne so much.
To my mother, who neither sought nor deserved
the resulting upsets in her life.
To my children whom I love dearly,
and who deserved a better start.

Contents

Prologue: A Visit to the Padre   ix

1   The Men From O'Cahan County   1
2   A Friend of Mr Hitler?   10
3   Daddy's Not Very Well   24
4   Sex and Schooling   44
5   You're in the Army Now   55
6   Iron Curtain, Green Line   70
7   Claiming My Inheritance   87
8   From Supermodels to Sugar Creek   103
9   A Girl with a Hammer   115
10 Politicians . . . and their Daughters   130
11 Viva Las Vegas!   151
12 Loadsamoney!   164
13 Little Brown Bottles   176
14 Blowing It   193
15 The Insurance Scam   214
16 Falling Apart   230
17 Grassed Up   247

18	You're Nicked, M'Lord!	260
19	Enter Mr Rocker	273
20	War at the Hall	286
21	Guilty	305
22	Inside	315
23	Plastic Gangsters	327
24	Nonces	339
25	Fighting the System, Meeting a Kray	356
26	Left for Dead	378
27	Meanwhile, Back in Hertfordshire . . .	388
28	Ali Brocket and the (Rather More than Forty) Thieves	403
29	A Changed Man	421
30	I'm a Celebrity, Stick Me in There	439
31	Oi, Charlie!	454
	Acknowledgements	463
	Index	467

Prologue: A Visit to the Padre

I'M A BORN OPTIMIST. FOR ME THE CUP IS ALWAYS half full, rather than half empty. I don't know why, but I'll always try and see the funny side of things. I'd rather laugh at a situation than cry. But there are times when crying is the only option.

By the middle of 1996 I was as low as a man can get. I'd been convicted of conspiracy to commit a fraud. I'd lost my wife, who'd become addicted to prescription pain-killers. My children had been taken away to Puerto Rico. My reputation and my fortune were in tatters. My girlfriend, whom I loved, and who'd sworn she loved me, had gone off with another man. My family home and my business were in the hands of a crazed class warrior who saw my personal humiliation as the first step on the long road to the total destruction of the aristocracy. What remained of my property was being stolen, and the police were refusing to investigate. And now I was banged up in Wellingborough nick, being threatened with death by an Asian prison gang.

I didn't know where to turn for advice or help. So I

went to see a priest. They have every possible denomination available in jail. I could have seen a rabbi, an imam or a Church of England vicar. But I chose a Catholic priest because in my experience, including army duty in Northern Ireland at the height of the Troubles, Roman Catholic padres are real men of the people. They're usually down-to-earth Irishmen, who've seen it all and done it all, and I wouldn't put it past them to have done the things they're not supposed to do, as well.

At Wellingborough, there was a room in the attic that had been tidied up and made suitable for worship. There were two or three little rooms next to it, and the Catholic padre had a regular clinic in one of those rooms: three hours a week for anyone who wanted to come and talk. I went along and introduced myself. The padre was a fit-looking, grey-haired man in his mid seventies. When he opened his mouth, he spoke, as I'd expected, in a broad Irish accent.

The padre listened while I recited my long list of problems. Then he said, 'D'ye know the Bible, now, Charles?'

I said, yes, I did, fairly well.

So he said, 'D'ye know the line in it that says, "Vengeance is Mine, sayeth the Lord"?'

Again I said, yes, I did.

He said, 'D'ye know what it means?'

I said, 'Well, it means what it says. Vengeance is His job, not ours.'

The padre said, 'No, it focken' doesn't. I'll tell you what it focken' means. It's the Lord's way of saying that what goes around, comes around. Because if you leave it long enough, you'll always see these people fock themselves.'

I thought this was pretty good, coming from a seventy-year-old padre, with his dog-collar on. But then, in my experience, your language does tend to slip a bit when you're in prison.

Then the padre spoke again: 'And there's a flip-side, too, which is that there's a reason for everything. You might not see it now, but there always is.'

And by God he was right in every single thing. Looking back, I can't think of anything that's happened to me, no matter how good or bad, for which there wasn't a good reason in the end, not one damn thing. The padre was right all the way down the line. And the best way to prove that is to start at the very beginning of the line.

– 1 –

The Men From O'Cahan County

TONY BLAIR ONCE USED MY FAMILY AS THE
perfect example of everything that was wrong with the
House of Lords. 'Consider the hereditary peerage of
Brocket,' he said in the Commons, where speech is privileged and you can't be sued for libel. 'The first Lord
Brocket bought the title from Lloyd George; the second
Lord Brocket was one of Britain's leading Nazi sympathisers; and the third Lord Brocket is serving five years for
fraud.'

Well, the last bit was fair enough. I was indeed
banged up at the time. But what about the other two
claims? Was our title purchased from Lloyd George,
and was my grandfather really a Nazi? Or are these
more examples of Mr Blair's often distant relationship
with the truth?

The answers lie in my family history, which begins
with an ambitious Irish brewer called Robert O'Cahan.
He was my great-great-grandfather and he came from

an old Ulster family. My grandfather later paid for a magnificent family tree, which claimed to trace the O'Cahans back to Fergal, Monarch of Ireland in AD 740, and back even further to Niall of the Nine Hostages, a mighty king who ruled Ireland, and led expeditions to Scotland, England and even Gaul in around AD 400, at the very end of the Roman occupation of Britain.

For many years, a great chunk of Ulster was known as O'Cahan's County. By the early nineteenth century, however, the O'Cahans were no longer the force they once were. True, they were minor gentry with a coat of arms, which featured three silver salmon and a cat holding the red hand of Ulster. But they must have been far from rich or powerful, because at some point in the 1840s Robert O'Cahan decided that there was no future for him in Ireland and emigrated to England.

Robert landed in Liverpool. I have a picture of him, a Victorian photograph, hand-tinted with colours. He's a tall, strong, faintly piratical-looking fellow, with vast, bushy sideburns almost meeting beneath his chin and a broad chest, covered with layers of waistcoats and overcoats, like a character from the pages of a Charles Dickens novel. And a character Robert O'Cahan most certainly was.

Within a few years, he had changed his name from O'Cahan to the far more English-sounding, and thus respectable, Robert Cain. By 1852 he'd also learned how to brew beer and set up his own brewery, selling Cain's Superior Ales. Huge sacks of barley, malt and hops were transported up to Liverpool from East Anglia and Kent, where they'd be shovelled into vast brewing vats by workers in stiff, heavy aprons.

The Cain's Brewery is still a Liverpool landmark, and so are the pubs that Robert Cain built to sell his beers. The most splendid of them all is the Grade 1 listed Philharmonic Dining Rooms in Hope Street. John Lennon once said that the worst thing about being famous was 'not being able to go to the Phil for a drink', and if you ever go there, you'll see why he missed it.

The Phil looks less like a pub than a massive Victorian mansion, complete with towers, an antique clock hanging over the pavement, and ornate black and gold gates. Inside, it's a riot of richly carved woodwork, copper panels, marble mosaic floors, stained glass, art deco lights and leather upholstery. The most famous feature is the gents' lavatory, which is so splendidly kitted out with marble urinals and toilets that women are allowed to go inside and gaze at its wonders, as part of a guided tour.

By the time the Phil was built, in 1898, Robert Cain was very old, very rich and very much admired by the people of Liverpool. His son Charles, my great-grandfather, was born in 1866 and educated at the Liverpool Institute, where Paul McCartney and George Harrison were both pupils many decades later. He went into the family business and merged it with another local brewery, Walkers.

Charles's first wife, Florence Nall, came from a smart Nottinghamshire family, who were a cut above the Cains. She told Charles that she would only marry him if she could keep her name. So Charles Cain and

Florence Nall became Charles and Florence Nall-Cain, which is still our family surname today.

They settled at The Node, a large country house in Hertfordshire. By now, Walker-Cain was one of the largest brewing companies in Britain. But as well as being a serious businessman, my great-grandfather was also a philanthropist. When the First World War broke out in 1914, he realised that there were not nearly enough facilities available to treat the huge numbers of men being wounded on the Western Front. So he toured the country, raising money to build and equip a fleet of ambulances, which were sent out to France, where they helped save countless lives. He was also a major contributor to the Liverpool Merchants' Mobile Hospital, which treated over 20,000 wounded soldiers and he gave money to funds for servicemen, nurses, widows and the Red Cross.

Charles Nall-Cain was made a baronet in 1921, in recognition of his genuine public services. That meant he became Sir Charles Nall-Cain and his heirs would also be 'Sirs'. Whether Lloyd George, who was Prime Minister at the time, made him pay for the privilege, I don't know: I've certainly never heard or seen any evidence to support that claim. But my great-grandfather certainly did not pay Lloyd George for the title of Lord Brocket, since he did not receive that honour until more than a decade later and from a different Prime Minister. And I wonder if Tony Blair is really the best person to lecture anyone about the probity of honours lists, or the exchange of political favours for cash.

Whatever the circumstances behind the baronetcy,

Sir Charles and Lady Nall-Cain, as they now were, left The Node and bought another, bigger house in Hertfordshire. Its name was Brocket Hall. Just twenty-two miles from Marble Arch, as the crow flies, and surrounded by a 5,000-acre estate, Brocket was the perfect stately home for the upwardly mobile Nall-Cains.

The first house on the site, called Watershypps, was built in 1239 for the Brocket family, merchants who'd made their fortunes trading with Spain. The house was rebuilt in 1440. In the 1550s, the then owner John Brocket received frequent visits from Princess Elizabeth, the daughter of Henry VIII, who was living under guard at nearby Hatfield House. During one such visit, in 1558, the princess was told that her elder sister Queen Mary had died and that she was now Queen Elizabeth I. As a mark of her warm feelings towards the Brockets, Elizabeth knighted Sir John later the same year, and the great oak tree down by the lake, under which she was standing when she heard the news of her ascension to the throne, is still alive today.

In 1746 Brocket Hall was bought by Sir Matthew Lamb. Fourteen years later, he commissioned the architect James Paine to design the current house. Sir Matthew's son, Sir Peniston Lamb, had the bad luck to be cuckolded by his wife, who became another man's mistress. Then again, he had the good fortune that the other man in question was the Prince Regent, later to become George IV.

Peniston was clearly an accommodating, patriotic chap, because he not only allowed the prince to stay at Brocket and sleep with his wife, but also set aside a special suite of rooms in which the adulterous couple could go about their business. Installed in 1783, the Chinese Suite was decorated to the prince's specifications, in his favourite oriental style, with beautiful wallpaper depicting garden scenes, peacocks and other exotic birds. Peniston even installed a race-course at Brocket to amuse the horse-mad prince.

Having done the nation the tremendous service of donating his wife to the heir to the throne, Sir Peniston Lamb rose up the aristocratic ranks, becoming first Baron Melbourne, then Viscount Melbourne. As a mark of his affection, the prince also gave Lady Lamb a portrait of himself, by Reynolds.

The second Lord Melbourne also married a flighty wife, the legendary seductress Lady Caroline Lamb. She had a passionate affair with Lord Byron, to whom she applied the famous description 'mad, bad and dangerous to know'. He was dangerous for Caroline, certainly. She quite literally lost her mind over Byron, who was far less devoted to her than she was to him. Still, Lady Caroline paid attention to her husband, too. One year, she livened a state banquet in honour of his birthday by squeezing into a giant soup tureen, had it carried into the Saloon and placed on the magnificent banqueting table, and served herself up, stark naked, as the dish of the day.

Lord Melbourne's reputation managed to survive the scandalous behaviour of his wife. He went on to be Queen Victoria's first Prime Minister, and an important father-figure in her life, before dying at Brocket in 1848. His sister, Emily Lamb, married another, even greater Prime Minister, Lord Palmerston, who also died at Brocket, while still in office, in 1865. He was, it is said, in flagrante on the billiard table with a chambermaid at the time.

You can imagine how irresistible such a magnificent house, steeped in history, must have seemed to a brewer's son from Liverpool. My great-grandfather loved Brocket Hall and he wanted to keep it in the family. So in 1921 he set up a trust into which the entire estate was placed. And now, with apologies – but trust me, this is important – a quick mini-lecture on trusts.

For the majority of people, their most valuable asset is their home. But they do not necessarily expect their children to live in it after their death. Usually, the house is sold and the proceeds distributed to the government in death duties, and then to the descendants, as per the will. But what do you do if you're the kind of family, like an aristocratic one, that wants to live in the same house for generation after generation?

Answer: you put the house, and the land around it into a trust. Now, the family does not own its estate. The trust does. Every trust has a board of trustees, who decide how to manage its assets. And it has beneficiaries, so called because they benefit from those same assets. In a typical, upper-class British family the main beneficiary is the eldest son. He gets the family title and the house and rolling acres that go with it.

But please note: our aristocrat may live in his stately home. He may invite his chums to go shooting on the estate. He may even have his smiling face plastered all over the teapots in the estate's gift shop, for all the day-trippers to buy. But he does not own 'his' property. His trust does. And the trust is not his property. It is, however, the aristo's responsibility, and that of his trustees, to ensure that the trust is kept in tip-top shape so that his son and his grandson and all subsequent descendants can benefit from it, too.

End of lecture, back to the story . . .

My great-grandfather, Sir Charles Nall-Cain, placed Brocket Hall in what came to be known as the 1921 Trust. Having seen the havoc that the slaughter of the trenches had wreaked on upper-class families – young officers being the soldiers with the shortest life expectancy of all – he wanted to make sure that his personal slice of English heritage was kept safe for his family, and the nation. Charlie, as everyone called him, was a great enthusiast. He plunged into everything from gardening (he and his head gardener Mr Paton won endless prizes for their splendid blooms) to golf and even aeronautics. Before the First World War, he'd helped found the Liverpool and District Aero Club, and he donated a plane to the city of Liverpool in 1917.

Charlie was the High Sheriff of Hertfordshire and mixed with the mightiest in the land. Both King George V and Edward, Prince of Wales regularly came to stay at Brocket Hall, which had some of the finest pheasant- and duck-shooting in the country. But throughout his life Charlie continued to be known for his generosity to the poor and the sick. As well as his efforts during the First World War, he was a major contributor to the Red Cross, and to several hospital charities, particularly in Liverpool. At the height of the

Great Depression of the early thirties, he also held events at Brocket to raise money for the unemployed.

All the pictures of my great-grandfather in our family albums show a warm, cheery, kind-hearted soul. A well-padded figure, with a bushy white moustache, broad smile and twinkling eyes, he always seems to be having fun, whether patting one of his dogs, turning up at a formal event in a fur-collared coat, top-hat and cane, or just standing contentedly outside Brocket Hall, his hands jammed into his jacket pockets. I have one photograph of him holding my father, who can't have been more than two or three, in his arms. As always, his face is wreathed in a smile. He must have been a splendid grandfather.

In January 1933 Charlie was given a peerage in the New Year's Honours List. The Prime Minister who advised the King to bestow that honour was not Lloyd George but the Labour Party's very own Ramsay MacDonald. On this occasion, I can say with absolute certainty that no money changed hands.

The newly minted baron took the title of Lord Brocket, after his house, Brocket Hall. He and Lady Brocket (his second wife, Anne Page Croft) celebrated by dressing up in party-hats done up with Christmas decorations to look like baronial crowns. But Charlie was only able to enjoy his new status for less than two years. In November 1934 he suffered a heart attack and died at Brocket, aged sixty-eight. He was succeeded by my grandfather, Ronald Nall-Cain, the second Baron Brocket. And now my family's story hits a discordant note.

– 2 –

A Friend of Mr Hitler?

MY GRANDFATHER WAS THIRTY WHEN HE INHERITED his title, and undoubtedly a gifted man. He was tall, handsome and, when he wanted to be, charming. He won a Blue for golf at Cambridge University, qualified as a barrister at twenty-one, and became the Conservative MP for the Liverpool constituency of Wavertree in 1930, with a 24,000-vote majority, aged just twenty-six. By then he was also a member of the board at Walker-Cain, and he stayed with the company when it later became Allied Breweries. But was he a Nazi sympathiser?

According to the older members of my family, my grandfather certainly made several journeys to Germany before the war, met Hitler, and actively sought an early end to the war once hostilities had begun. I was always told that he was one of a number of young men, either aristocrats or junior politicians, who were trusted to take private messages from the

British government, led by Neville Chamberlain, to the Hitler regime – messages deemed too sensitive to be carried by the usual King's Messengers. Brocket's surviving children, my aunt and uncle, have always felt certain that he was a patriotic man, who would have joined up and done his bit were it not for a heart condition that made him unfit for active service.

It is certainly not impossible that my grandfather could have been used as a conduit between Whitehall and Berlin. He had been a Tory MP and still sat in the House of Lords. He was a close personal friend, even a confidant, of Chamberlain, and knew Lord Halifax, the Foreign Secretary very well, too. As a peer of the realm, he would have been taken seriously by the Germans. And his desire for peace was shared across all levels of British society, right up to the start of the Second World War. The word 'appeasement' is taken as an insult today. But for people who had lived through the horrors of the First World War, the thought of another global bloodbath was so repellent they would go to almost any lengths to avoid it. At the end of September 1938, when Chamberlain arrived back from meeting Hitler in Munich, promising 'peace for our time', he was met at the airport by massive, cheering crowds.

But there is another side to the argument. There seems no doubt that my grandfather moved within a circle of extreme right-wing aristocrats. The list of peers who either opposed war with Germany or even supported Nazism includes the then Dukes of Westminster, Wellington, and Buccleuch, along with the Marquess of Londonderry, the Earl of Galloway, Lord Lothian, Lord

Mount-Temple and Lord Redesdale, father of the famous Mitford sisters, two of whom (Unity and Diana, the wife of the British fascist leader Oswald Mosley) were also pro-Nazi.

In the chaotic wake of the First World War, the Russian Revolution, the stock market crash and the Depression, many people looked for simple, clear-cut answers to the overwhelming problems all around them. Left-wing intellectuals turned to communism, supporting the Stalin regime in the Soviet Union. They turned a blind eye to Stalin's purges, his labour camps, his secret police and even his slaughter of more than 20 million of his own citizens, because they believed in his socialist principles and they saw him as a bulwark against fascism.

The same thing happened, in reverse, on the right. Many saw communism as the greatest threat to society and believed that Hitler should be supported, since he hated communism, too. They admired the way he had rebuilt the German economy. They were impressed by the visible signs of Nazi self-confidence, from the swagger of the Nuremberg rallies to the sweep of the brand-new *autobahns*. And they weren't especially bothered if the price of 'progress' was oppression of the Jews.

One prominent upper-class Conservative, a close relative of the Duke of Marlborough, wrote in 1920 that the 'movement among Jews' was a 'worldwide conspiracy for the overthrow of civilisation'. In 1937 he wrote admiringly that: 'One may dislike Hitler's system and yet admire his patriotic achievement. If our country were defeated, I hope we should find a champion as indomitable to restore our courage and lead us back to our place among the nations.' And the name of this apparently anti-Semitic fan of Adolf? Winston Churchill.

I don't say any of this to excuse Nazi sympathisers. I've been to Auschwitz. I've seen the evidence of cold-blooded, calculated genocide. I'm simply trying to explain how people could have been seduced by the apparent successes of Adolf Hitler, and closed their eyes to his evil.

My grandfather may have been one such person. He certainly belonged to the Anglo-German Fellowship, an organisation with many virulently anti-Semitic members that went far beyond simple friendship between two nations. The Fellowship was never as rabidly pro-Nazi as some other pre-war organisations, but it certainly served the interests of Hitler's government, and fuelled its propaganda by giving Nazism an air of respectability.

During the thirties, Brocket Hall was used for meetings of pro-German supporters. In 1936 my grandfather is also believed to have hosted a dinner party for Joachim von Ribbentrop, the German ambassador to Britain (later to become Hitler's Foreign Minister), at Knoydart, a 60,000-acre Scottish estate that his father had given him as a wedding present.

Grandpa was also an extremely close friend of the Prince of Wales, who became King Edward VIII in January 1936, before abdicating later that year, whereupon he took the title of the Duke of Windsor. Edward has frequently been accused of harbouring Nazi sympathies. He travelled to Germany in 1937, as a personal guest of Adolf Hitler, and German intelligence officers made strenuous attempts to recruit Edward to their cause while he was exiled in Lisbon in the early years of the war.

Edward, of course, married Wallis Simpson, an American divorcee. It is always assumed that Edward was forced to abdicate because the establishment would not countenance the idea of a monarch marrying a divorced woman. But intelligence reports prepared for the US President of the time, Franklin Roosevelt, suggest that the real reason the government did not want their King marrying Wallis Simpson was that she had strong pro-Nazi beliefs.

Her influence over the weak-willed Edward could have undermined Britain in any war against Germany. FBI files also suggest that while Mrs Simpson was having her affair with Edward, she was also sleeping with another friend of my grandfather's: Joachim von Ribbentrop. Had the Queen of England been both a Nazi sympathiser and a senior Nazi's mistress, the consequences would have been devastating.

Documents captured after the war suggest that German intelligence officers agreed with the FBI: they, too, believed that Mrs Simpson's politics, rather than her marital status, were the real reason she was not allowed near the throne of England. Swastikas, sex and high society were mixed in a potent brew. And Lord Brocket knew all the key players. One of the most powerful bonds between Britain and

Germany was the social connection between aristocrats in both countries.

My grandfather knew many members of Germany's smartest families, who often came to shoot on his estates. They were as opposed to the prospect of war as their counterparts in Britain. Yet many German aristocrats were not well disposed towards the Nazi Party. In fact, they despised Hitler. This wasn't a matter of morality or politics, but sheer snobbery. The Prussian nobility regarded Adolf as a jumped-up little working-class oik. Not a patch on the dear old Kaiser.

I wish I could say my grandfather shared their disdain for Herr Hitler, but the evidence suggests otherwise. In the words of Professor Richard Griffith, the leading expert on the pre-war British far right: 'Brocket was a particularly convinced pro-Nazi.'

In September 1938, just before Hitler's meeting with Chamberlain in Munich, my grandfather attended the last of Hitler's gigantic Nuremberg rallies, at which almost 1 million Nazi faithful, dressed in brownshirt uniforms and clutching tens of thousands of swastika banners roared their love and support for the Führer.

My grandfather might just have used his visit to Nuremberg as cover for delivering secret British government messages to Hitler – if that was, indeed, his role. But in April 1939, less than five months before the outbreak of war, he made another journey to Germany, accompanied by the Duke of Buccleuch and Major-General John Fuller, a military theorist whose revolutionary ideas about tank-based warfare were ignored by the British army but adopted by the Germans as the basis of their *blitzkrieg* tactics.

The three men were honoured guests at Hitler's fiftieth birthday party. And this was surely not a visit that my grandfather made on Chamberlain's or Halifax's behalf. Cabinet minutes from April 1939 clearly state the determination of the British government to make the least possible acknowledgement of Hitler's birthday, short of outright hostility. The last thing they wanted to see was two peers and a retired general lining up to pay their respects.

After the war began, in September 1939, my grandfather only avoided internment as a potential enemy sympathiser after a family lawyer lobbied a government minister on his behalf. I have heard family stories that he was involved in the plotting that led up to the extraordinary episode in 1941, when Hitler's deputy, Rudolf Hess, flew to Scotland on his own, freelance peace mission.

Knoydart, his Scottish estate, was requisitioned by the army and used as a training base for commandos and secret agents during the war. Grandpa was not a popular man north of the Border. His management of Knoydart, which sits in glorious countryside between Loch Nevis and Loch Hourn, typified the widespread unrest between Highlanders and absentee English landlords in the post-war years when unemployment in Scotland was rife. His Lordship's gamekeepers were told to make sure that no one intruded upon his acres, be they hill-walkers, shepherds, or children playing on the beach. In the immediate post-war years, when a Labour government ruled and men who had fought against fascism expected a fairer society, the old ways of the aristocracy were deeply unpopular.

Finally, in November 1948, seven local men invaded the Knoydart estate and staked out smallholdings, which they then seized. The seven squatters, who rapidly became celebrities in Scotland, claimed that the Land Settlement Act allowed them to farm under-used land. Their lawyer wrongly told the men that they were bound to win a legal action to keep 'their' land. So the Seven Men of Knoydart, as they were now known, marched off the land and into court – or, to be precise, a room at the West Highland Hotel in Mallaig – where my grandfather's lawyer promptly knocked their case for six.

Now, you may be wondering why I'm going to such lengths to reproduce all the evidence against my grandfather. Hardly seems like loyalty to the family, does it? Well, there are three reasons. In the first place, the point of this book is to tell the truth, or as near as I can get to it. In the second place, I don't want anyone claiming I'm covering things up. And in the third place, I'm not desperately enamoured of his subsequent behaviour towards his future heirs. Or, to put it another way, towards my father and me.

In 1927, when he was twenty-three, my grandfather Ronald married Angela Pennyman, the pretty, vivacious daughter of the Reverend W. G. Pennyman, vicar of St Mark's Church, North Audley Street, London. Being a vicar is a perfectly respectable profession, and North Audley Street is in the heart of Mayfair, making it as smart as a parish can be. But in the snobbish days of the twenties and thirties, a vicar's daughter was not the sort of girl whom the brilliant son of one of the country's richest, smartest families would be expected to marry. So the new Mrs Nall-Cain set about moving herself up the social scale as far and as fast as possible.

Angela went out of her way to act like a woman of breeding, or, at least, what she thought a woman of breeding should be. It wasn't long before her airs and graces were causing comment among everyone from local shopkeepers to lords and ladies. People at Brocket used to tell me, 'She was posher than the Queen!'

In November 1934, with the death of Charlie Brocket, Angela ceased to be Mrs Ronald Nall-Cain and became the second Lady Brocket. She must have been thrilled. But not half as thrilled as her husband. The new Lord Brocket didn't just get a title. He got some serious cash. The question is, where did it come from?

You may recall that my great-grandfather had set up the so-called 1921 Trust to preserve the Brocket Hall estate for the benefit of all future Lord Brockets. I was told all about that trust soon after I inherited the title in 1967. Then, in February 1996, one week before I was due to be sentenced, I was invited to a meeting with my father's former solicitor, Gilbert Rowberry, who was still hard at work at the age of ninety.

'Do you know about the 1925 Trust?' he said.

'No, no, Gilbert,' I said, in the patronising tones that a man in the prime of life reserves for a charming old boy who's clearly losing his grip, 'it's the 1921 Trust.'

'No,' said Gilbert, 'I mean the 1925 Trust.'

I sighed in exasperation. 'It's 1921, Gilbert, 1921!'

This time it was Gilbert's turn to be irritated. 'There's nothing wrong with my brain or my memory,' he said. 'There was a second trust, created in 1925. You clearly know nothing about it.'

So then Gilbert Rowberry told me the extraordinary story of the missing Brocket trust. It seems that my great-grandfather Charlie decided that it wasn't enough to give his descendants a beautiful home. He wanted to give them the means to preserve it for posterity. So in 1925 he put £1 million – a staggering sum, worth the best part of £100 million today – into a second trust. This was the 1925 Trust and had it still been in existence when I inherited the title, my entire adult life would have been completely different. But I had never seen a penny of the money. What had happened?

To put it bluntly, my dear old grandpa appears to have waltzed off with the lot. Soon after inheriting his title, he set about stripping the 1925 Trust that his father had set up. First, he dismissed all the existing trustees and replaced them with the ever loyal Angela, who dutifully signed whatever papers he put in front of her without a murmur of doubt or dissent. She had vowed in church to obey him, after all.

Over the next two decades, my grandfather used the money from the family trust to fund an astonishing spending spree. He collected stately homes the way other people collect parking-tickets. He'd already been given Knoydart, of course, as a wedding present. Now he bought Bramshill, a huge Jacobean house near

Camberley that was three times the size of Brocket and is now a police training college. He bought Carton, an Irish mansion in County Kildare, the former home of the Dukes of Leinster.

He also picked up Kinnersley, a castellated house near Oxford; Inkpen Hall, a Queen Anne house near Newbury, Berkshire; and Cashel Palace, an archbishop's old residence in Cashel, County Tipperary. He had London mansions in Wilton Crescent and at 55 Park Lane, conveniently located near his father-in-law's church in North Audley Street. When the famously extravagant Lord and Lady Docker suffered financial problems, my grandfather bought their yacht. He and his family holidayed in Monte Carlo and Cap Ferrat, down the coast on the French Riviera. You could say he lived pretty well.

Along the way, Lord and Lady Brocket had three children. The eldest was my father, the Honourable Ronald Nall-Cain, who was always known as Robin. Then came my uncle David and my aunt Elizabeth. My father longed for my grandfather's approval and affection. I have a picture of him as a very little boy, taken during one of his father's election campaigns. He's looking at the camera like a real-life Christopher Robin, holding a sign that says: 'VOTE FOR DADDY'.

If only Daddy had voted for him.

In 1947, when he was eighteen, my father was due to inherit £60,000 under the terms of his grandfather's will. In those days of post-war austerity, that was enough money to give a young man an extremely good lifestyle. But my grandfather refused to pay up.

A year went by. My father tried again. Still my grandfather refused to give him the money. When he turned twenty, my father tried for a third time. He had done his national service in the Life Guards, but had been invalided out, suffering from crippling headaches, though no one had been able to diagnose their cause. Since he could no longer have a military career, he wanted to go into farming.

Specifically, he wanted to follow in his father's footsteps. For my grandfather had a famous herd of prize Aberdeen Angus cattle. An entire room at Brocket Hall was covered, floor to ceiling, with rosettes won by these splendid beasts. Now my father wanted to buy a farm and build up a herd of his own. So could he have his sixty grand, please?

Most parents would be touched if a child showed such a passionate interest in something that mattered to them. But not my grandfather. Once again, he refused.

My father went to see a solicitor, Gilbert Rowberry. Gilbert told him that this was not a difficult legal issue. He was indisputably entitled to the money. His father was one of the wealthiest men in the country and could easily afford to pay. A single letter should sort it all out.

But it didn't. On the contrary, my grandfather was appalled to discover that his son had dared to challenge him by consulting a lawyer. So far as he was concerned, he was the head of the family, his word was law, and damn what anyone else said.

My father knew he was in the right, and he refused to back down. He told my grandfather, 'If you don't pay me the money, I'll sue.'

The response was instant: 'If you even think of suing me, you are finished as my son.'

I suppose my grandfather must have looked at his tall, slender, sickly boy and assumed that he would be a pushover. Big mistake: my father stuck to his guns and began legal proceedings. He was now at war with his own father. And, to make matters worse, he had made an enemy of his mother, too.

Angela Pennyman may have been a vicar's daughter, but after fifteen years as Lady Brocket she had become convinced that nothing but the smartest bride would be good enough for her son, or reflect well enough on her. Ideally, she wanted him to marry someone of royal blood. The Brockets had been great friends of King Edward VIII. Perhaps their son could marry Edward's niece, Princess Margaret.

Whether there was ever the slightest chance of a romance between my father and Margaret, I really don't know. She was the right age, being a year younger than him. They must have gone to many of the same society balls. And as the next in line to the Brocket title and fortune, Robin Nall-Cain was certainly a splendid catch for any aristocratic beauty, even a princess.

My grandmother certainly had ambitions for a royal wedding. As an old family friend recently told me with a sigh, 'Your grandmother was a good girl, but misguided. The problem was she so wanted your father to marry Princess Margaret.' But that wasn't what happened. Two decades after his father had married a vicar's daughter, my father fell for a vicar's granddaughter. Her name was Elizabeth Stallard: my mother.

Elizabeth was a respectable girl from a good family. Her father ran a successful engineering business called the English Drilling Equipment Company, or EDECO. Her mother was a talented artist. They lived in a large white house in Crowborough, Sussex, with a library filled with valuable old books and wonderfully illus-trated maps of faraway countries.

But the Stallards weren't good enough for the Brockets, and my grandparents told my father as much in no uncertain fashion. It made no difference.

My father's defiance simply grew stronger. Shortly after his twenty-first birthday, he did indeed take my grandfather to court. When it became obvious that my father was not going to back down, my grandfather finally paid him the £60,000. But Grandpa never forgot or forgave the anger and humiliation he felt. And though he and my father had a few brief meetings over the following years, that was effectively the end of their relationship as father and son.

My father left home and bought a farm by the banks of the River Severn, at Maisemore, in Gloucester. He started rearing his Aberdeen Angus cattle. He married my mother, though, rather sadly, I cannot recall ever seeing a picture of their wedding. And then, on 12 February 1952, I came on the scene.

Daddy's Not Very Well

MY VERY FIRST MEMORY DATES BACK TO WHEN I WAS four. Our family dog, Snipe, a soppy springer spaniel, gave birth to six puppies, right between the pedestals of my father's desk, on the floor of what we used to call the Blue Room, because it had a blue carpet. I always felt cosy in the Blue Room. I loved the reassuring smell of my father's cigars, which seemed to hang in the air, whether he was in the room or not, and Snipe clearly felt just as at home there as I did.

Being a little boy, I loved events that happened down at my level, so I was fascinated by the six little creatures that emerged from Snipe's tummy. Soon the smell of warm milk pervaded the Blue Room. I spent two happy weeks playing with the lovely, cuddly puppies, until one day one of the farmhands arrived with a great, big hessian sack. Snipe retreated to the basket under the desk, curling herself protectively around her brood. Then a large weathered hand reached down and one by one put four of the little creatures into the huge sack. I was petrified.

'What are you doing?' I asked.

'We only want two of these pups so four must go.'

My world was in turmoil. These little animals were my friends. I wondered with increasing alarm what happened if a human family had too many children.

I hurried outside to catch up with the farmhand, who was walking across the lawn towards the kitchen garden, 'What are you going to do?' I asked again, not really sure that I wanted an answer.

'The kindest way is to drown them.'

I thought of my four tiny friends in their dark prison and the dull splosh as the water rose to cover their little mouths. I secretly prayed for them to be clever enough to hold their breaths when the sack went in the water. For the rest of the walk I was too scared to say anything, as if I was taking part in some unmentionable crime.

We stopped next to a leaking water butt. At first, I was afraid to go too close but my concern for my little friends overcame my fear. I stood next to the farmhand as he started to push the sack under the water. It bubbled like my big sponge and to this familiar sound was added a terrible new one, as my little friends squeaked. Then the noise suddenly stopped, as if on command.

After what seemed like an age, the farmhand pulled the sack out.

'Can I see them?' I asked, praying I would spot movement.

'They're gone now. No point,' he said matter-of-factly.

Unable to say a single word, I followed the farmhand to the Blue Room, where Snipe was cowering in her basket, looking absolutely miserable, with her two remaining puppies. The hand reached down again and I was too frightened to ask what might happen next. The two trembling little creatures, were plucked out and I followed as they were carried back out to the woodshed where all the logs were split.

Delighted that the water butt was to play no part in whatever was to happen next, I felt a little braver. 'Why are we here?' I asked.

'Spaniels have their tails docked.'

'Please, what does docked mean?'

'It means cut off, lad.' Before my confused thoughts had a chance to sort themselves out, one big hand had placed a puppy on the chopping bench and another brought the axe crashing down on the little tail.

With the curiosity that is an inevitable part of every child I examined the pathetic remnant of the puppy's tail. Strangely, it hardly bled at all.

The second puppy was docked, then both were returned to their mother. Much to my relief, they soon seemed to forget about the whole episode but Snipe still seemed sad at the disappearance of her four other offspring.

So that's my first memory, and there are those to whom I have told the story who think it's significant that it should concern death and loss rather than happiness and love. But that's quite enough psychological speculation. Let me show you around my childhood home.

*

Maisemore stood on slightly raised ground, above the floodplains of the River Severn. It was reached down narrow country lanes, with high banks topped with hedgerows rising up on either side of the road. The house itself was a modest, white-painted Georgian building at the end of a short drive. It was very nice, but compared to the vast mansions between which the rest of my father's family divided their time, it was absolutely minuscule.

As you walked into our house there was a large entrance hall. To the right was the drawing-room, a smart, formal place with puffed-up cushions on the sofas and chairs that were not to be disturbed or squished by young boys. We hardly ever went into the drawing-room unless we had guests, and even then I always felt it was chilly and unwelcoming.

My father's study, the Blue Room, was to the left of the front door as you came in. It contained his desk and also the family television. I vividly remember us all huddling round the set, one day in 1957, when I was five. Suddenly, the announcer said the name of our home!

Daddy appeared on the small screen, in his herring-bone brown suit, plus-fours and cloth cap, holding a rope attached to a huge black bull. I wasn't sure what he was doing there, but I knew it was part of something of which we should all be proud. Even now, when I think of my father, I see him on that old-fashioned, black-and-white TV, just a flickering image on a tiny screen.

Back out in the hall, a staircase led up to a first-floor

gallery, ringed by a balustrade. I used to sit there in the evenings with my brother Richard, who was ten months younger than me. We'd stick our heads through the balustrade to try and see what the grown-ups were getting up to downstairs.

Richard and I had a bedroom with a blue lino floor and beds either side of the door. My parents had their suite, with their own bathroom, at the back of the house. But the most fascinating room upstairs was the family bathroom, which we children shared with our long succession of nannies.

Most of the nannies were useless. We never quite knew how we managed to drive so many of them out of the house, but it may have had something to do with a game that Richard and I liked to play. We used to hide on the top shelf of the airing-cupboard that opened onto the bathroom, waiting for the nanny of the day to have her bath. We'd lie there, trying desperately to keep quiet, peering out through a crack in the door as she undressed and slipped into the tub.

The sight of a female body, so different from ours, was completely fascinating, thrilling in ways we couldn't begin to understand, and enough to reduce us to helpless giggles. But our careers as under-age peeping Toms came to an end when one nanny, who may just have got wise to what we were up to, took far longer to disrobe than we'd expected, causing us to overheat in the stifling cupboard and give up our game for good.

Mornings at Maisemore began with fresh milk being brought in from the milking-sheds to the dairy, just behind the kitchen, where it lay in huge metal saucers,

arrayed on a slate slab. My first job of the day was to
stand on a big box, so that I could reach the saucers of
milk and skim the cream off the top. I'd put some in a
Kilner jar for storage, then pour the rest into a churn,
powered by a wooden handle, so that it could be turned
into butter.

Every day, during term-time, I'd go to the local pre-
school, which I hated and where I was always bolshy to
the teachers. Milk was a big feature of the day there,
too. It came in little bottles, holding one-third of a
pint. It was warm and sickly by the time we came to
drink it and to this day the smell of milk puts me back
in that lino-floored schoolroom. Perhaps that's why I
hardly ever drink the stuff. If you come to my London
flat and you want white coffee, you'll have to make do
with Coffee-Mate.

The time wasted at pre-school made weekends and
holidays on our 200-acre farm all the sweeter. The farm
manager, Mr Adamson, was a seriously good man and
his wife was any child's idea of heaven, plying us with
delicious home-made cakes and pies. Mr Adamson,
though, could offer something even more enticing than
food: he gave us access to all the farm's tractors and
machinery, like the turnip mangles in our barn – a
wildly clattering mass of pulleys, belts and gadgets. Many
happy hours were spent in this thrilling mechanical
world, and it gave me a love of engineering that's stayed
with me ever since.

These were still early days for my father's herd, and
he was probably having to spend more to set himself up
than he could yet hope to earn back. But his cattle

were steadily acquiring a fine reputation. He had not mended the rift with his parents, but as their eldest son he could expect to inherit the title of Lord Brocket and the house that was entrusted to the holder of that title. Thanks to his £60,000 inheritance, he'd been able to buy a working farm and he'd even treated himself to a second-hand Bentley motor. The future should have been rosy. But it was not. For though he was not yet out of his twenties, my father was dying of cancer. The headaches he had first suffered in the army and that had steadily worsened were not caused by migraines or nervous tension. They were the harbingers of a fatal brain tumour.

The evidence of just how serious his condition really was appeared in the autumn of 1958. The harvest at Maisemore had just been completed and my father was feeling exhausted. He called his sister, my aunt Elizabeth, who was staying at Carton, in Ireland. He asked if he could visit her: he needed a rest. Liz was nervous, frightened of what her father might say if he discovered that his son and daughter had conspired to defy him. But she could hardly turn away the brother she loved, so she invited him over.

My father flew to Dublin airport and drove to Carton, arriving in time for drinks. The racehorse trainer Vincent O'Brien had popped over to say hello, and the booze and conversation were flowing until, without any warning, my father collapsed and passed out on the floor. A doctor was sent for and quickly confirmed that there was something seriously wrong. For once, my grandparents showed some concern.

They had my father flown to London, where he was rushed to the Middlesex Hospital.

There he had an exploratory operation, which discovered a tumour at the top of his spine. The doctors had grim news. The cancer was terminal, his decline and death inevitable.

It's taken me more than forty years to realise that I never really came to terms with my father dying. Just before Christmas 2003 I went to see a psychiatrist for the first time in my life – a long-overdue visit, some may say! I'd been making a total disaster of my relationships with women, because I found it impossible to commit myself, even to women I knew I loved. I wanted to. I tried to. But then I'd start to go into reverse.

To help solve this problem, the shrink wanted to know about my relationship with my father. But it soon emerged that I had virtually no memory of him at all.

The shrink asked me how I'd interacted with my father. I told him that I wasn't sure: I didn't know my father that well. He said, 'You must have. How did you get on?'

I said, 'I dunno. All right, I think.'

He said, 'What images of him do you have in your brain?'

I said, 'Well, I remember my father on our farm, wearing a cloth cap and plus-fours. And I remember him standing by a Land-Rover, because I've got a photograph of him like that. I remember him on television, with his prize bulls. And I've got a photograph of him in the sitting-room, smoking one of his prize cigars. But that's all.'

So he said, 'Okay. Now, how did you interrelate?'

I still didn't know, so he said, 'Do me a favour. Ask your mother, then come back and tell me what she says. And I bet I know what her answer is.'

So I did, and my mother said we got on famously. Dad and I laughed and joked, because he had a hell of a sense of humour. He loved to see the funny side of life – so much so, in fact, that it sometimes drove my mother mad.

But I told the therapist, 'I don't remember any of that.'

He said, 'Well, you've just cut that out because it's painful and you don't want to remember it.'

We started to talk about how, whenever I get too close to people, I start to get really cold feet. Subconsciously, I'm terrified that I might get hurt, because of course I was hurt, as a child, by the loss of the father I loved. The trouble was, I'd never dealt with that loss and that pain. In a typical upper-class family, you're not encouraged to face these things. It all comes from the old days when you had go out and run the empire. When the call comes that your father has died in one of the outposts of the empire, or in a war, in a trench or something, you're not supposed to be sad about it. You say, 'He was a fine chap,' and move on.

But now I know that I've got to come to terms with what happened to my father, my family and me. So what follows is as much a journey of discovery for me, writing the story, as for anyone else reading it. The problem, though, is that one remembers the wrong bits of the story. For example, I know my mother took me to visit my father at the Middlesex Hospital, where he returned for more operations over the next few years. I know we stayed at a friend's flat and that I slept on the floor. I can remember feeling the rumble of underground trains as they powered through their tunnels, directly below the flat, and being fascinated by the thought that there were people somewhere beneath me, whizzing to and fro through the earth. But I can't remember the hospital ward, or what it felt like to see my daddy lying in bed, wrapped in bandages, doing his best to be cheerful.

How much can any child know or understand at the age of six? I did not know that my father would rapidly become unable to work on his farm, that he was losing his sense of balance, that he would spend many of his days lying on a sofa, or staying in bed, and that all his beloved cattle, into which he had put so much work and hope, would be sold off for a pittance. And besides, my father never, ever talked about dying. Perhaps he thought he might not. I just sensed that something was wrong, that Daddy was not well and that Mummy seemed upset. And then I was sent away to school.

You might expect me to say that I was bitterly homesick, cried every night and was left with scars that will haunt me for ever. But in fact I remember this as a good time. I'm not sure I could have coped if I'd stayed at home full-time. The atmosphere was becoming quite oppressive as the strain imposed by my father's illness, combined with our growing money troubles, put my mother under terrible pressure.

At my little boarding-school I could get away from

the black cloud hanging over the family and spend my time fooling around with a house full of other children. It was only a small place. There must have been about twenty boarders, plus a few day boys and girls. Note the word 'girls'. The school was mixed and we boys were actually in the minority. So the other reason I liked the school so much was that I had developed my first crush.

She was called Elizabeth. She was very lively, she had short, blond hair and I thought she was yummy. I spent most of my time behaving like an idiot trying to impress her. We stole secret hugs whenever we could and soon everyone knew about us.

The biggest obstacle in this relationship was access to the girls' dormitory. I really liked talking to Elizabeth and the other girls, but it was a high-risk operation. The girls' dormitory was strictly out of bounds and the headmistress was always on the prowl. Sometimes she'd catch me and the punishment was instant: a bar of soap forced into my mouth until I gagged or even vomited on this waxy, smelly, foul-tasting substance that seemed to linger round my mouth for days, no matter how often I got out my toothbrush.

A soapy mouth was a small price to pay for getting close to my first girlfriend and, anyway, I had a secret defence. All my life I've been embarrassed by my big teeth. I was positively goofy as a young boy. But, for once, my gnashers came in handy. They stopped the bar from completely disappearing down my throat, even if they did act like a cheese grater, gouging out extra soap as the bar was pulled out of my mouth.

When I got back home for the holidays, my father's

chest was in plaster. I don't know why, given that the cancer was in his head. He must have had some sort of exploratory operation. But he passed it off with his normal bravado. In the evening, when we assembled in the Blue Room to watch TV, he would strike a Swan Vesta match across his plastered chest to light his favourite Churchill cigar. The lovely, fragrant smoke would drift in my direction before it faded away into nothing in the air.

My father had boxes of beautifully coloured fishing flies. They were so gem-like, that I had taken it for granted that they were very valuable. One day, Daddy sat next to me and patiently explained how the different flies suited the appetites of different fish. Then we went out on to the lawn where he showed me how to cast a fly. This proved too much for my little arms, but he told me that one day we'd go fishing together in Scotland. I longed to be able to catch my first salmon with him.

A few years ago, I was on holiday in Spain. At a supper party, I heard someone say, right out of the blue, 'I recognise that voice!' I turned and saw a woman in her sixties, looking intently at me. We were introduced and as soon as she heard the name Brocket she said, 'I used to look after your father.'

It turned out she'd been his nurse at the Middlesex Hospital and then cared for him at Maisemore until his death. My father obviously felt he could pour out his heart to her because he wrote to her, first from his hospital bed, and then from Maisemore, when he'd gone home to die after the doctors realised that there was nothing more they could do for him. His old nurse had kept his letters and the next day she brought them round for me to read.

The letters gave me a sense of my father, in his very own words. The humour everyone had always told me about was there, but so was an aching sadness that broke my heart. Though his parents had flown him back to England, they had shown little interest, let alone concern for him, thereafter. My father could not understand their indifference. He was desperately confused about the way he'd been pushed out of his family, particularly when he'd not done anything wrong. He did not know why his parents did not love him, why his mother, even more than his father, seemed so cruel to him.

Sadly, the letters revealed a growing tension in my parents' marriage. I think the strain was simply too much for them. My mother, after all, had married very young and was still in her mid twenties. She should have lived a life of luxury and ease. Instead, she was having to cope with a dying husband, a collapsing farm, three small children – for I now had a second little brother, David – and parents-in-law who were content to let their elder son die without lifting a finger to help him, or his family. No wonder she was often tired and unhappy.

What is, perhaps, more surprising is that amid all her troubles my mother was able to come up with a business idea that would later provide our only financial support through some very difficult times. The mighty Aberdeen Angus cattle had gone, but in their place

Mummy erected two huge single-storey buildings, which eventually housed 75,000 battery chickens. Their breasts and drumsticks paid for my education.

When I was eight, the time came for me to go away to a new prep school. It was called Spyway and was run by two brothers in their late fifties, Geoffrey and Eric Warner. Spyway was a severe stone building some 800 yards back from the top of the cliffs to the west of Swanage, in Dorset. The school had no central heating and the only sources of warmth were small fires in three of the classrooms. Our beds were the plain, metal type, suitable for hospitals, barracks and other grim institutions, that flooded the country during the war years and added to the austerity of the place.

The bathroom was a large room with three baths down each side and one in the middle. The floor was concrete. Every morning cold baths were run full to the brim and we were paraded outside the room, lined up naked. On command we had to get into a cold bath and submerge ourselves up to our neck. If we didn't, the matron would push us under with a broom. Some mornings it was so cold that ice had formed on the surface of the bathwater, which had to be broken by the first boy in.

The headmaster, Geoffrey Warner, was a fitness fanatic. Every Sunday morning after chapel, he'd order us out on walks to Corfe Castle and back, a round trip of some eight miles. To our little legs that seemed like a trip to the end of the world and back, but the prefects ensured that no one turned back before they reached the castle.

Not surprisingly, we all became very fit and were thus prepared for the other sports for which Geoffrey was such an enthusiast. I played a lot of rugby and liked it, but the Spyway regime also included boxing, which I absolutely hated. I can still remember the weight of the huge boxing gloves and the fear of stepping into the ring, knowing what was coming next. Week after week I had to fight the same boy, George Ellis. While I was a long, skinny string bean, he was a short, scrappy, fiery little chap. Within seconds of the bell going for the start of round one, he'd flatten me with punches I couldn't even see coming.

I didn't want to punch George and I certainly didn't want him to punch me. I knew by then that my father was ill and that his illness, whatever it was, had something to do with his head. But here we were being told to punch each other's heads, repeatedly, as hard as we could, without any protection whatsoever. I was petrified that I might get ill, the same way Dad had done, or – even worse – make someone else as ill as him.

If other boys weren't hitting me, the teachers were. Both brothers were disciplinarians. Geoffrey Warner used a cane and Eric a highly polished wooden hairbrush. We could scarcely make up our minds which was the more painful but the hairbrush won by a small margin. I seemed to be constantly in one or the other of their studies having punishment meted out to me. The pain of the beating was always followed by the embarrassment of returning to the class, creeping to my desk with all eyes on me, and then being unable to sit down.

My favourite place in the whole school was the carpentry shop, which was run by Eric Warner. I've always been good with my hands. I love carpentry, engineering, design – anything to do with physical objects – and Eric awoke a lifelong interest in furniture-making. I spent endless hours in the workshop. It was like a refuge for me, somewhere I could be alone and just get on with something I loved.

I was quite a lonely, unhappy boy. The situation at home was getting worse by the month and Spyway did not provide the sort of warm, friendly environment I'd experienced at my first boarding-school. I wouldn't say that I was unpopular, but I was definitely not part of the gang. I also had a complex about my looks. I thought I had goofy teeth and goggle eyes and my classmates seemed to agree. Their nickname for me was Goldie, because they said I looked like a goldfish.

By now, there was no way of escaping the fact that my father was going downhill. When I went home for the holidays, he would often be away, and my mother would be with him, leaving us in the care of nannies, or the lovely Mrs Adamson, the farm manager's wife. On one occasion, I didn't go home at all, but was sent off to Sussex to stay with my mother's parents.

The start of my second year at Spyway brought me company in the shape of my younger brother Richard. And then, a few weeks into the autumn term of 1961, when I was nine years old, my life changed dramatically. Geoffrey Warner summoned me to his study. He told me that my mother would be coming tomorrow to collect Richard and me and take us home. My first thought was that I was being expelled. I tried to imagine what I had done wrong but could come up with nothing that would warrant being taken out of school.

The next day my mother arrived in the Bentley. She'd been driving us home for half an hour before she told us that Daddy had died. Though I'd known he was ill, this came as a total, horrible surprise. I'd always thought he'd get better. When you're a kid, people don't die, especially not your father. He was only thirty-two years old. I instantly regretted that I had not spent more time with him and got to know him better. I felt deprived because of what might have been and cheated, too. If I had known, I would have spent more time with my father and less time messing about on the farm.

Richard was devastated, too. Big tears began to roll down his cheeks and in my confusion, painfully aware that I was the eldest, I desperately tried to think how a grown-up would behave. So I said to him, 'It's very sad but there's no good crying over spilt milk.' I'd heard grown-ups use the phrase often, so I thought it was what you were supposed to say.

For the rest of the journey hardly a word was spoken. I don't think Richard ever forgot or forgave what I'd said. It must have seemed so callous, and I knew it was wrong as soon as I opened my mouth. I wished I could unsay it. I tried desperately to think of some way to comfort Mummy. But I couldn't think of anything, and so we drove on in silence.

Daddy was interred in the family crypt at Brocket Hall. It was a small, quiet, family funeral. My mother thought it best that Richard and I did not attend, something I have always regretted. We never had the chance to say goodbye to him. He simply ceased to exist, as if he'd just been a temporary guest in our house. The crypt at Brocket is sealed. You have to crowbar up the paving stones, then go through a secret entrance to find the tombs below. But there is a small stone memorial to my father outside the chapel and I go there sometimes, to pay my respects, and just be close in death to a man I knew so little in life.

Whatever my regrets, I know that my mother was just trying to do what she thought was best to protect us from being upset. What my grandparents did next, though, was a calculated insult. A short while after his funeral, there was a memorial service for my father, held in the splendour of Gloucester Cathedral. My grandparents did not attend. Having paid no more than lip-service to looking after their son when he was ill, they then proved that he meant nothing to them by not going to his memorial service. And they did nothing at all to help his widow or her young children.

In fact, they went further than that. Though I did not yet know it, my grandfather planned to disinherit my father's side of the family. My grandparents, who claimed to care so much about their family and its social standing, who had themselves inherited every penny they had, did their best to ensure that all future Lord Brockets would be completely penniless. The money, though, is not the real issue. It is just the symbol of what really hurts: their total rejection of my father, my mother, my brothers and me.

What drives someone to go out of their way to harm

their own flesh and blood? I cannot conceive of anything that would drive me to do that to my children.
And if it sounds as though the scars are still raw, that's
because I remember the effect that my father's death
had on my mother and us children.

Mummy was shattered. She wouldn't talk to us about
what had happened. She'd spend hours alone in her
room, utterly miserable and depressed. I'd go in and see
her sometimes, when I was home from school. The
sight of her lying in bed, just like Daddy had done, was
deeply unsettling. I began to fear that she was getting ill,
just like he had done. Now she, too, was going to die
from this mystery illness.

Sadness enveloped the entire home like a blanket.
One day, I happened to notice my father's little box of
fishing flies. I picked it up, slowly opened the lid and
stared blankly at those rows of beautiful flies. Their
bright colours seemed to fade before my eyes. Who
would take me fishing now? Who would show me how
to do all those things that only fathers do?

There were so many questions. And by the time I
was eleven, another one had come along: where were
we going to live? Death duties had to be paid and the
farm would have to be sold. Father's machines were
lined up with numbers on them, like old cows put out
to grass. All the rosettes that his cattle had won were
packed up in a large box and sealed. Daddy might as
well have been in that box. It contained all that he had
achieved in his short life on this earth, and if anything
ever brought home to me man's mortality that was it.
Nelson had a column as a reminder to us all of his

existence. Kings had statues. My father just had this nondescript box of rosettes, sitting on a dusty floor, soon to be lost for ever.

Goodbyes were said to everyone and I gave cosy Mrs Adamson a final big hug. It was time to go. We were moving to a quaint, compact Tudor cottage called Fruiter's Gate, on the edge of Dorney Common, just across the Thames from Windsor and a couple of miles from my next school, Eton College. My mother had done her sums. If she kept the chicken-sheds, she could earn enough to keep us afloat. As the car drew away from Maisemore I looked out of the back window, wondering what would become of the place. We were off to a new existence.

— 4 —

Sex and Schooling

I WAS GENERALLY ASSUMED TO BE TERMINALLY THICK. At Spyway, Eric Warner decided that I should take the Common Entrance exam for Eton a year early. That way, if I failed I could have another go the following year. Amazingly, however, I did not fail. So I went to Eton a year early. Most of the other new boys were thirteen, but I was only just twelve. Something else marked me out from the vast majority of my classmates. I was not a virgin.

Her name was Heather. She lived in the next village and, in the finest family tradition, she was a vicar's daughter. She was sixteen, giggly, and almost as tall as me in her heels, which is saying something because I was over six feet, even at twelve. Heather had wavy, shoulder-length brown hair, but the thing I remember most is her wonderful mouth. I've always thought that a woman's mouth is her most important feature — including teeth, by the way: if a girl has lousy teeth, I go no further – and Heather had lovely, sensuous lips, which made her brilliant at kissing.

Heather and I became friends during the summer holidays before I went to Eton. I have no idea at all what she saw in me. I was still as convinced as ever of my butt-ugliness and assumed – as I did for many years to come – that if I ever managed to persuade a girl to take the slightest interest in me it was purely out of my luck, or her kindness. But I liked the fact that Heather was older than me and felt flattered by her attention.

We spent hours talking about our lives and our feelings. My heart used to pound every time I saw her. Completely unable to handle all the new emotions coursing through me, I'd get nervous, say silly things that I didn't mean at all, get my limbs hopelessly tangled and generally make a big, gawky fool of myself.

She must have forgiven me, though, because one afternoon we went down to the fields on the banks of the Thames. We cuddled, we canoodled, and slowly, but inevitably, one thing started leading to another. My hands explored her body, going to wonderful, exciting places I'd only ever seen in tacky pictures in the porno magazines boys would smuggle into prep school.

I felt as if I were about to have a wonderful meal, filled with foods I'd never tasted, but which I knew were going to be delicious. But I was worried about my inexperience. Shyly, I confessed that I'd never done this before. Heather told me that she hadn't, either. But, somehow, instinct guided us in the right direction.

At school, boys had talked about sex as something that happened in an instant. But when Heather and I made love, it seemed to go on for ages, and I wanted it to last for ever. There we lay in the long grass, out of breath and, in my case, glowing with manly pride. I felt as though I'd grown ten years in the last few minutes.

We made love two or three more times over the following weeks and then our passionate teenage love affair petered out, as these things do.

So the holidays ended and off I went to Eton, the most famous school in the world and also, in many ways, the most misunderstood. For one thing, it's not really a school in the normal sense so much as a small town, whose ancient buildings, chapels, classrooms and boarding-houses stretch down a maze of streets, lanes and passageways. It is a big, intimidating, ferociously competitive place, filled with boys who all seem impossibly confident.

I wondered what I could say about myself. How about 'I'm the son of a dead farmer, who had a fine collection of rosettes'? Or 'My mum pays for my fees by selling battery hens'? My maternal grandpa was a fine engineer but I knew nothing about my father's father, except that he had a title. My mother never talked about him and I certainly didn't feel remotely special or superior – quite the reverse, in fact. We weren't at all wealthy. My mother couldn't afford to splash money around, like other parents at Eton did.

Perhaps I found this new world intimidating because I was almost a year younger than most boys in my intake. Or perhaps all the boys at Eton felt as insecure as I did behind their brash façades. Either way, I didn't really enjoy my time at Eton, a fact made worse by the constant bullying I received from a pair of boys in my house, whom I'd better just refer to as Smith and Jones. And of course, I was beaten on a regular basis. The drill was always the same. Misdemeanours would be followed by a summons to see the headmaster, who would greet me with the words 'Well, dear boy, shall we get the business stuff over with? Trousers down, then we can have some sherry.'

I sang bass in the school choir, where I met another new boy, Carron Snagge, son of the BBC's Boat Race commentator John Snagge. Like his father, Carron was a keen oarsman, or 'wet bob', as they're called at Eton (as opposed to 'dry bobs', who choose to spend their summers playing cricket instead). Carron and I weren't exactly Redgrave and Pinsent, but we were decent oarsmen, beating all the other teams in the school and winning our colours, or 'cap'. On weekend afternoons, we'd take our boat several miles upstream to an island called Queen's Ayot, where there was a snack-bar, housed in an old shack, where we could drink as much beer as we wanted and eat delicious fruit-cake.

My other great love at Eton, as at Spyway, was the huge workshop known as the School of Mechanics. It was a treasure-trove of materials and machines where one could build anything from a simple footstool to a fully operational car. My own speciality soon became disco equipment. I'd noticed that boys were keen to buy hi-fi sets and I reasoned that there must be a market for smart, well-made systems which incorporated a second record deck and were powerful enough to blow the windows out of parents' homes.

I started sneaking up to London to buy all the electronic components I needed – valve amplifiers, fancy Wharfedale speakers and brushed aluminium controls – then carried out the work in the School of Mechs. For the speaker and amplifier cabinets I chose African mahogany, French-polished to a rich, dark shine. Once I'd sold my first set of disco equipment, word spread and, before long, I was making hundreds of pounds and was able to afford a serious, top-of-the-range hi-fi of my own. I'd soon have somewhere decent to play it, too.

For my mother was finally becoming happier again and recovering her old sense of fun and laughter. Our little house at Fruiter's Gate had a warm, comforting atmosphere, with friendly neighbours all around. The chicken unit was producing a good profit, removing her financial worries. Best of all, she was in love.

An admirer called Colin Trotter was seeing more and more of her. But one morning, as I was helping my mother make her bed, I noticed that she was clearly upset. She said that she had just told Colin that she could not marry him, and asked him not to see her any more. She believed that it was unfair to ask any man to look after three children who were not his own.

'Do you love him?' I asked.

'Yes,' she replied, 'very much.'

'Well, ring him up and tell him you will marry him. Go on, do it now.'

She hesitated for a moment and gingerly picked up the phone. The conversation was short but when she replaced the receiver tears of happiness flooded down her cheeks. Another new phase in all our lives was about to open up.

As all our things were being packed up and the little house, of which we had all grown so fond, was put up for sale, Richard and I returned to school knowing that we would soon have a stepfather.

Back at Eton, I added bicycles to my manufacturing business. I reckoned that I could get the fancy European components I needed from the foreigners employed as domestic staff at the school, build a full racing bike from scratch, sell it at £23 (well below the price of a shop-bought model) and still make a decent profit. My first machine, designed to appeal to flashy show-offs, was sprayed bright red with silver stripes. It was sold before the paint was dry. The next machine was snapped up even faster. Soon I had two flourishing businesses. My great-great-grandfather Robert O'Cahan, founder of the family brewing fortune, would have been proud of my entrepreneurial instincts.

Meanwhile, I was about to receive a visit from another member of my family. One day, I was summoned to my housemaster's study and told that my grandfather, Lord Brocket, was coming to visit. I was not sure what to think. I'm told he saw me once or twice as a toddler, but I had never knowingly met him. I'd never had a Christmas present or birthday card from him. I certainly had no idea that he had treated my father so badly.

That Saturday, a huge, black, chauffeur-driven stretch-limo pulled up outside the house and Grandpa introduced himself. We talked about nothing in particular and he made no mention of anything to do with him or his affairs. Five minutes later, he said he had to go, gave me a £5 note and left.

Feeling enormously pleased with myself, I ran as fast as I could down the High Street to bank it in my post office savings account. Little did I know that, so far as my grandfather was concerned, that £5 note would be my entire inheritance. Looking back, and knowing what was to come, I can't quite work out what my grandfather was up to. Had a guilty conscience pricked him? Was he curious to see what his son had sired? Or was he just confirming the wisdom of his decision to cut us all out of his life?

By now my mother had married Colin Trotter and moved to his home, Mells Park in Somerset. Colin is a kind and honourable man, and we were very lucky to have him as a stepfather. He made over various parts of the house and outbuildings to us boys. I even had my own flat at the top of the house. Colin always insisted that Richard and I had to work for every penny he gave us, but he was incredibly generous in giving us jobs to do at top rates of pay.

I soon had a little half-brother Rupert, whose shock of blond hair could often be seen bobbing up and down in his pram as he was wheeled around the grounds. My own preferred mode of transport was a vehicle that defied all description, built by one of the farm mechanics, known only as 'the Thing'.

As if the noise from my disco gear and the rumble of the Thing were not enough, I now started shattering the peace of the countryside by letting off huge explosions. I'm not sure how I discovered the knack of creating home-made explosives, although I do know that the mix of potash, sodium chlorate and diesel I came up with was exactly the same as the IRA's favourite bomb-making substance, known throughout Northern Ireland as Co-Op.

Around this time Colin was having problems with moles wrecking his lawns. My first solution to the mole question was gas. I put one end of a hosepipe up the exhaust pipe of the Thing, and the other end down what looked like the front entrance of the mole settlement. Then I started revving the Thing's engine.

In theory, the deadly exhaust fumes would choke all the moles, forcing them up to ground level, where they could be shot, bashed, or otherwise whacked. The practice was rather different. After five minutes, foggy fumes started rising out of the ground, and hovered over the lawn in a noxious toxic fog. Suddenly, the Thing's chugging ceased as the engine boiled over. Not one mole had bolted out of anywhere.

Well, I wasn't putting up with that. Richard and I mixed enough Co-Op to blow up the Tower of London and filled up the mole holes with it, ramming each mini-bomb down tight with a piece of wood as a stopper. A trail of Co-Op was left above ground as a makeshift fuse.

We lit our end of the fuse and stood back to see what would happen. Suddenly, the entire area erupted. Sods of earth flew through the air and bombed-out mole tunnels spewed forth white-hot flames. The lawn was left looking more like the Somme than Somerset, and that was the end of making Co-Op. It was banned by

Colin before we wiped out the whole family, along with all the moles.

Back I went to Eton, my businesses and my sporting pursuits; by now I was in the Third Eight at rowing, as well as the school shooting team. Then one day in 1967, when I was fifteen, my housemaster, Mr Lawrence, summoned me to his study. As always, I assumed I must be in trouble. Instead Lawrence said, 'I have some news that may be both good and bad. Your grandfather has died and your name has changed. You are no longer Nall-Cain. Your name is now Brocket.'

I reflected on this sudden bit of news. It didn't seem very good. I quite liked my proper name and I thought of all the things that sounded like Brocket, like Bucket, Rocket and, of course, Fuck-it. It never really occurred to me that I wasn't just Brocket, but Lord Brocket. I knew of course that my grandfather was a lord, but I hadn't given much thought to the fact that, with my father gone, the title would pass straight to me. That may sound odd. Under normal circumstances, as the eldest son of the eldest son, an awareness of my future responsibilities would have been drilled into me almost from birth. But with my father dead and my grandparents estranged from me, that process simply did not happen. I had no memory of ever going to Brocket Hall and Mother had always said that we would have to sink or swim by our own efforts. As I would discover over the next few months, she was absolutely right. Despite the clear intentions of the first Lord Brocket, that his successors should have Brocket Hall and the means to support it, my grandfather's will left nothing – not Brocket, not a single penny, not even a trinket or keepsake. His hatred of his son and heirs persisted. That fiver was his one and only gift to me, alive or dead.

Still, I had one compensation. I attended the one school in the world that regarded lords as perfectly normal. At Eton, where earls and viscounts are commonplace, a mere baron is no one special, so my title made no difference whatever to my schoolboy status, other than giving my friends the chance to take the mickey out of my new name, exploiting every one of the variations on Brocket that had occurred to me, too.

Not all my schoolmates, however, were so light-hearted. My old enemies Smith and Jones had one last surprise in store. Houses at Eton are run by groups of prefects known as 'Library'. New recruits are elected by existing Library members, who celebrate their decisions by rampaging through the house, grabbing the successful candidates and either de-bagging them, or dumping them in baths filled with freezing water or even baked beans. My election was rather different.

Unbeknown to the rest of the Library, Smith and Jones had run not a cold bath but a boiling hot one. I was thrown into the scalding water. By the time I was pulled from the bath, I was covered in burns and needed emergency hospitalisation, plastic surgery and months of recovery in the school sanatorium.

Twenty years or so after that horrendous night, I happened to be at a ball at the Café Royal. By then I was rich, famous and married to one of the world's most beautiful women – a very far cry indeed from the shy, awkward, petrified schoolboy I'd once been. My wife Isa and I were talking to a friend of mine, when another man I vaguely recognised came up to me, smiled ingratiatingly and said, 'Hi,' in a manner that suggested he knew me, and desperately hoped that I knew him.

'Who was that?' asked my wife after the man had disappeared back into the crowd.

Before I could say a word, my friend answered for me. 'His name,' he said, 'is Smith. And he is pure evil.' I might have changed over the decades, but my old school bully clearly had not.

I finally left Eton aged seventeen. With all my time devoted to business enterprises and sport, work had taken a back seat. Even in those less result-conscious days, seven O-levels and one A-level were not much of a return. So I was sent to a crammer called Applegarth, near Godalming, Surrey, to add another two As.

There, for the first time, I began to get a degree of self-confidence. This was due to two factors. First, I rented a room from a lovely couple called Mary and Brian Brennan, who really made me feel at home with their family. And, second, there were two girls who worked as cooks at Applegarth. They were both in their mid twenties, both bloody tasty and they both fancied me. What's more, they proved it. Perhaps I wasn't quite so goofy, after all!

– 5 –

You're in the Army Now

THE BOMB HAD GONE OFF IN BELFAST'S CENTRAL
bus station. The IRA had stuffed it into a litter-bin,
next to a queue. When it exploded, the casualties were
almost all women and children. Now it was my job to
lead the men who were cleaning up the mess. Treading
through a grisly, blood-soaked scrapyard of tangled
metal, smoking rubble and human remains, we collected the little hands, legs and even complete breasts,
like parts from some macabre puzzle, and put them in
plastic bags. People can talk about the struggle for freedom. They can romanticise the taking of innocent lives
for the sake of political power. At that moment we
stared into the face of the terrorist and saw him for
what he was.

It was 1972, and I was serving as a lieutenant in the
14th/20th King's Hussars. The men I was commanding
ranged from tough old campaigners to young lads still
in their teens. But none of us had ever seen anything

like this, or even imagined that it could be possible. We had to find a way to cope, without being overwhelmed by the sights and smells around us, the feel of the flesh in our hands. I told my men, 'Don't think of them as human beings. You've all seen meat in a butcher's shop. Does it upset you to handle it? No. Just imagine you're dealing with that.'

My family's ancestral homeland of Ulster had been turned into one giant battlefield. Every day, I would get into my Ferret armoured car and lead my squadron into the Catholic housing estates that were the IRA's strongholds, knowing that someone, somewhere would be aiming an Armalite rifle and taking a pot-shot at me. On quiet days, we'd go for a ride in the country, patrolling down lanes where the snipers weren't so common, but every culvert, every roadside ditch could contain a bomb, primed to explode on our approach.

And yet I don't think I've ever been as happy, before or since, as I was during the five years I spent in the army. It hadn't been my first choice of career. After leaving my crammer in 1969, I'd decided to pursue my love of design by training as an architect. I signed up as an assistant in a practice in Bath, which specialised in restoring old buildings. I learned how to read plans, survey buildings and find my way through the maze of different tasks that building and rebuilding require. But by 1971 the construction and property industries were mired in recession. There simply wasn't enough work to guarantee me a job. I needed to look somewhere else.

The army seemed to offer the chance to travel the world at someone else's expense, while getting the best training in man-management on offer anywhere. So I signed up in the 14th/20th King's Hussars. As a smart cavalry regiment, their job was defined by one senior general as 'adding tone to what otherwise would be a mere vulgar brawl'. They sounded perfect, and so in 1971, at the age of nineteen, I enlisted at Mons Officer Cadet School in Aldershot, Hants.

Mons had originally been set up to deal with young men doing national service, who needed to be turned into officers as fast as possible. So it didn't bother preparing men to become the generals of the future. It just turned out efficient junior officers. As a consequence, you could be through Mons and serving with your regiment within six months.

Of course, the only way the army could prepare men to lead troops into battle that quickly was to train them at maximum intensity, all the time. Mons was a high-pressure place, and that became obvious from the moment we cadets arrived in our civilian suits, carrying our regulation brollies. We were immediately lined up on the parade-square, feeling super-smart and bursting with military potential.

Our sergeant major, however, had other ideas. He thought we were the most pathetic rabble that he had ever laid eyes on. He walked up and down the ranks, his nose about an inch from our faces, shouting in a voice that was loud enough to be heard in the next-door town. His various obscenities involving our doubtful parentage and poor prospects of ever achieving officer status, let alone perpetuating the family line, were always ended with the regulation 'Sir!' delivered with withering contempt.

As he came opposite me he stopped. His nose an inch from mine, he yelled, 'I've never seen such a long, tall, paralysed piece of piss in my life! ... Sir!' And with that he moved on down the line.

As at prep school, we worked to a strict routine. Every morning we had to strip our beds and fold our sheets and blankets with such precision that the resulting block would resemble pieces of plywood stacked up in a pile. The sergeant would measure the bed block with a measuring stick and push it on the floor if it wasn't up to scratch and usually if it was. Black bayonets had to be polished to chrome-like surfaces and boots had to be 'bulled' using a hot spoon, polish, a candle flame and spit. Eventually they came up like mirrors.

There was, of course, a method to the army's apparent madness. Our group of cadets learned to work together, trust one another and stand up for one another, come what may. We'd be sent on ten-mile runs in full fighting uniform, with packs on our backs, and we'd all come back as a unit, even if it meant dragging one another past the finishing-post. We were sent on week-long exercises, when we'd be deprived of sleep for the full seven days, fed on iron rations of chocolate and tinned fruit-cake – the richest high-energy food there is – and still be expected to lead the men under our command.

By the time I left Mons, I was Second Lieutenant Lord Brocket. But there were still a few important lessons to be learned. I was posted to Bovington Camp, near Blandford in Dorset, to acquire the specific skills required to command armoured vehicles and point their guns in vaguely the right direction. This was obviously an important task. But Bovington taught me something just as important, but less obvious: the vital importance to a junior officer of knowing how to have fun.

The army is the ultimate work-hard, play-hard existence. British forces have a natural ability to be blasé about facing adversity and life-threatening situations, brushing them off as if they were nothing. But you live fast because you really could die young. We may have seemed like a bunch of delinquents to an outsider, but we needed frivolity to balance the life-and-death tasks for which we were being trained. That's why, for example, we punished one fellow officer who we felt was being altogether too serious about his gunnery studies, by locking him in his room – with a herd of sheep that we'd smuggled into our barracks.

This, though, was just the start. We had bigger, higher targets in our sights. Every morning, the camp commandant arrived on the dot of nine and took the modern, steel-doored lift up to his office. As any assassin could tell you, it is always dangerous to stick to a fixed routine, since it gives one's enemies the chance to prepare an ambush. As the commandant now discovered.

One day, working with the very same team spirit that had been drummed into us at Mons, the junior officers got to work. First the lift was summoned to the top floor. One of the team, stationed by the lift's power-supply, switched off its electricity. A keen young officer in the Gunners jumped through the hatch and sealed the edges round the lift doors with black masking tape and did the same with the floor. This sealed the lift, and made it watertight. The Gunner then climbed back out of the lift and his place was taken by a fire hose, which was put through the hatch and turned on, full blast.

In no time, the lift filled with water. The pressure of the water pushed the masking tape against the walls and floor of the lift, sealing it even tighter. Now came the tricky bit. As the minutes went by, all sorts of people came up to the lift doors in the lobby, pressed the button and . . . nothing happened. The power was still off. Assuming the lift was out of order, they walked upstairs.

Then, at 0900 hours precisely, the CO marched in. A whispered warning was radioed from the lobby to the power-supply. The juice was switched back on. When the commandant pressed the button, the lift descended towards him. It arrived at the ground floor. The doors opened. The masking tape gave way. And then suddenly a tidal wave of water exploded from the lift, picked up the CO and hurled him bodily against the far wall of the lobby. At this point, one of the conspirators walked by. Seeing his commandant lying in a shocked, sodden huddle, he straightened his uniform, walked up to the senior officer and, in his politest possible tones asked, 'I say, sir. Something wrong with the plumbing?'

When my time at Bovington was up, I reported to the Hussars at Tidworth, near Salisbury, to take

command of a troop of armoured cars. I was now confronting something for which not even the finest
training in the world can fully prepare a young officer:
the moment when you have to stand in front of your
men for the very first time and assume command. I
knew that the men's basic assumption, not to put too
fine a point on it, would be that I was an upper-class
twit. So I thought, Okay, I'm going to let them know
that I'm a nice guy, but also that I'm firm, and I do
know my stuff.

Now, they can only discover whether you know
your stuff over a period of time. Being firm, again,
takes time. But if I could show them straight away that
I'd got a sense of humour, then I'd be halfway there. A
suitable opportunity to demonstrate my wit occurred
on my first exercise with my troop of Saladin armoured
cars, near Thetford, in Norfolk. As we set off down the
road in convoy, I stood with my head poking proudly
out of my turret wanting desperately to lean out of the
turret and yell to motorists, 'Hey, you, this is my troop!'

At one of our positions, we discovered an apple tree
and promptly stripped it. It was then that an idea
occurred to me. Saladins sport a respectable 75mm
main armament. We only had blanks but what would
happen to a barrel full of apples? Tittering like school-
girls, we elevated the barrel, loaded a blank up the
breech and filled the barrel with apples.

The other side's line of advance was due to pass
through some trees, only 200 yards away. I lowered the
gun to horizontal and aimed at a clearing in the trees.
Excitement mounted as we heard an armoured car

approach and, taking into account the apple flight time, I aimed at the front of the advancing Saladins, which was commanded by David 'Bowsie' Bowes-Lyon, the Queen Mother's great-nephew, a delightful and mild-mannered man.

'Fire!' I shouted with great authority and the apples exploded from the gun barrel with an almighty bang.

Bowsie's Saladin came to a standstill. As the cordite fumes cleared away, we could see no sign of movement. It was only then that it occurred to me that fifty apples travelling at several hundred miles an hour might do some serious damage to a human body. Bowsie was totally motionless in the turret.

I suddenly realised that I might just have done terminal damage to a cousin of the Queen. 'God, I think we've killed him,' I said as we accelerated towards our crippled opponent. I jumped out of the turret to find Bowsie completely puréed. His beret and headphones were all dripping with sweet-smelling goo, as were the antennae, most of the turret and the driver's head.

'You ordered a packed lunch?' was all that I could feebly think of saying as I helped Bowsie down out of his perch.

'More like apple crumble,' muttered my driver.

'Christ, I think I've gone deaf. All I can hear is ringing in my ears,' said Bowsie, banging the side of his head. After a while the ringing diminished and his hearing returned along with his sense of humour.

It took a while for me to give orders with some confidence. All military orders are given in a sequence: situation, mission, execution. So it's 'The situation is . . . we're all in the shit. The mission is . . . to take that hill. The execution will be . . . blah-blah-blah.' But I used to get my knickers in a twist about giving commands in the correct, logical sequence. In the end, I just reduced my orders to common sense. I'd say, 'This is the situation. This is what we're supposed to do. This is how we're going to do it.' Once the guys realised that I knew what I was doing, and had a reasonable brain for tactics – particularly devious tactics – they actually quite liked following me.

I met one of my old soldiers the other day at a regimental get-together. 'It were fuckin' funny bein' with you, Lord Brocket,' he said. 'We 'ad no fuckin' idea what were gonna happen next!'

I didn't dare tell him the truth, which was, of course: neither had I.

In November 1971 my squadron of Hussars was posted to Hong Kong, then still a British colony and a paradise for anyone in the British army. The standard of living was incredibly high as everything was so cheap. Married officers lived in palatial houses with servants who provided round-the-clock service, and the country clubs gave you everything that was not available at home. There were even five 1959 MGA open sports cars, reserved for the use of officers.

We spent our days guarding the border with communist China, apprehending refugees and handing them back, which I hated. (There simply wasn't room in Hong Kong for all the refugees that a dictatorship of one billion people could produce.) And then, every afternoon at five o'clock, when our duties were done, we piled aboard to make a nuisance of ourselves in downtown Hong Kong. For a young lad on his first posting, it was absolute bliss. And then we received new orders. We were summoned back to Tidworth, to begin training in urban warfare. We were being sent to Northern Ireland.

In 1972 the Troubles in Ulster had reached the point of open warfare on the streets. The IRA were setting off bombs all over Northern Ireland and on the British mainland, with the stated policy of terrorising civilians and killing as many soldiers as possible. Meanwhile, thirteen men and youths had been shot by the Paratroop Regiment on Bloody Sunday. So when we got back to Tidworth, we cut down on the fun and games. This time, the training was deadly serious.

By now we had new vehicles. Our Saladin armoured cars had been swapped for smaller Ferret scout cars armed with only one .30 Browning heavy machine-gun, with a section of railway line welded across the front of the car for barrier clearance.

In July 1972 we drove up to the Liverpool docks, where Robert O'Cahan had landed 130-odd years before, and got on board a foul-smelling troop-ship going in the opposite direction. And from the moment we docked at Belfast, we knew we were entering a war zone. We could feel the menace as we unloaded our kit, and had for the first time the uncanny sensation of knowing that somewhere nearby snipers were watching us, training their gunsights on our backs.

Few people in the army actually volunteer to go into

action but most soldiers need confirmation that they can react sensibly under fire. In short, they want to be tested. So although we were all fearful of what lay ahead, we were secretly pleased to be in the thick of things. Nothing, though, compares to the sobering effect of sitting in an armoured vehicle, surrounded by live ammunition, knowing that exercises are over and this is real.

The machine-gun in the commander's turret was capable of shooting right through a building and had 200 rounds of live ammunition hanging from it. The spare bins were full of more rounds.

Our submachine-guns were fully loaded, with spare magazines taped back to back for quick reloading, and the grenade-launchers were primed. In my belt was a 9mm pistol.

I put what few possessions I had brought with me in my room in a prefabricated hut at Aldergrove Barracks, where we were based, and then checked in at squadron headquarters. The next morning, when I reported in for my patrol briefing, the squadron leader, John Rawlings, looked sombre. He told me that a fellow officer, a man I knew well, had just been killed.

'How?' I asked.

'Sniper got him with an Armalite. Armour-piercing, passed through the turret armour, through his temple, bounced off the inner wall of the Ferret and went through the driver's shoulder.'

'How's the driver?' I asked.

'He remained conscious long enough to drive the car to the hospital then passed out. He'll be okay.'

'Christ, John, I had dinner with him only the other day' was all I could say.

I was given my patrol orders and went to the hangar for last-minute checks, so vital when your life depends on everything working correctly. I gave the order to mount up and we set off on our first patrol in a formation that enabled our arcs of fire to cover one another. We very soon had to deal with our first sectarian killing. The troop corporal and I stared at the body lying at our feet by the side of the road. There was a small, neat hole right between his eyes.

'It's funny how there's a blue stain around the hole,' the corporal said.

'Powder burns,' I said absent-mindedly. 'They must have held the gun right against his skin.'

I lifted the man's body up and the whole of the back of his head fell away and splattered into the gutter. As we waited for the Red Cross wagon, I thought about what had happened. I'd always wondered how I'd react to the sight of my first dead body. I'd been worried I might lose control in front of my men. But when the moment came, I was surprised to find that it was an impersonal feeling, just business. It was only when the bodies belonged to people you knew, or to helpless children, that personal emotions began to emerge.

Some days later, I experienced another first: my first IRA riot. These were organised with cynical, calculated precision. The so-called 'protesters' would be arranged with women and children massed at the front, to act as a human shield for the gunmen who were positioned right behind. From the IRA's point of view, it was a no-lose strategy. If we held our fire, for fear of hitting the civilians, the gunmen could march up to us, completely unopposed. If, on the other hand, we lost our discipline and shot at the chanting, stone-throwing mob, then the IRA's political allies could claim that they were the victims of an atrocity.

But make no mistake, the IRA were out to kill us – and me, a fellow Irishman. They would station men in the houses on either side of the route down which the protesters would march. With more gunmen at the back of the march, this created a three-sided killing zone, a bit like a funnel, into which the troops would be drawn. We lived with an ever-present fear of snipers and we very soon learned that a sharp 'crack', as opposed to a 'bang', meant that a bullet had just passed over our heads and we had only a millisecond before the reloaded round would be on its corrected trajectory.

One day, having returned from one of our patrols, I jumped out to let the mechanics prepare our Ferrets again for the next 'crash out'. Sitting on my commander's seat, the sergeant major exclaimed, 'Jesus, you were lucky today, sir.' Turning back, I saw him rubbing his finger over the tip of a bullet that was protruding from the inside armour.

'Armour-piercing Armalite,' he said. 'Must have hit an inconsistency in the metal that stopped it going right through.'

If anything made me realise that survival depends on luck, then this was it. That bullet didn't have my name on it but the next one could and the same went for all of us. There was nothing I or anyone else could do about it.

This being Ireland, there were always a few funny moments. One useful little gadget on the Ferret armoured cars was an induction coil that, when switched on, pumped a huge voltage through the armour. The idea was to get rid of any unwanted passengers. During one riot an irate protester whipped out his penis and peed on one of the armoured cars to demonstrate his contempt. Quick as lightning, the commander threw the switch and the massive current was conducted back up the golden stream, straight to the place from which it was flowing.

The man was gripped by uncontrollable convulsions. He started shaking the weapon of his contempt so violently that it looked like he might pull the whole thing off. Finally, the pee stopped flowing, the current was broken, and one sorry rioter went hobbling off down the street, muttering incoherently and apparently unaware that his battered manhood was still hanging out of his pants.

That kind of story, to be told over many celebratory drinks back in the officers' mess, was a rare break from a conflict that was growing bloodier and more ruthless. For nights on end we would return from patrol to throw food down our throats before getting some sleep, only to be woken up an hour or so later to deal with a 'situation'. The men never complained and just kept going on autopilot. Whenever we could stop somewhere safe for ten minutes or so, we would curl up on the vehicle batteries or against the ammo boxes and get some kip.

When serious riots were building up, the troop would be held back in reserve until the order came to go in. This waiting period played havoc with our nerves and I found that I needed a pee every five minutes. But as soon as the order came and we were going in, we totally forgot our nerves and became the professionals that we were expected to be.

I escaped from Ulster without a scratch, but there were countless close escapes. Just before our tour of duty ended some joker dropped a bomb on the back decks of my Ferret as I was passing under Elizabeth Street Bridge in Belfast. My dinner jacket, stowed in an ammunition bin (well, one never knew when formal wear might be required), was riddled with holes and the headphones and beret on my head were blown away. If I had been an inch higher out of the turret I would have lost the top of my head instead of just what was on top of it.

Iron Curtain, Green Line

MONTHS OF CONTINUAL DANGER IN NORTHERN Ireland were followed, as is the army way, with six more months of naff-all in barracks at Tidworth. Then, in June 1973, we were on the move again, this time to Germany.

Thirty years ago, the Soviet Union seemed impregnable. No one could have imagined that the communist occupation of Eastern Europe would be over in fifteen years, without a shot being fired. Tens of thousands of British and American troops were based in Germany, waiting and training for World War Three. And the front line was the border between East and West Germany, part of the infamous Iron Curtain.

Our sector of the border was in the mountain region of Bad Harzburg, about 120 miles due west of Berlin, and was snow-covered for much of the year. I was given command of a border patrol. Having done the same job in Hong Kong, I thought I knew what to expect. I piled my men into two Land-Rovers, loaded up with submachine-guns, cold-weather gear and cross-country skis and set off for the border. A few miles short of our target we got out. The last bit of the journey was done on foot. So we trudged through the snow and then, finally, we came to our destination – and gasped in sheer astonishment.

The enormous, intimidating fence ran like a jagged black scar across the snowy landscape. At regular junctures, the fence had 'goon towers' filled with machine-gunners hungrily searching for an excuse to spit their message of defiance to the world. The fence stopped for nothing, ignoring natural barriers and even dividing villages in two, like an axe splitting a piece of wood.

As we got closer, the layout of the actual border became apparent. Standing on high ground, we could look down and see each line of defence that the Red Army and its East German vassals had erected. The first sign of the border, for anyone trying to reach the West, was a concrete road. This was for rapid deployment if there was an escape attempt. Jeeps and their crews were kept on a state of permanent alert in underground bunkers every three miles. Then there was a ten-yard stretch of earth that was kept raked to check for footprints. Next was a single strand of wire to which an angry, half-starved German Shepherd was shackled on a running leash so that it could attack any escapees. Then came a line of anti-tank obstacles followed by a section of minefield. The fence itself had high-voltage wires through it, alarm wires and anti-personnel grenades that looked like innocent plastic bicycle horns but spewed a deadly blast that could shred a human body. The proper West German border was another ten yards the other side of this fence and was marked by simple concrete posts every fifty yards or so.

The sheer effort that had been put into this fortification took our breath away. I simply couldn't imagine how anyone could escape through it all. But, as we would soon discover, there were plenty of East Germans who were desperate and determined enough to try.

At least in Germany, as opposed to Hong Kong, our job was to welcome asylum-seekers and not to send them back. Occasionally the border alarm would go off, telling us that someone had tried to get over the fence. We would race to the point, hoping that we could be of some help. One night, we watched a scene from *The Great Escape* brought to life in front of us as a man raced across the minefield on the far side of the fence. We willed him on, our hearts pounding, our mouths bone-dry with tension, praying that he would make it, but expecting his legs to be blown off at any moment.

Miraculously, the man got through the mines, but now the German Shepherd was after him, hurtling down the wire to which its leash was attached. The salivating dog, its teeth bared like the fangs of a wolf, was gaining on the man with every stride as he desperately raced for the shelter of the anti-tank obstacles. We could hear the growling of the dog, the pounding of feet on the ground and the desperate gasps as the man tried to drag more air down into his burning lungs. He threw himself over the last few yards as the dog was suddenly jerked to a standstill, unable to stretch its leash over the metal and concrete obstacles.

Now, though, the stakes were ratcheted higher again. The alarm had been raised, and we all knew that the 'crash-out team' of East German guards would already be on their way. The man had about fifteen seconds before they got to him and shot him dead. Obviously exhausted, but dragging his body to the limits of his endurance, he threw a flimsy rope ladder over the fence. A blast of explosives ripped through the cold air as the grenades on the fence exploded. But when the smoke cleared the man was still there, huddled at ground level, right up by the fence, too low for the blast to kill him. Someone must have given him inside information about the wall's defences, a serious criminal offence in the totalitarian East German state.

The man got up again and started climbing his little ladder. But now the guards arrived. As the man clambered up the fence with agonising slowness, soldiers were tumbling from their vehicles and cocking their weapons.

We could see them getting ready to fire, but there was nothing we could do. Shooting at the other side, from their border would be taken as an act of war. But before his pursuers could shoot, the man flung his coat over the razor wire on the top of the fence. Driven by adrenaline and desperation, he hurled himself over, lacerating his clothes and skin on the razor wire, then landed on the ground on our side of the wall.

Even now, his escape was not complete. East German territory extended for ten more yards on the western side of the fence, and we were not allowed to set foot upon it. But nor could their troops move one inch on to our side of the line.

So now we were in a stand-off, a deadly game of chicken. The East German soldiers kneeled in the firing position and aimed their guns at the man, and us. I gave my troopers the order to do the same. A tense, electric silence fell on us as we waited to see who would lose their nerve first, break their orders and start a deadly firefight.

Meanwhile the man lay between us, his chest heaving, his breath coming in little sobs. I wondered how good his inside information really was. Did he know the rules of the bizarre, yet deadly, game we were playing? All he had to do was cover the last few yards of ground, get to the concrete posts that marked the actual border, and he would be safe.

The seconds ticked by. The eyes of the gun-toting soldiers tightened with fear and tension. Suddenly, the man made his move, dashed for the border and collapsed at our feet, weeping helplessly. The East Germans kneeled there for a few seconds more, still in the firing position. Then their officer barked a command. They stood up and moved away. A man had come in from the cold and both he and we had lived to tell the tale.

Of course, there are some things in life more frightening for a soldier than an escape over the Iron Curtain. Like a royal visit, for example.

The colonel-in-chief of our regiment was HRH The Princess Anne. She was twenty-four years old, newly married to Captain Mark Phillips, just two years away from an Olympic gold medal and, in every sense of the word, an extremely fit woman.

Naturally, such a lovely princess would require a presentable young officer to be her aide-de-camp (a fancy term for a personal assistant) for the duration of her visit. This ADC would have to be impeccably behaved, reliably efficient and, above all, guaranteed not to do anything daft. The finest minds in the 14th/20th Kings Hussars considered the problem. And Lieutenant Lord Brocket was deemed just the man for the job.

There was frantic preparation for the visit. The regiment would be on parade and the correct way to address HRH had to be impressed on the men. Corporal Grimshaw, one of my troop's great characters, who sported a full handlebar moustache of which any Victorian Hussar would be proud, asked, 'Sir, what should I do if she sort of stops, like, and says something to me? Like when she comes round the tank park to see us? Do we curtsey or something?'

I explained that it was not the done thing for burly great soldiers to curtsey. 'Just stand to attention, give a slight bow of the head and answer her question, adding "Ma'am" at the end.'

Since I was her ADC, the princess wanted to meet my troop. They lined up on parade and she went down the line. She stopped in front of 'Chalky' White, a tough, battle-hardened trooper, rarely seen without a fag hanging from one corner of his mouth, who had served with me all the way from Hong Kong to Bad Harzburg. As they exchanged a few words it suddenly struck me that I had not given him any instructions about how to greet a member of the royal family. And surely he couldn't make the same mistake as Grimshaw? I mean, he couldn't possibly . . . actually . . . and then he did. His knees bent, his hands fluttered by his side, his head bobbed, and cavalryman Chalky White give a perfect, ladylike little curtsey.

The royal visit entailed trips to see several military and civilian installations. The princess was as forceful and unabashed as her reputation suggested. At one of our destinations, we were overrunning the time set aside for her visit. 'Ma'am, we must leave here now,' I said. 'There's another school to visit, and all the children are waiting.'

Her Royal Highness gave a sigh and muttered, 'Not another fucking school!' All the troopers in earshot gave an approving smirk: they liked the idea of a princess who spoke their language. When we got to the school, of course, the princess received her flowers with a charming smile, was attentive to one and all, and did her stuff in admirably professional style.

The visit ended with Princess Anne joining the regiment on exercise for a live firing demonstration. For all our laid-back attitudes, the regiments in the armoured corps secretly took soldiering very earnestly and we were proud of our legendary ability to hit a target with speed and precision. So this was a serious display of our nation's military firepower. But there was no reason not to have a cocktail party while we were at it.

Our sergeant major, 'Singe' Powell, set up an officers' mess tent on the edge of some woods and organised supplies of champagne. It occurred to Singe that Her Royal Highness might like to powder her nose, and she could hardly be expected to use the bushes and holes in the ground that sufficed for the rest of us, so he erected a special royal loo.

This consisted of a standard army latrine – a hole in the ground some five feet deep, with a 'thunderbox' over it – to which Singe had added a sophisticated, feminine touch: a hessian screen that he had painted pink to preserve the princess's modesty.

That, though, was not quite the end of Singe's inventiveness. On a noisy firing range, a Tannoy system is a vital safety feature to guarantee communication. So a Tannoy speaker was removed from the range, placed halfway down the hole and attached to a microphone via a cable covered with leaves. Singe stood by the microphone, expectantly, like a commentator waiting for a race to begin.

We had our drinks, the inevitable moment arrived and the pink loo was visited. Singe waited for a moment for the royal bottom to settle upon its throne. Then he spoke into the microphone and his indignant voice emerged from the speaker, deep in the bowels of the earth: 'Oi! D'you mind, ma'am? We're still digging down 'ere!'

Her Royal Highness leaped up like a cork exploding from a bottle and her head popped up above the top of the hessian screen. For a second we feared we might be in for one of those fearsome royal scowls that she has inherited from her father. Frankly, we probably deserved it. But, to her great credit, the princess saw the funny side, burst out laughing and joined us all for lunch. So far as the regiment's officers were concerned, she'd displayed humour, pluck and a thoroughly down-to-earth attitude. We were mightily impressed by our colonel-in-chief.

Having undertaken one official duty, I was now called upon to do another. The chief constable of the Hertfordshire Police thought it would be a good idea for his county's youngest peer to take the salute at the passing-out parade for his latest batch of police cadets. I was given leave to go back to England, put on my smartest dress uniform, complete with ceremonial sword, and inspect my county's coppers-to-be. 'Youngest peer takes salute', reported the local paper, adding that I gave a brief speech in which I declared that, 'As members of the force, you will have the very important job of upholding the law and defending the freedoms of the British people.' Little did I know how seriously they would take my advice, or how personal the consequences would be.

I was ordered to Berlin where I found myself part of the guard at Spandau Prison, Berlin, where the only prisoner was Hitler's old deputy, Rudolf Hess, the man who'd parachuted into Scotland (perhaps at my grandfather's invitation: who knows?) more than thirty years before.

Spandau Prison was an imposing orange brick building in the Western sector. As I gazed down from the guard office at the jail's solitary inmate, an old man tending the plants and flowers that were his greatest joy, I could not help but feel sorry for him. Whatever his crimes as one of the founding fathers of Nazism, his presence here had little to do with justice and everything to do with power politics. As long as Hess lived, the Russians could demand a share in guarding him. And so long as they had men in Spandau Prison, they had an official foothold on the Western side of the Berlin Wall.

Rudolf Hess finally died in August 1987, aged ninety-three. Barely two years later, communism collapsed, the wall came down and the mighty Soviet empire disappeared. Spandau Prison was demolished. Today the visitor can see no evidence of any of this. It is almost as if I imagined it all. It is, perhaps, proof that events unfold in ways that are often completely unpredictable. But then, who'd have guessed that twenty-odd years after I was in one jail, guarding a prisoner, I'd be in seven other jails, being guarded as a prisoner myself?

In the meantime, off we went for one last overseas posting, this time to Cyprus, which the Turks had invaded in August 1974. By the end of the year, half the island was in Turkish hands and half in Greek. The so-called 'Green Line' between the two sides was patrolled by United Nations forces. So we slapped some white paint on our Ferret armoured cars, put on our blue UN berets and set off to the eastern Mediterranean for guaranteed sunshine and almost certain action: just what a soldier likes best.

When we reached Cyprus, we were told the rules. The Green Line was divided up into sectors, each allocated to a troop of UN soldiers. Within his given sector, the troop leader could patrol in any way he saw fit but his main objective was to report any incidents, react to them if possible and ensure that the Green Line was not moved forward by the Turks, who still had designs on the half of the island they had yet to conquer.

That seemed simple enough – or would have been if this had been a purely British army operation. But all our objectives had to be carried out within the remit of the UN, and this was the core of the problem facing the UN both then and now. My lads were professional fighting soldiers, hardened by experience in Ulster and elsewhere. But of the forces alongside us, only the Canadians were also pros. The soldiers sent to Cyprus by the Swedes, Dutch, Irish and Danish were all civilians serving as part of their national service. And their response to the situations they encountered and the orders they were given was very different to ours.

The Swedish troop leader, who supplied me with fresh coffee, and the Dutch troop leader, who donated his tinned pâté, were good company. But one was a bank manager and the other ran a restaurant. Both had families to think about and as the Dutch restaurateur explained, 'If shit hits the fan, Charles, we will get the hell out of it.' We professional soldiers might regard casualties as an unfortunate but inevitable aspect of being part of an army. But casualties were certainly not part of his everyday life or that of his men and, understandably enough, they had no intention of changing that.

The inevitable result of this mixed-ability force was that the Green Line was a movable feast, except where the British and Canadian troops opposed the Turks. On one occasion, military intelligence wanted some pictures of a Turkish radar installation. I was known for being a keen photographer, so they asked me to bluff my way into the Turkish camp, take some pictures using my 900mm lens and sneak out.

I took two Ferrets on the mission. We cruised up to the main entrance of the base at a sedate 30 mph, with curtseying Chalky White at the wheel of my vehicle, only to find that the guard in the guard hut was dozing with his machine-gun across his lap. I quickly fired off a few pictures, said in the intercom, 'Okay Chalky, tread on it. We're out of here.'

We sped back down the road. But on the last left-hander, just before the Green Line, Chalky stamped on the brakes. Some 200 yards ahead of us, two Turkish battle tanks blocked the road, pointing their very big guns at us. And they were accompanied by a large detachment of troops.

There was no way out of this. We had no right to be there. The only thing to do was to play the dumb, lost officer, which my men would think came naturally to me anyway. I told Chalky to coast down to the road-block and he halted ten yards from our reception committee. I dismounted, went forward to the Turkish officer who seemed to be in charge and saluted. I was surprised to find he was a full colonel.

'What are you doing here?' he demanded in perfect English.

I put on my best chinless-wonder voice. 'Awfully sorry, old boy. I'm new to the island and a little lost. I say, is this a restricted area?' I said, feeling certain that they could not have seen me take the pictures.

Ignoring my question, the colonel said, 'Was there a guard on the gate when you went in?'

I wondered what the point of the colonel's question could be, but replied, 'Yes, there was.'

The colonel said nothing. He just pulled out his German-made Luger pistol, put it to the side of the head of the soldier on his left and shot him at point blank range. The soldier slumped to the ground, quite dead.

If this was meant to get my attention, it worked.

'My men will search your vehicles,' the colonel said. This was a statement of fact, not a question. The search took only a few minutes and when my camera was found it was given to the colonel, who asked me if I had taken any pictures in the area.

'No,' I said with great conviction as he opened the back and pulled the film out to expose it.

The colonel handed the camera back to me and looked me in the eye. 'Don't come back here again,' he said. Then he gave a command and the tanks rumbled backwards, clearing a space in the road. We drove on, past the dead soldier lying in the dusty road, with his blood and brains splattered across the tarmac.

All along the Green Line, the two forces were poised in an edgy, angry stalemate. The local Turkish commanding officer, a difficult and aggressive character, decided to teach us a British lesson by mounting a full-scale advance over the border.

I knew that it was coming, and I knew I ought to alert UN HQ. I was rather loath to do this, however, because I knew that the UN would almost certainly back down. Besides, our four .30 Brownings packed a hell of a punch. They could go through half a dozen people at once, as well as through light armour.

As I was wondering what to do, a Turkish officer in a Land-Rover came forward from his lines with a white flag.

'Jesus, that's a bad sign,' I said out loud to no one in particular. 'We haven't even started anything and they're already surrendering.'

The officer came up to me, saluted and said very firmly, in a tone that invited no argument, 'You will move or you will be killed. You are now in Turkish-controlled Cyprus.'

'I'm afraid that won't be possible,' I said. 'The Green Line stays where it is. Those are my orders.'

'Then you will all be killed,' he said.

The officer left in a cloud of dust and I muttered, 'Well, it's shit or bust.' Then, more loudly, 'Mount up, everyone.'

The clearing in front of us was some 500 yards wide, with scrubby woodland either side leading all the way up to the Turkish line. That was the direction from which the attack was bound to come, since the woods were virtually impenetrable. It also presented us with a natural killing ground. Perfect Ferret country.

We formed up in our standard formation: two Ferrets in the middle, two parked in the woods, to cover us from the flanks. I told the men, 'No firing until I give the order, even if we are shot at. We don't have enough ammo for a big scene, so every round must count.'

I told Chalky White to drive my Ferret up and down our lines. Guns were cleaned and rechecked. We had been doing this for an hour and a half when there was a tremendous crashing noise as a group of bushes on the Turkish line were flattened to reveal an entire company of infantry on foot backed up by an assortment of armoured vehicles and crews carrying anti-tank rocket-launchers.

'Oh, shit, you've done it now, sir,' said Chalky from the driver's hatch.

We parked the two middle Ferrets facing the Turks, making it clear that we were not going to budge. The Turks moved into our killing zone and stopped some 200 yards from us, and for a moment I thought they were going to fire. After a moment the commander, a major, drove up to me, across the open ground, in his armoured car.

I waited for him to stop. But he did not. Instead, he rammed straight into the Ferret. The impact threw me forward, smashing my nose into the turret armour. As blood streamed down my face, the major got down from his vehicle, with his pistol drawn.

'Christ,' Chalky whispered. 'He's going to shoot us.'

Chalky reached for his submachine-gun stowed on his right.

'Don't do anything. Just sit still,' I told him, but I cocked my pistol, all the same.

The major stopped and ordered, 'Move your vehicle.'

'No,' I said.

In pure rage the major blasted his pistol, emptying his magazine into our tyres. As the shots rang out in the hot, dusty air, I prayed that the men in the other Ferrets wouldn't take this as an order to open up. If they did, there was going to be a blood bath.

'Chalky,' I said, 'drive forwards ten yards and then back again, just to show him that these are "runflats" and we don't give a fuck.' Chalky obeyed the order, chuckling as he did so.

The major then came alongside my turret. Through clenched teeth he said, 'If you do not move you will be shot to ribbons.'

'Major,' I said, 'if you look into the woods you will see two Ferrets with their Brownings pointing right down your lines of infantry. One word from me in this microphone and most of your men could be killed. You may kill us, too, but at what cost?'

The major listened to me in silence, then he stormed back to his vehicle and within a few seconds two detachments of his men scurried off towards the two other Ferrets, parked up in the woods.

The major turned to me with a triumphant smirk. 'Now what do you say? Your armoured cars are surrounded by my men!'

Just then, a voice came over my radio from one of the Ferrets. 'I have a Carl Gustav [anti-tank rocket-launcher] pointed right at me. Over.'

'How far away is it? Over,' I replied.

'About nine fucking feet. Over.'

'No need to worry, then. They won't fire. They'd be killed in the blast if they did. Out.'

'Thanks a fucking bunch.'

That frank exchange of views between a junior

officer and a sergeant happens to be recorded for posterity on official United Nations tape. For, unbeknown to us, this radio transmission had been intercepted by UN HQ, who were suddenly shaken from their usual deep lethargy.

Moments later I got another message, this time from HQ. Helicopters were on their way with the UN commander on board, accompanied by various other top brass.

Within minutes the air was alive with choppers as the UN general jumped out. I dismounted and saluted him. I briefed him on the situation and strongly suggested, as much as a humble lieutenant can suggest anything to a general, that the Turks should withdraw, call it a jolly interesting manoeuvre and go home.

After much gesticulating and shouting that is exactly what happened. As we went back to our positions I was proud of my men and their calm, unflinching professionalism.

I'd now been in the army for five years. I would happily have made it my career. But I had other work to do. My inheritance was calling. I was needed at Brocket Hall.

And so, with great regret, I resigned my commission and said my farewells to the men. I flew to Heathrow with a letter in my pocket that I will always value. It was from the colonel of the regiment, Colonel Forte Allen. It said how sorry he was that I was leaving the regiment and ended by remarking that if I did not drive everyone mad I was classic material to make a general. General what, he didn't say.

– 7 –

Claiming My Inheritance

I CAN'T SAY THAT I HAVE A TREMENDOUS AMOUNT of respect for judges. None of the ones that I have come across have done me any favours. In fact, they've gone out of their way to make my existence as difficult as possible. And the first judgement I encountered, no one could make head or tail of.

As you remember Ronald Brocket, the golfing, shooting (alleged) Nazi sympathiser had decided that it was not enough to persecute his oldest son and his grandchildren while he was alive. He wanted his vengeance to extend beyond the grave as well. So, shortly before he keeled over dead from a heart attack while shooting on the grouse moors of Scotland, leaving a widow and two surviving children, he drew up a will that was specifically designed to exclude my father's side of the family – in other words, my brothers and me – from any of the family's property or wealth.

He had, of course, already dismembered one family

trust and spent the proceeds on assorted stately piles in the UK and Ireland. But, there was still the first, 1921 Trust, which contained the actual Brocket Hall estate. The entire estate amounted to roughly 5,000 acres.

Think of it like an archery target. In the middle was the bull's-eye: the house itself, its immediate surroundings and outbuildings. Next came an inner ring of about 1,500 acres, split between 900 acres of beautiful but entirely unproductive parkland, which cost a fortune to maintain, plus 600 acres of semi-productive land, rented out to a protected tenant. Finally, there was an outer ring of 3,500 acres of prime farmland, whose income would normally go towards the upkeep of the house.

My grandfather repeated his old trick of dismissing existing trustees, replacing them with his wife and getting her to sign any paper he put beneath her nose. He left the 3,500 acres of farmland to my uncle David. The house and parkland, however, he left to the National Trust.

But there was just one tiny problem: the Hall wasn't Grandpa's to leave. Whether he liked it or not, it was held in trust for all future Lord Brockets. And my grandfather did not own the trust. He was merely the beneficiary – as he certainly knew, being not only a Brocket but also a qualified barrister, who perfectly well understood the legal status of trusts.

None of this meant anything to me, of course. When I became Lord Brocket, I was a schoolboy of fifteen. The first indication I had of the depth of the family split had come during the school holidays, just after I'd inherited the title. My mother sat me down, told me what had happened, and showed me some letters, all tied up in a large bundle, between my father and grandfather. She felt it was her duty to let me read them, though it clearly upset her. She was far too self-controlled to cry in front of her son, but I could see how deeply she'd been hurt by it all. For my own part, I was utterly shocked that any parent could cut themselves off from their child as my grandfather had done.

Within a year of his death, the will appeared and the full extent of his intentions became clear. My mother was incensed. She went into action, determined to challenge the will and regain my inheritance. She hired Gilbert Rowberry, the lawyer who had successfully helped my father sue my grandfather for the £60,000 to which he was legally entitled almost twenty years earlier. Essentially, this was the same fight, but on a much bigger scale. My grandfather had attempted to deny me something that he had no right to deny. The problem was proving it.

We did, however, have one stroke of luck. After my grandfather died, but before his will was formally read, the National Trust changed the rules under which they would accept property from individuals. They had noticed that the aristocracy were using bequests to the nation as a cunning means of dumping their huge, old, draughty stately homes, which cost a fortune to maintain, while keeping all the money-making bits of their estates for themselves. So the National Trust decided that they would only accept properties that were self-supporting.

'We'll take Brocket Hall,' they said. 'But we want £1 million to go with it.'

Naturally, I couldn't help them on that one. I was making a few bob selling disco systems and flashy bikes to Eton schoolboys, but it certainly didn't amount to a mill. So who would get Brocket Hall?

Teams of lawyers were rustled up by everyone concerned with the whole grisly business. Years went by, with m'learned friends pocketing vast fees in their usual way (I ended up with a legal bill for £70,000: enough, in the late sixties, to buy almost any house in London). Finally we put the case before a judge. He was, to put it mildly, a bit of a character.

The final judgement was so unintelligible, both in its writing and its delivery, that no one had the faintest idea what any of it meant. After the case was over, the judge shared a taxi back to his chambers with one of my trustees. When they got there, the taxi door was opened and the judge simply fell out of the cab and collapsed in a heap on the kerb. He was a rather large bloke, so the trustee had a seriously difficult time dragging him to his feet again and leading him, step by step, back to his chambers.

He got the judge in through the front door, only to discover that his office was on an upper floor. There was a very old, small lift, and because the judge was so big, there wasn't any room for anyone else to get in with him. So the trustee went to the building's porter, got him to put a basic wooden chair in the lift and they heaved the judge on top of it. Then they pressed the 'Up' button and went upstairs to meet the lift at the top of its journey.

But when the lift arrived and the doors were pulled back, they discovered that the judge had become hopelessly wedged between the chair, the sides of the lift and the floor. It took for ever to drag him out into the corridor. And this was the man deciding my fate.

It was now 1970, three years after my grandfather had died, and still nothing was settled. I was eighteen years old. I was curious to see the house that was causing all this fuss. My grandmother, meanwhile, was curious to see me. As I have only recently discovered, she had longed to see her grandchildren but had been forbidden to do so by my grandfather. Now that he was gone, she must have wanted to make contact: she invited me to lunch. Unaware of her motivation for seeing me, I paid my first visit to the house from which I took my new name: Brocket Hall.

I drove up the A1 from London and pulled off at the turn for Welwyn Garden City. Then I drove down a road bordered by a line of fifties ribbon-development housing and drab, scruffy fields. This did not seem like a very promising setting for a stately home. But then, on the right-hand side of the road, I saw two red-brick gatehouses astride the main entrance to Brocket Hall.

As I drove through the gate I suddenly, and quite unexpectedly, entered a very English vision of paradise. The drive fell away downhill, through rolling parkland, dotted with trees, towards a classical, Palladian bridge that spanned a narrow stretch of water between two ornamental lakes. Beneath the bridge, water tumbled over a weir in a frothy, silvery rush. Then the ground rose again and there, on top of a hill, on the far side of the lake, stood the house itself. The whole landscape was magically beautiful. The effect of entering it from such a dreary approach was as though one had been sitting in a bland, unexciting theatre, and then suddenly the curtain had risen to reveal a wonderful stage-set, half a mile deep.

Brocket Hall is not, I have to admit, as awe-inspiring as Blenheim Palace, Chatsworth or Castle Howard. There are no long colonnades, no massive classical porticos, no towers, domes or castle walls. It's a square, red-brick building. But precisely because it's not especially vast or intimidating, it's a proper, welcoming home. Even the colour of the bricks seems warm and reassuring. Some country houses feel like museums that you might want to visit. Brocket Hall feels like a house where you would actually want to live.

I thought it all looked breathtakingly beautiful. If you want to know my emotions at seeing my family home for the first time, the answer is simple. It was love at first sight.

I walked up to the door and was greeted by the one and only member of the domestic staff. She led me into a simple entrance hall, at the far end of which was a Roman arch. I walked through it and stopped short. The whole heart of the house opened out into a magnificent grand staircase, running up through the centre of the building in a real architectural extravaganza. Or, at least, what would have been an extravaganza if it hadn't all been painted plain white.

The absence of colour and the scruffiness of the paint (applied, I suspect, when the house was used as a maternity hospital during the war) gave the place a faded, almost ghostly air. This was made all the eerier by the sound of a piano, playing the strains of Tchaikovsky's *Swan Lake*, which floated on the air from no particular direction, almost as if the music were emanating from the fabric of the building.

I was led upstairs to my grandmother's first-floor sitting-room. She looked old and unwell, and by her side was a small, tinny speaker from which the music was coming. We ate a meagre lunch and then she showed me around the house. At last we came to the grandest room, the ballroom, which is known as the Saloon. In one corner was a Steinway grand piano. A frail, elderly woman was sitting at the piano, playing into a microphone that stood beside her. So that was the source of the music!

As I left Brocket that afternoon, I wondered whether I would ever live there. Despite her desire to meet me, my grandmother appeared to have remained utterly loyal to her husband's wishes and the legal action over my grandfather's will seemed bound for the Court of Appeal. That, though, was going to take even more time and money, and the prospect of yet more expense seemed finally to concentrate everyone's minds.

At last, the various parties got together to see if a deal could be sorted. My lawyer gently pointed out that Grandmother was technically guilty of a criminal offence for conspiring with my grandfather to empty the 1921 Trust, since her signature was on every document. She was told, 'Sort this out, or face the music.' Things became a little easier after that.

In 1973 the various parties signed a Deed of Compromise. It stated that Brocket Hall would be returned to the 1921 Trust. My uncle David agreed to give up any claim to the Hall, kept all the other properties he'd been left (including the 3,500 acres of farmland surrounding the Hall) and became a Brocket trustee. Weeks after my 21st birthday party, which was held at the Hall, my grandmother moved out and went to live in a small flat in Mayfair, which she filled with mementos of her former life. She lived a sad, lonely, diminished existence there, before dying of cancer. Finally, I became the beneficiary of the family trust, although all that now remained was the house, its contents and its surrounding, unproductive 1,500 acres.

So there would once again be a Lord Brocket at Brocket Hall, just as my great-grandfather had always intended. My feelings when I inherited the place were mixed. I was thrilled, of course, but at the same time I was overwhelmed by a sense of responsibility. I knew that I had to find a way to pay for the place, because one thing was for sure: if I didn't come up with a bright idea the trust would go bust, Brocket would have to be sold and all the effort that had been made to recover my heritage would have been entirely wasted.

By the time the Brocket lawsuit had been sorted out, I'd begun my five-year stint in the Hussars. Whenever I could, I'd head back to Brocket. From our barracks in Germany, for example, the round trip for the weekend was 1,160 miles. I bought myself a Mercedes and ate up the miles on the *autobahn*, dashing for the Dutch coast and the ferry to Dover.

Life at Brocket Hall was far from glamorous. I moved my gear into my grandmother's old first-floor flat (the upper floors, I discovered, had been converted into three more flats and let out to tenants). There were only four, very basic bedrooms, but I had people to stay most weekends. Years of neglect had left the whole place totally overgrown. So every morning we men would don our combat gear, load up the tractor and trailer with chainsaws and attack the jungle that surrounded the Hall. Meanwhile, the unfortunate girls who'd been conned into coming along with the promise of a weekend at a stately home would be left to cook up enough food to quench the massive appetites worked up by a full day's worth of hard, manual labour.

By 1976, when I left the army, it was not enough just to spend the odd weekend at Brocket, larking about with my friends. I had to be there full-time. Ironically, though, when I landed back in England, the first person I met at the airport was another soldier.

Major Swannell had been hired along with his wife to look after Brocket Hall. Aside from them, the total staff for a massive house and a 1,500-acre estate comprised two woodsmen to manage the grounds, a daily for the Hall and an elderly maintenance man called Tomlinson. A splendid figure, with a magnificent, silver handlebar moustache, the major had won two Military Crosses (the second-highest soldier's medal, outranked only by the VC) during the Second World War. He had also been captured by the Japanese and treated with terrible cruelty in a prisoner-of-war camp, an experience that still gave him constant nightmares. He and his wife possessed a devotion to Brocket Hall that was equalled only by their patience towards its young master.

The major greeted me at the Arrivals gate with a great big smile that made his moustache shimmer up and down. Then he snapped to attention, as was his habit, asked how I was, and we drove off towards Brocket.

I had a strange feeling at the thought of finally taking up permanent residence and setting off down a very uncertain road. Failure was unthinkable, yet success would be hard to come by. My trustees and relations, ignoring the fact that our money had been made by creating a business from nothing, had acquired a very British dislike of trade. Yet I was sure that the solution, whatever it was, would have to be a commercial one. But as the car swept through the gates and the breathtaking beauty of the park and lakes unfolded before me I knew, without doubt, that this was a place worth fighting for. I would not let it go.

Before I could find enough money to run the house, I first had to make enough to live off. So I went to work for a London estate agent's firm. My salary was a princely £1,400 per annum and my daily transport was the estate's battered old Renault 4 van. This was a far more distinguished vehicle than it looked. Not only did it live in the garage of a stately home, but it frequently took me to debates at the House of Lords, where I was now entitled to sit.

The van's parliamentary appearances came to a sorry end when I returned from work one day. I rolled up the drive and came to a halt, with a satisfying scrunch of gravel, by the front door where the major was standing, ramrod straight, ready to greet me. He stepped forward to open the car door, pulled the handle ... and the entire door fell off its terminally rusty hinges and clattered to the ground.

It is at moments like these that the British show their true worth. The major did not flinch. In fact, he did not allow the slightest flicker of alarm, or even surprise, to cross his face. He simply saluted, wished me good evening, and led the way into the Hall, handing me a large gin and tonic which he had already prepared. Soon afterwards, I bought myself a motorbike and started going up to London on that instead.

Not for the last time, I became increasingly aware of the gap between people's perceptions of my situation and the truth. The public image was of a rich and privileged young lord, with a stately home and the world at his feet. The reality was a worried man, rattling around an increasingly rickety old house, wondering what on earth to do next. My low point came in the autumn of 1976.

The summer that year had been one of the hottest and driest on record – fantastic for sunbathers and cricketers, but no good at all for the old beech and cedar trees that had stood in the park at Brocket Hall since 1760. The trees' wood became parched and brittle for want of water. Their roots became loosened as the earth around them turned virtually to dust. When autumn announced its arrival with a blast of hurricane-force winds, they were helpless.

I had a large house-party staying when the storm hit. After dinner we gingerly stepped out on to the drive. My old army friend Richard Dashwood was swept aside like a piece of rag and two of the four great cedars that line the left side of the front lawn came crashing down. I was so cross and upset that tears ran down my cheeks. I just felt so powerless. The cedars were lying on their sides, almost in one piece, with their huge root structures intact and pointing forlornly to the sky. All they needed was a giant hand to reach down from the sky and stand them up again, like a parent picking up a fallen child, but everything bowed before that mighty wind that night.

The next morning we all stood on the front lawn and stared in silence at the devastation that surrounded us. After breakfast we got the one elderly tractor that we owned, slung the chainsaws in the trailer and started the long job of clearing up. But perhaps that hurricane, blowing away the old, was a harbinger of new life to come at Brocket Hall. For not long afterwards I had my first real money-making idea.

It struck me that the grand rooms at Brocket Hall were both very beautiful and very empty. No one ever used them. I thought they would make perfect back-drops for making films or taking photographs, particularly since we were so close to London. People could get here quickly, work in spectacular surround-ings and not worry about getting in anyone else's way.

I approached an agency in London called Locations Unlimited. Its boss, Annie Glanfield, was a delightful woman, who made a special effort to bring film business to the Hall. In no time at all we were attracting Hollywood icons such as James Mason and Bette Davis, and Britons ranging from rock stars such as Sting to theatrical knights such as Sir John Mills, Sir John Gielgud and Sir Ralph Richardson.

Suddenly, money was pouring in. Our basic fee for using the Hall was £1,000 a day, plus £100 overtime, plus extra charges for the use of telephones and electricity. I was soon making more in any one day at Brocket than I was paid a year for selling property in London. So I quit the job and devoted myself full-time to running Brocket. My dedication was total. In 1977, I even handed over my own bed so that Joan Collins could have cinematic sex on it during the filming of *The Stud*.

My grandmother must have been turning in her grave. I'd been using her old bedroom, still done up like a thirties boudoir, with pale yellowy-cream floral wallpaper, and matching flower-painted furniture. It wasn't the sort of decor you'd expect for a young bachelor, but redecorating my bedroom was the last thing on my mind. Someone must have thought that the room was just perfect for a seductress in suspenders, however, because Joan was soon looking absolutely spectacular, romping away in sexy lingerie for the camera's benefit. As the owner of the property, I reserved the right to observe any filming, to make sure no damage was done to the fabric of the house. Naturally, I felt it was my duty to pay particularly close attention to the filming of this particular scene.

Joan and I met again, more than twenty years later.

By then, she had swapped a career in low-budget British sex flicks for mega-stardom in *Dynasty*. I went up to her and said, 'Hello, Joan. The last time I saw you, you were having sex in my bed.' She didn't take very kindly to that!

Joan Collins wasn't the grandest actress to ply her trade at Brocket Hall. One of our early films was a re-make of *The Corn is Green* with Katharine Hepburn and Bill Fraser, directed by George Cukor. The shoot was due to begin one morning, but the cast and crew were late arriving, so I told the major that I was pop-ping up to the pub for lunch. When I got back I found the local constabulary about to carry off Katharine Hepburn, one of the greatest actresses in Hollywood history, under suspicion of breaking and entering.

Miss Hepburn, who was seventy at the time, had arrived at the Hall under her own steam and rung the front doorbell. Sadly, the intercom system was hope-lessly antiquated, and the major had not heard the bell. At this point, other actresses might have thrown a fit, and stormed back whence they came. But Katharine Hepburn was made of sterner stuff. She simply opened the kitchen window and started clam-bering in.

This had set off a burglar alarm, which summoned the police, who had arrived with admirable speed, as they did in those days. When I saw the great movie star in the grasp of the Hertfordshire constabulary, I asked what had happened.

Miss Hepburn said, with all the dignity that she

could muster (though she was spluttering with indignant rage), 'I told this officer, I am Ka . . . Katharine Hep . . . Hepburn and—'

The officer interrupted, 'Yes and if she's Katharine Hepburn, I'm Father Christmas.'

I could see the problem at once. It wasn't the prospect of being arrested that annoyed her, it was the fact that she had not been recognised by the man who had arrested her.

'Er . . . officer . . . I'm afraid she is Katharine Hepburn,' I said.

The policeman's mouth moved up and down like a stranded goldfish's. Finally, when his brain could form actual words, he gabbled his apologies and then added, 'Could I have your autograph?'

Brocket Hall soon became a favourite location for magazine fashion-shoots, as well as movies. So there were soon gorgeous, leggy models swishing about the place, as well as movie stars. Some of the models, however, weren't there to model the latest fashions.

One of the still photo-sessions was for a French magazine called *Lui*. I hadn't really paid much attention to the booking: it was just another name in the diary and another few bob in the bank. Then, at the end of the day, I wandered into the Saloon to find a well-endowed lady pianist sitting at the Steinway in a G-string and not much else.

The Saloon, of course, was the room in which Lady Caroline Lamb had been served up stark naked as the surprise dish at her husband's birthday dinner, so you could say that the topless pianist from *Lui* was just carrying on a fine tradition. Sadly, however, that was not the way my trustees saw it.

At the next trust meeting, under 'any other business', a trustee said that he had a very serious business to discuss. We all prepared ourselves for some bad news and he said that there had been some 'pornographic' photography in the Hall. He knew, he said, because, 'I have been put in possession of a copy of *Lui*.' We all wondered how.

I explained that I had not known that the magazine was even vaguely pornographic and that I would not let it happen again. It was not the last time that my elders' remarkable awareness of the contents of dirty mags would come back to haunt me.

From Supermodels to Sugar Creek

LUCKILY, MOST OF THE PUBLICATIONS THAT USED Brocket as a backdrop were a little more respectable than *Lui*. *Cosmopolitan*, for example, chose the Hall as the backdrop for a big photo-spread in 1978. At the beginning of the day, while everyone was still arriving, a willowy blonde girl came up to me and asked if she could use the telephone to call Paris. I was wearing a pair of old jeans and a green army sweater, so she assumed I was the gardener. She certainly didn't put on the kind of flirty, giggly, eyelash-batting act some models did when confronted with a twenty-five-year-old bachelor who had a stately home and title at his disposal.

There was something else different about this girl. Even by modelling standards she was outrageously beautiful. The day's work had yet to begin, so she wasn't wearing a scrap of make-up, but that just made her seem even lovelier, with the natural elegance of a young Grace Kelly. Statistically, I can tell you (having seen her modelling card), she was five foot nine tall. Her vital statistics were 33-24-35 and she took a size 8 or 10 dress. But who cares about numbers? This girl was utterly breathtaking, and her beauty scared the life out of me.

I may have looked like a total scruff. but she seemed frightfully sophisticated and worldly. We started talking, and she told me her name was Isa Lorenzo. She was nineteen. Her father was Cuban, her mother German, and she shared a Paris flat with a model called Andie MacDowell (the same Andie MacDowell who'd later star in *Four Weddings and a Funeral*). The more we talked, the more I realised that Isa did not have the been-there-done-that, blasé attitude that so many gorgeous girls possess. Quite the reverse, in fact: there was a real freshness about her. She came across as being very innocent, fragile, almost naïve.

I took her over to the old Bakelite telephone – a real antique, even in the seventies – that served as Brocket's contact with the outside world. Isa, who'd grown up in the United States, thought this was a charmingly old-fashioned touch. Then she gave me a look of supplication that made my heart pound, the same way it had when I was a boy of twelve, seeing my girlfriend Heather. 'I've taken out my contact lenses, to give my eyes a rest,' Isa said. Then she smiled shyly: 'I'm blind without them. I can hardly see the phone. Could you dial the number for me, please?' So I did. And then I asked her if I could write it in my address book, too. Yes, she said, I could.

A few months went by before I called her. I was incredibly busy at Brocket and Isa was working flat out. She was, I would later discover, one of the top five models in the world, regularly appearing on magazine covers, shooting commercials for cosmetic companies and commanding fees of thousands of dollars a day.

Finally, however, we made contact and she seemed pleased to hear from me. We met up, we made love. And then we settled into a funny sort of routine that was neither a simple friendship nor a full-blown romance – just something mutually convenient and pleasurable.

Isa and I would get together every few months, if she were in England, or I had the chance to go abroad. She was like a gorgeous golden cat. She loved to lie stretched out across a bed, or a floor, preening herself – almost purring – while I stroked her lovely, naked body.

Like any man, I loved the thought that this fabulous creature had given herself, however temporarily, to me. I loved taking her places and watching the looks on the faces as we walked in: the men goggle-eyed, the women trying to look cool, but casting envious, competitive glances from the corners of their eyes. Isa was a woman who made clichés come true. Rooms really did fall silent when she walked into them. Jaws would drop. And if she felt like a cat, so did I: the one who'd got the cream.

So why wasn't I passionately in love? Why wasn't I getting down on my knees and begging this astonishing woman to be with me all the time, for ever?

Looking back, we didn't have that much in

common. Isa certainly was not stupid. She had been planning to become a doctor until swept away by the instant success that followed her first few, light-hearted modelling assignments. But she liked to talk about the world she moved in: the prettiest dresses, the best designers, the hot new photographers, the smartest jewellers, the latest gossip from the fashion business. Those were all subjects about which I knew absolutely nothing.

And the same applied in reverse. I like to think I'm extremely imaginative, but my creativity is all to do with making things or starting businesses. I've always liked current affairs, politics, long conversations where you take an idea and ask, 'What if . . . ?' And that wasn't Isa's kind of thing at all.

So we kept our conversation light, pleasant, non-committal. We often laughed, because Isa was giggly and free-spirited. But we never argued, and that in a way said it all. We didn't really care enough to fight.

And there was something else. In those days, the English upper classes set very high store by the ability to 'muck in'. Money was far less important then than it is now, and – thanks to 98 per cent tax rates at the top end of the scale – there was much, much less of it about. So people didn't expect to be pampered. That was why my friends were perfectly happy to come to Brocket for the weekend and spend it up to their knees in mud and brambles. It was all a jolly good laugh and besides, primitive as Brocket was, it was no worse than most other freezing-cold, draughty, shabby stately homes.

Isa, however, came from a very different culture.

Her father had migrated to America from Cuba. Now he had a successful business making the metal cases for ballpoint pens. The Lorenzos were prosperous, rather than super-rich, but they still had a nice waterfront property in Merrick, Long Island, a smart suburb of New York, with a motor-boat tied to the jetty at the end of the lawn. Isa grew up taking comfort for granted, the way most Americans did then, and many British people do now. Once she had reached the top of the modelling tree, being paid an average $5,000 a day (a huge amount back then), she became even more accustomed to getting five-star, first-class treatment all the way.

I first realised the problem when I invited her to come sailing with me in the Greek islands, in the summer of 1979. We'd spent several weekends together by this point, without doing more than scratching the surface of our relationship. Now my old landlords from Applegarth crammer, Brian and Mary Brennan, had invited me to join them on their forty-eight-foot yacht. They said I could bring a friend, so I invited Isa and, to my delight, she agreed to come. We flew to Corfu, joined the boat and settled into a nice routine.

Every day we'd have a leisurely breakfast, explore whichever island we happened to be moored at, swim by the boat and then catch the afternoon wind to sail to the next island. We would then have dinner ashore, drink way too much retsina, and fall asleep on the deck in the early hours of the morning. All in all, it was a fine way to spend a summer fortnight and Isa loved the beautiful islands and the crystal-clear sea just as much as the rest of us. She made a fine sight, stretched out across the deck, sunning herself in her bikini, too.

But although the Brennans' yacht was a lovely way to get about the Adriatic and Aegean, it certainly wasn't luxurious. The rails of the boat were usually hung with the washing that Mary Brennan had hung out to dry: 'For God's sake, woman, we look like a travelling Chinese laundry,' Brian would yell as we sailed scruffily into port. There were times when alarming leaks appeared in the boat, necessitating emergency repair work by the on-board mechanic – i.e. me – to prevent us going down with all hands.

It was all great fun, if you like that kind of thing. But Isa didn't really, and I began to understand why when I got a taste of the life to which she was now becoming accustomed. For I was not the only man in Isa's life. She was also having an on–off affair with an immensely wealthy Italian called Carlo Cabassi. And life with him was very different indeed from what I could provide at Brocket Hall, or on my friends' sailboats.

Carlo was a typical Milanese playboy, from a wealthy family. He could buy Isa anything she wanted, take her anywhere she wanted to go. If she fancied an African safari, he could – and did – whistle up his private jet and fly her off to Angola or Kenya. And if that enabled him to pick up an uncut diamond or too, so much the better.

There was, however, a catch. Carlo Cabassi had a very Italian view of fidelity, which is to say he did not think it applied to him. Isa was not the only girl in his life. As I was about to discover.

One weekend, I flew to Milan to be with Isa. She had work to do in the city, negotiating with agencies who were bidding for her contract, and had borrowed a friend's flat for us to stay in. Cabassi invited us both to dinner at his apartment. 'Carlo and I have broken things off,' Isa had told me. 'But we're still very good friends and he wants to get me back.' Isa agreed to go straight to Carlo's from her final business appointment. So he sent a car to pick me up from the flat.

A large, armour-plated Merc pulled up outside our flat, and two men emerged carrying submachine-guns. For a second, I thought Carlo had ordered a hit on me. But then I realised that there were so many terrorists, anarchists, gangsters and kidnappers roaming round the country that heavy-duty protection was a must.

I got into the car and we drove to the large, old apartment building where Carlo lived. As the car slid past the electrically operated gates, and I was ushered into the lift, I felt as though I were being lured up to a deadly rival's lair. I entered the huge, lavishly decorated penthouse, expecting to be met by a slim-hipped, super-smarmy vision of Italian cool, only to find that Carlo was a chubby, friendly, welcoming man who went out of his way to make me feel at home. All the same, I was uncomfortably aware that he knew I was sleeping with his girl, and that he wanted her back for his exclusive pleasure.

What also became clear, within seconds of walking into Carlo's pad, was that he lived like a sultan. There were beautiful women everywhere, like sweetmeats laid out on a sumptuous buffet. But when Isa walked in, she made every other woman in the room look dumpy and plain. She was utterly spellbinding. As she later admitted to me, she knew that Carlo had a harem of girls, but that she was his favourite. He flirted with the others, made love to them as the fancy took him, but always returned to her.

For the next few days, I entered into Isa's and Carlo's world, as one party followed another, in yet another stunning apartment or house. Wherever we went, there were copious supplies of two commodities, women and cocaine – both equally free and equally available. Carlo spent his time doing his best to charm Isa, a gift that came sickeningly easily to him. As I watched him work, his line or argument became clear: a brief dalliance with an English milord was an amusing diversion for a beautiful girl, but her home was with him.

And he was probably right. Isa wanted to be admired and pampered. She often used to joke that 'I want a sugar daddy,' someone to give her all the finest things in life and indulge her love of fashion and shopping. With servants to take care of everything, she would never have to lift a finger. In return, she would be the ultimate arm-candy, a perfect wife and, in time, the gracious mother of beautiful children. For all his faults, that was what Carlo Cabassi could give her. But, of course, he wasn't going to change. All her luxury would have come at the price of knowing she would be constantly betrayed.

That, though, was not my problem: not yet, at any rate. Since she had no objection to the arrangement, I was perfectly happy to keep seeing Isa at irregular intervals, enjoying our time together and leaving it at that. It seemed to suit the way we both felt about each other and, more than that, she was so beautiful, so exotic, that I always felt that she was ultimately unattainable. A woman like that is like a living fantasy. You daren't let yourself care too much about her, because you can't imagine her being part of your everyday existence.

And speaking of my everyday existence, I remember once, in the early days at Brocket, my mother came across me by the drive, painting the white stones that ran along either side. I was wearing my usual jeans and army top. My mother was horrified. 'What are you doing?' she asked. 'You can't be seen outside like this. You must wear a three-piece suit.'

'I can't wear a suit to paint stones,' I replied.

My mother, however, was insistent. 'You must,' she said. 'It's what people expect.'

The major, my maître d', heard about this little exchange. 'A woman with fine standards, Lord Brocket's mother,' he declared. 'But not very practical.'

And that, in essence, was the trouble I faced when trying to find a long-term solution to the Brocket problem. All the time that models and actors were trooping in and out at £1,000 a day, I was racking my brain to find an even better way of using the Hall's existing assets – its location, setting and grandeur – as the basis for a profit-making enterprise. One obvious solution was to start a hotel. I reckoned I could fit thirty bedroom and bathroom suites into the building's upper floors. But what did I know about running a hotel?

My trustees, meanwhile, were trying to think like

nineteenth-century peers of the realm. They wanted me to go to Cirencester Agricultural College to learn the noble art of estate management. But my portion of the estate by itself was never going to provide the income needed to run Brocket Hall, no matter how many degrees in estate management I acquired.

The argument came to a head when I suggested that we should build a hotel elsewhere on the estate, so that the house itself would not be disturbed. Initially, the trustees approved the scheme and we applied for planning permission. But then they changed their minds and told me that if I didn't go to Cirencester they would withdraw the planning application. When I refused to go, they carried out their threat and withdrew the application. So now we had reached an entirely pointless stalemate. Without the trustees' consent, I could do nothing. But whether they liked it or not, I was in the Hall. Once again, my family was on the brink of tearing itself apart.

Looking back, I think my grandfather's treatment of my father had put a sort of poison in the family. Everyone must have known, even if they did not want to admit it, that a wrong had been done and that some people had profited from that wrong. With that knowledge came guilt, and with that guilt, perhaps, resentment: no one, after all, appreciates feeling bad.

Finally, after endless arguments, I persuaded the trustees to scrap their plans for packing me off to Cirencester and let me go to America instead, to see how they ran leisure and tourism businesses over there.

I travelled the States from New York to Florida,

right across to California, and everywhere I went the atmosphere was vibrant, full of hope and possibilities, a total contrast to the economic gloom and overbearing pessimism that permeated England in the seventies. Americans felt that anything could be done if you wanted to do it badly enough. Faced with a new idea, we'd think of a million silly reasons why it couldn't work. They'd concentrate on the one good reason why it would.

When I wandered into American companies, all wide-eyed and gormless, carrying my folder filled with pictures of Brocket Hall, people didn't say, 'Go away. I can't be bothered.' They tried to find ways of helping me out. As I travelled around, I made contacts who would generate huge amounts of business for me over the following years. And I noticed the development of a new kind of hotel, known as a 'retreat'. Instead of renting out rooms to lots of individual guests, retreats catered for one client at a time.

Any organisation that needed somewhere private and undisturbed for its conferences could simply hire the entire place. That way, no one else could get in their way, or spy on them, or even object if things got a little loud over dinner. And from the property's point of view, it was much easier to deal with a few big clients, who were guaranteed to fill the place, than have to worry about lots of little ones.

Now, I happened to have a large property that was twenty miles from central London, the heart of British business, finance and government. It was close to Heathrow, and there was even a private airfield just outside the estate. The 1,500 acres of grounds ensured total privacy. My thirty bedroom suites, upstairs, should be enough for most corporate needs. And there was plenty of space downstairs for conference-rooms. Best of all, the property would be free. So I'd be spared the single biggest capital cost that would normally be attached to a business of this kind.

The other lesson I learned was about the power of a brand. These days, everyone knows about branding. But in the seventies, Britain was still light-years behind America in understanding that kind of basic, competitive, business approach. So it came as a surprise to me when I visited an exclusive resort south of Houston called the Sugar Creek Country Club.

Sugar Creek consisted of luxury homes discreetly scattered round a golf course, with a fancy clubhouse slap-bang in the middle. First you made money selling the homes, then you made more by running the golf club. And the Sugar Creek logo was used on everything from the development's very own Sugar Creek Bank, to the Sugar Creek logos on the caps and golf umbrellas on sale at the club store. It suddenly struck me that I could brand Brocket Hall, just like Sugar Creek. At last, I knew how to save my family home.

— 9 —

A Girl with a Hammer

AS I SAT BACK IN THE TAIL END OF THE ECONOMY section of the TWA flight from Los Angeles to Heathrow I felt real excitement. For the first time since my first visit to Brocket I had a clear idea of what to do with the place and I knew that it would succeed. All that remained was to convince my trustees to let me do it, and a bank to finance my plans. When I thought of that, all my American, can-do optimism evaporated. I could just see the jaundiced look on the trustees' faces, as if to say, 'Not another bright idea.' And I could imagine the bankers who'd demand proof that the concept would work before they'd lend me any money.

At the next trustees' meeting, round a table in the library at Brocket Hall, I talked through my idea. I described the market for meetings venues and my belief that it was about to spiral. I pointed out how shoddy the facilities and services were at virtually all British hotels; that privacy was almost non-existent; that the needs of the people holding their conference were forgotten if the delegates were just a few among many guests.

I told them that Brocket Hall was perfectly suited to conferences. I pointed out that the fact that it was outside London, with no restaurants or theatres on the doorstep, meant that all the guests' spending would be on-site. I explained that staff could be hired on a part-time basis, keeping costs down. I underlined the massive advantage of free business premises. I put my heart, my soul and my passion into the proposal. At the end, there were a few harrumphs, lots of reasons why this might be far too risky for the Brocket trust to consider. And, by the way, please would I be a good boy and go to agricultural college?

Of course, there was another alternative. One of the trustees was a senior merchant banker called John Elton. In 1979, just as we were all arguing about what to do next, he announced that he thought he could secure a sale of the Hall and park for £7 million. Was I interested? He told me not to give an answer at that moment but to do so at the next meeting.

Seven million quid is a pretty handy sum of money today, but twenty-five years ago it was a massive fortune, especially for a young man of twenty-seven. Elton's offer was certainly tempting. But I thought of other young peers who'd inherited huge fortunes and still managed to blow the lot. I could see myself doing the same. Then I thought of Brocket Hall. I imagined making a go of it, and the satisfaction I'd get from filling the place with people and activity again. My decision was firm and I told the trustees that Brocket must not be sold.

To be fair, they accepted my decision and agreed to provide a small amount of capital to start the initial works. The lion's share, however, would have to be raised commercially from banks, who soon turned out to be as reluctant as I had feared to support a new idea. Then there was the tricky matter of planning permission. The local planning officer was surprisingly supportive of the plan but the left-wing firebrands on the council were far less inclined to help an aristocrat (bad!) make a profit (worse!) from his inherited stately home (appalling!).

While assorted British worthies competed to find reasons why the whole Brocket Hall scheme either could not work or should not be allowed to do so, I just got on with repairing and renovating the fabric of the house. And I soon discovered that eighteenth-century mansions are a lot harder to fix than your average suburban semi.

Part of the problem is the way these places are built. Imagine, for example, that you have a fine library, whose bookshelves and furniture were made by Thomas Chippendale himself, arguably the greatest furniture-maker of all time. A bit of this library's ceiling collapses, owing to a water leak in the room upstairs. You have to do something about this, because the library is one of only two in the entire world furnished by Chippendale and is therefore a priceless work of art in itself.

You take a look at the ceiling and find not the standard joists, boards and plaster, but a complex construction involving two layers of thatch, dried mud slurry, wooden laths, coated plaster and separately applied plaster mouldings. This provides fantastic heat and sound insulation, but it also traps water, allows fungus to grow, and then gives the fungus an easy means of spreading through the entire ceiling via all the hollow reeds from which the thatch is made.

So then you have to replace the whole ceiling, which means holding it all up on giant hydraulic jacks and in no time at all you've spent £7,500 in 1979 money: call it £50,000 today. And if that sounds bad, try changing a lightbulb. Or, in the case of Brocket Hall, a giant chandelier.

The chandelier in the Saloon, one of the finest in the country, was made by Perrys of Whitefriars in 1768. It weighs about 400 pounds (or 180 kilos, if you're metrically inclined) and has thirty-six candles. Problem: crystal chandeliers only have that magical, sparkly appearance when immaculately clean. And they're seldom as clean as you'd like because (a) the crystals attract dust like a magnet attracts iron filings and (b) it's jolly hard to clean a socking great chandelier fifteen feet above the ground. Obviously, it would be easier if the chandelier could be lowered to ground level. But how do you lower a chandelier that weighs as much as two fully grown men?

The answer I came up with was to go to my local commercial vehicle parts supplier and buy an electric winch designed for hanging broken-down cars off the back of recovery vehicles. We installed the winch in the floor space above the Saloon, re-hung the chandelier on the end of the winch line and soon the whole glittering monster was rising majestically up and down at the touch of a switch.

Meanwhile, using the skills learned from my time with Mr Robert's architectural practice in Bath, I had redrawn the layout of the second floor to create sixteen bedroom and bathroom suites. With a large felt-tip pen, I marked the walls that we could take out without the entire building collapsing. I then held a series of week-end parties where the only duty of the guest was to get suitably cranked-up on Pimms or cheap Italian vino, then grab a sledgehammer and demolish the felt-penned walls.

I had no idea how popular these parties would become. There's a natural vandal lurking deep within all of us and there were endless volunteers eager to inflict as much damage as possible. Revealingly it was the women who seemed the keenest to beat the living day-lights out of the place. Impeccably raised Sloane Rangers were suddenly given the chance to forget their duty to be sweet and charming and they rose to the challenge with gusto. One particular girl, whose beauty was legendary, smashed her way clean through a wall, stepped proudly through the hole, sledgehammer in hand, and flashed me a wicked, murderous grin. I made a mental note to treat her with more caution in future.

The sewers were another problem altogether. To start with, I wasn't sure that there actually were any. I knew that when the flush was pulled everything disap-peared. Where to, I had not the faintest idea.

A local surveying company quoted me many thou-sands of pounds just to map the pipes and sewers of the

Hall. But I didn't have that kind of money. So I did the only thing possible. I invited my poor, long-suffering friends to yet another weekend house-party. Then I sent the housekeeper out to scour the shops for miles around to find the maximum different varieties of coloured lavatory paper, while I hired a large number of walkie-talkies.

On the Saturday morning, I assembled my troops – sorry, guests – and explained the situation. There were fifteen operational loos on five different floors in the Hall. Outside in the grounds and around the Hall I had found about the same number of manholes. The furthest manhole was 400 yards away down by the lake. So which loos connected to which manholes? Or were they not, in fact, connected at all?

The problem could, I felt, be solved with use of the loo rolls and radios. The guests were split into two groups. The first lot were sent to stand by the loos with a radio and a roll of coloured paper each. The second lot had to stand guard by all the opened manholes, peering down into the drains. Then we started flushing the loos, one colour at a time.

As a former Hussar officer, I did the job with proper military efficiency. Speaking into my walkie-talkie, I'd give the order: 'Flush the pink paper!'

From somewhere deep in the bowels, as it were, of the house, a voice would crackle in my ear: 'Flushing now with pink paper. Over.'

There would then be a wait of as much as a minute while the flushed paper made its way along our mysterious pipework and then another voice would pipe up –

this time from out in the grounds: 'Simon here. Pink paper has passed through my hole. Over.'

I'd plot Simon's position on my map until I heard another voice: 'Richard here. Pink paper through my hole. Over.'

I'd duly plot Richard's position, link it with Simon's and the drill would go on until I had plotted the entire route that all the loos took and discovered two complete drainage systems, heading south and west of the house. Neither of them, though, would be able to handle the waste generated by a retreat hotel, with thirty bathrooms all in full use. So I plotted a new system that I knew I would have to build in the near future, finance allowing. And then, suddenly, after countless fruitless visits to British banks, finance actually did allow. Finally someone was willing to lend me money. Someone with 'American' in their name.

A man called Arthur Jordan, from the domestic banking side of American Express, drove out to see Brocket and stayed the night. At the end of it all he said, 'Three things are needed to make a success: a new concept, a niche market and location. You've got all three, and a fantastic house and park to go with it.' With these words he backed my proposal and gave me a loan of £326,000. I raised extra funds by selling some of the cottages on the estate (people claimed they were over-priced at £17,000: I bet they don't think that now). Now I had enough to start work in earnest and, what's more, the local authority granted me planning permission. At last it was all beginning to happen.

I was thrilled, but also apprehensive. I knew that this was my one and only shot at restoring not only the family seat but also the family fortunes. I knew that my idea was the right one and I knew that I'd get the job done with the finance available, even if I had to work every night to do so. I also knew that my family didn't expect me to succeed.

Their scepticism wasn't entirely unreasonable. Every single bit of the Hall needed renovating. The wiring, for example, had been installed in 1928 and was all encased in lead. The plumbing was one of the world's great mysteries. Within the main house, most of the pipes were made of old lead and had sprung leaks – invariably in the least convenient, hardest-to-get-to places.

The exterior woodwork of the Hall needed a coat of paint badly and many of the windows on the second and top floor had rotted completely. The roof was leaking and covered in broken slates. The guttering overflowed, and leaked water into the house whenever there was heavy rain or snow. The whole of the inside of the house needed new plasterwork, new lighting and new paint. And painting's not easy when you've got to slap it on a palatial stairwell three storeys high.

One of the decorators acquired the nickname 'Bish-Bosh' because, as he put it, 'There's so much fuckin' wall to paint that all I 'ear when I get home is the saahnd of me blinkin' brush goin' bish-bosh, backwards and forwards, all night fuckin' long.'

Everything was on a massive scale. The amount of

carpet we needed was so large that it had to be laid out on the front drive, cut up and then taken into the rooms. At one stage, most of the front drive area was carpeted. Just at this time a prospective American client drew up in front of the hall.

'Gee, now that is unusual!' he declared, with wide-eyed wonder.

'Not really,' I assured him. 'In England, we believe that all proper stately homes should have their drives re-carpeted every ten years.'

I didn't employ an architect or even a contractor. There wasn't enough money in the budget. Besides, I knew a bit about architecture, I knew a lot about keeping a troop of men busy and contented and since I was living on site, I could keep a check on the work and materials throughout the day.

My apartment was frequently left without power, light or hot water, and I had to do my cooking on a little camping-gas stove. But at least I didn't have to go far to see right through the building. Most of the time I was able to stand in my little dining-room and look up through two floors to see the roof above me, or down below to see the stone flags of the entrance hall. And the benefit of being so intimately acquainted with the project was that I got to know every square inch of Brocket Hall. I knew what was and was not possible, what worked best and how much it should cost. And I knew the men who could do it, too.

Other people, though, found the scale of Brocket Hall harder to grasp. One day, trying to decide whether our new central heating should be oil- or gas-fired, I wandered into the local Eastern Gas showroom and sat at the desk of an officious-looking woman with horn-rimmed glasses. She did not treat me like a valuable customer, but as a deeply suspicious individual who needed to be interrogated as fiercely as possible to prove himself worthy of state-owned gas.

'You're interested in gas heating?' she said, as though this was, in itself, a sign of a dodgy character.

'Er . . . yes,' I replied.

'Domestic or business?' she barked again.

Tricky question. It was my house, but it would soon be my business. 'Well, domestic at the moment but—'

'Domestic, then,' she said, cutting me off. Next she asked, 'Square footage of the premises?'

Oh Lord, I hadn't a clue. I did a quick sum in my head and said, 'About 85,000 square feet.'

The woman slowly removed her glasses and gave me a look of utter contempt. 'If you can't take this seriously then I don't see that I can help you,' she sneered. 'Next!'

So oil it was, then.

Finally, towards the end of 1980, Brocket Hall was almost ready to open its doors as a residential conference venue. All I had to do now was to equip the place with china, glass, cutlery, sheets, blankets, leather desk-sets, and all the branded items from laundry bags and 'Do Not Disturb' signs to enamelled boxes. Oh, yes, and the kitchen: I'd rather forgotten about that. I got in touch with a bunch of tasty characters who sold reconditioned, second-hand kitchen gear from under some railway arches in the East End of London. I turned up with a van, haggled as if my life depended on it and bought all the equipment for the princely sum of £2,000. 'Quality!' as they say in that part of the world.

A kitchen needs a cook. Enter Werner Newhold, an excellent Austrian chef. To cut down risk, I did not pay him a salary. Instead, he charged me for the meals he cooked and I then sold them to guests, with a mark-up to cover my expenses and profit. I had a similar arrangement with the wine suppliers. That way I would not incur any costs until bookings took place. As long as I kept my fixed costs down I could not fail to make a success of the business. Or so I hoped.

As well as Werner, I needed kitchen, household and office staff, and I was lucky enough to recruit a group of people whose enthusiasm and loyalty was the single biggest factor in Brocket Hall's success. We all knew we couldn't compete with established, five-star hotels when it came to the comfort of the rooms, or the slick professionalism of the service. We knew that Werner, however hard he tried, couldn't match the Michelin-starred chefs at the finest London restaurants. We knew we were only beginners.

But we could work harder than the competition, try harder to please our guests and go further to make their stay enjoyable. The attitude among the staff, who all referred to me as 'LB' (I was only 'Your Lordship' when we had guests to impress), was fantastic. Many hotels suffer from petty fiddles by the staff, but the team spirit at Brocket Hall was too strong for anyone to milk the system. We all knew that the enterprise was being run on a shoestring and this helped to bind us together. If mistakes were made we moved heaven and earth to rectify them and the clients knew it. After a while, it was almost as if our regular visitors had become part of the team. They were as determined as we were to make the place a success and would go out of their way to put more business our way.

The Brocket spirit was epitomised by Jean Lenderyou, who replaced the major as our maître d'. Originally hired by Werner as a waitress, she turned out to be the most wonderful organiser and diplomat, equally adept at rustling up precisely the correct number of staff for each event, or greeting guests at the front door and showing them to their rooms. Jean's welcome was so warm that she immediately endeared herself to all the guests and she was absolutely tireless. At one in the morning, she'd be cleaning out the fireplaces and relaying them. If a party went on into the early hours, Jean would supervise the whole affair, then keep on working through the next day despite our protests.

For the office side of the operation, I hired Felicity Buxton, a bubbly woman in her mid twenties who'd been working at Knebworth House, a nearby stately home known for its massive rock concerts. Felicity, or 'Flick' as everyone soon called her, was supposed to market Brocket and help in the office as I couldn't spell or add properly. But she was bursting with enthusiasm and ideas and would turn her hand to anything. Our approach to life was very similar and we hit it off right from the start.

Now that we were up and running, I had to rustle

up some business. To grab people's attention, I printed a brochure that was mostly photographs. I wanted something that would catch a PA's eye and make her show it to her boss. Then it had to be appealing enough to pique his interest. Shiny photographs would always do that better than words ever could.

But I didn't only stuff glossy booklets into envelopes. I got out and trod the pavements of the City, knocking on doors, taking every meeting I could, and never going anywhere without a briefcase filled with business cards and brochures. I just never knew when I might bump into a potential client.

Businesses weren't my only targets. It had struck me that Brocket Hall would make a perfect setting for political summits, so I badgered government departments as well. One day, Flick put down the phone at the end of a call and started leaping round the office, shrieking as happily as if she'd just won a jackpot. She'd been speaking to a colonel in the Foreign Office. He wanted to come and inspect Brocket to see if it would be an appropriate venue for a forthcoming European summit.

Flick gave the colonel a guided tour. As he walked around the outside of the building, he naturally examined all the doors and windows, to check the building's weak spots. Now, it happened that there was a photoshoot going on during the day: 'fashion' was how it was described in the diary. So there was no reason to worry as the colonel looked through the window, into the kitchen, where the fashion crew was working. Or so Flick thought.

Except that this was one of those occasions when 'fashion' wasn't really the right description of what the photographer had in mind. On the kitchen's centre table there was a blonde girl, wearing the traditional chambermaid's outfit. She had a white pinnie round her waist, a look of ecstasy on her face, and no knickers on her naked rump. Her backside was poking up in the air. Behind her was a man in a butler's uniform. He was wielding a large cucumber.

Flick saw our first government contract disappearing along with the cucumber. She did her best to carry on as if the scene on the kitchen table was somehow not really happening. But an army colonel is not an easy person to fool and anyway he's seen most things in life, so he doesn't get fazed by a spot of soft porn. He spared Flick's embarrassment by roaring with laughter. Then, calm as anything he asked, 'Will the same crew be on duty when the ministers are staying?'

I dare say he hoped that the answer would be 'But of course.'

After years of frustration, I was on the verge of real success. Then something happened that was to affect my life in years to come more fundamentally than I could possibly have imagined. One of the tenants in our upstairs flats had been an ex-Scots Guards officer, turned car-dealer, called Graham Duncan. Knowing that I shared his interest in classic sports cars, Graham had introduced me to an elderly motor engineer he knew called Jim Bosisto, who claimed to be an expert on Ferraris and Maseratis.

Graham had kept a couple of Maseratis at Brocket

Hall, and Bosisto had often been around the place, tinkering with them. Now he told me that he'd found a Ferrari in Bristol that was going dirt cheap. Bosisto suggested it would be a good buy and, flushed with the excitement of the progress we were making, I agreed.

The Ferrari was a dark metallic blue coupé. It was rusty. It was unreliable. But as I drove back from Bristol, feeling the quality of the car's handling and listening to the sound of its twelve-cylinder engine, I thought I was the king of the road. It was as if I'd been given a hit of some fantastic drug. I felt wonderful. I was completely hooked. From then on, I was a sports-car addict. And, as with so many addictions, it would prove to be my undoing.

Politicians . . . and their Daughters

WHAT WAS IT JANE AUSTEN SAID? 'A SINGLE MAN IN possession of a good fortune, must be in want of a wife.' Well, I didn't yet have a fortune. But I was single, and titled, and my family home was visibly shaking off its cobwebs and rising from its slumbers. I really felt as though things were looking up. Fairly soon, though, the rest of the family would start wondering when I'd get married and father the heir-and-a-spare that every landed family, from the Windsors down, requires.

First, of course, I'd need a wife. It wasn't easy finding a suitable candidate, because I was working seven days a week at Brocket, but every so often I managed to get out and about. At one local party I met a strapping blonde girl called Annabel: good figure, terrific long legs, sweet little button nose. She was just seventeen and still at school, but she didn't seem to be bothered that I was ten years older than her and we happily began a lusty holiday fling.

This was only slightly complicated by the fact that Annabel's surname was Heseltine. Her father, Michael Heseltine, had just returned to power as the Environment Secretary in Margaret Thatcher's new government, which I, as a Tory peer, was pledged to support. I'm not quite sure whether it was good or bad form to display my loyalty by sleeping with a Cabinet minister's daughter. But I had to smile when I saw a recent article by Annabel, who is now both a successful journalist and a happily married woman, headlined: 'Yes, posh girls ARE better lovers!' It described how her years at girls' boarding-schools had contributed to 'our reputations as girls who were probably up for it'.

Well, it's not often that newspaper articles are entirely accurate, as Annabel well knows, having once written a conspicuously inaccurate one about me. ('I have my career to think about,' I'm told she declared, when a mutual friend upbraided her for her wilder distortions.) But in this case, she was being completely truthful when she said that, 'Weekends were spent at our parents' country homes where childhood games of musical chairs were replaced with musical beds.'

I remember one such weekend with particular clarity, if only because I can still recall the leathery taste of my feet in my mouth. I'd spent the weekend at the Heseltines' magnificent home in Oxfordshire, a grand place, even to those of us with substantial homes of our own. As we sat down to Sunday lunch, Michael fixed me with the deeply suspicious stare that fathers tend to give a young man who's been sleeping with their teenage daughter, particularly if they suspect she enjoyed it.

The lunch was quite a formal affair, with lots of guests sat round a magnificent dining-table. I was doing my best to keep the lowest possible profile, but then there came the sort of lull in conversation you often get in the middle of a good meal. The sun was streaming in, glittering on a pair of silver candelabra that stood in the middle of the table. Between the two candelabra, there was a cobweb, stretching horizontally across a gap several feet wide. Suddenly, a girl spoke up: 'Look at that cobweb. I wonder how on earth the spider gets from one side to the other.'

I looked at the web and started thinking. This was the sort of practical, mechanical problem I really loved. I soon worked out what the answer must be. 'Well,' I said, 'I think the spider must start from the ceiling. It comes down on to one of the candles, then swings across on to the other one. You know . . . like Tarzan.'

A deep, glacial silence descended on the room. Heseltine knotted his eyebrows and looked at me with a look that was certainly intended to kill. For a second I was baffled. What had I done wrong? And then I remembered.

Michael Heseltine's nickname, which he hated, was . . . Tarzan.

My fling with Annabel ceased soon after that. I would however, meet her father many times again, the last of them in circumstances neither of us could have anticipated. Meanwhile something happened that was far more important, and yet utterly unexpected. I met the woman of my dreams.

I'd gone to a London theatre to attend the 1980

Annual General Meeting of the Historic Houses Association, an organisation for people who own historic homes. The atmosphere was businesslike, the surroundings were dull. Sex and romance were the last things on my mind. And then, across the far side of a packed foyer, I saw one of the most perfect creatures that I have ever laid eyes on. She was petite. She had brown hair, eyes that were big mysterious pools, high cheekbones and a full, voluptuous mouth. I think I fell in love there and then.

For the next hour, all thoughts of country houses vanished from my brain as I desperately tried to engineer a way to bump into her without looking too obvious. Eventually we got talking. Her name was Judy. She told me she came from South Wales. Her family had been miners, but her father had left the valleys and was now a lecturer at Sussex University. She must have inherited his intelligence, because she'd graduated from Cambridge, two years earlier, with a Double First. Now she was a banker, helping with the finances of one of the stately homes.

Judy had one of the most infectious laughs I had ever come across and an enquiring, constantly active mind. There was nothing dry or self-consciously highbrow about her intelligence. Like me, she could see the funny side of things. She shared my belief (one that had helped keep me sane during the stickier moments of my army career) that sometimes the only way to cope with life is to realise that it's fundamentally absurd.

Judy and I seemed to know exactly what the other was thinking. We talked for hours, everything and everyone around us completely forgotten. At the end of the meeting, when she agreed to see me again, I couldn't believe my luck. All the way home I thought of her, knowing that I was in love, and reminding myself time and again that it wasn't all a dream. She was almost too perfect to be true.

Over the next few weeks Judy and I got to know each other and I discovered that she was even better than I had imagined. She would stand her ground and speak her mind, making me question ideas that I had always accepted without really thinking, just because they were part of my upbringing.

Judy was an excellent pianist and would play for hours on the Steinway in the ballroom at Brocket Hall. Night after night we would sit by the fireside with a bottle of wine and talk into the early hours. We were becoming very close, but then something began to dawn on me: I was terrified by the depth of my love for Judy. These were uncharted waters and I wasn't sure that I wanted to venture any further into them.

I didn't want anyone to look too deeply into my soul, for fear of finding someone unworthy of them, someone with such a hunger for a loving relationship that it would show as a sign of weakness. I had spent so long acting the jovial clown that, faced with the holy grail of real love, I had no idea what to do with it.

Let me give you an example of what I mean about acting the clown even if unwittingly. A couple of years before I met Judy, I went to stay with my uncle David at Carton, my grandfather's old mansion in Ireland. While I was there, I was invited to play in a game of polo. I'd played polo in the army, but it had been years since I'd last done any riding, so I needed to get in some serious practice. Because I wasn't used to being in the saddle, the friction from my stirrups left me with inner thighs like a pair of raw, red, steaks. I was in agony. How was I going to climb back into the saddle, let alone play a polo match?

'No trouble at all, old chap,' said Hugh Dawnay, the man who'd organised the whole thing. 'Give you some horse pain-killer. If that doesn't sort you out nothing will.'

He handed me some foul concoction, washed down with a tumbler of whisky. By the time we mounted up, I was completely numb from the waist down, which is a problem if you want to use your legs to control a nimble polo pony. Somehow I managed to stay on board. In fact, things were going brilliantly until I found myself at the front of a string of players, all galloping hell for leather for the goal, standing up in the saddle, bums aloft, like jockeys in a race.

The man behind me had the ball and was swinging his mallet, ready to whack it as hard as possible. I'd just turned around to see where he'd hit the damn thing when I felt a mild stinging sensation between my buttocks, accompanied by a feeling a bit like the anal equivalent of having a stone stuck in your shoe: that uncomfortable sense that something is there that shouldn't be.

It's tough enough to see your own backside at the best of times. It's a damn sight harder when you're stuck on top of a pony bolting towards the far end of a polo field. So it wasn't until we hurtled between the goal-posts to the sound of cheers, mixed with helpless laughter, that I was finally able to regain control of my mount, reach round behind me and discover the cause of my discomfort and everyone else's hilarity.

The ball had rocketed over my pony's hindquarters, continued on its upward trajectory and smashed into my anaesthetised rear-end, where it lodged between my buttocks. There it stayed as I hurtled down the field and between the posts, thereby scoring quite possibly the most absurd goal in the entire history of polo.

That's the Brocket everyone expects. I make a total prat of myself on a polo field, then I wallow in the humiliation by telling the story in the pages of a book. And I've always been happy, too happy perhaps, to go along with that image.

I'll entertain. I'll amuse. It's loving that's the problem. Even, as I was rapidly discovering, loving Judy. That was incredibly hard for me to do. Needless to say, acting the prat was effortless.

I once went to meet her at her flat in Milner Street, South Kensington, opposite a pub called the Australian. I arrived in my battered old Renault 4 van – the one that wasn't supposed to leave Brocket because it was so totally decrepit – just as a crowd of flash young executives were gathering outside the pub for lunch. Judy came out to see me and, for some unimportant reason I've long since forgotten, we started arguing. To emphasise what she was saying, Judy prodded me in the chest.

'Don't you do that,' I said.

'Oh yes, I will,' said Judy, prodding me harder.

I'd had enough and started to get back into the van. Judy told me to stay and argue the point, whatever the hell it was. She grabbed the sleeve of my shirt, which came away in her hand.

I was hopping mad because I'd got dressed up specially to look presentable for her. Standing in a one-sleeved shirt, with the young execs on the pavement of the pub beginning to taking notice, I yelled, 'That's my best shirt, you bugger!'

Judy wasn't standing for that. She grabbed the other sleeve and pulled it off too.

My favourite shirt was now a thin cotton waistcoat. I yelled at Judy again. So she grabbed hold of my shirt for a third time, and yanked the front as hard as she could. It came away in her hands, leaving me wearing nothing but a collar, with the tie still in place and a couple of shards of fabric hanging either side.

I did my best to rise above my battered appearance and deliver some cool, dismissive, argument-ending line. Then, with my chin held high and a look of triumphant, masculine arrogance, I sat down in my van and started to drive off. The crowd outside the pub was now twice the size and they were all cheering and clapping.

I smiled smugly, assuming that their approval was directed at my brilliant handling of the situation. It was only as I drove off, to the sound of a belching engine and rattling body-parts, that I realised the truth. They were all applauding Judy for her total demolition of some sad, bad-tempered tramp in a ratty, broken-down old motor.

Looking back, I want to applaud her too. Judy was fantastic for me. She knew me better than I knew myself. She'd worked out what was wrong with me decades before I even began to, and she loved me enough to break down the walls I'd built around my heart.

The intensity of our arguments was only matched by the pleasure of making up afterwards. We were both physical creatures and the sexual chemistry between us was so intense, so passionate, that there were times when it was almost too much for us to control. Little by little, all my insecurities shrank away until all that was left was love.

The one small irritation was that my mother did not really approve of Judy. I don't think the problem was her relatively humble background, more that Judy wasn't the sweet, passive, adoring and not remotely challenging girl that mothers seem to dream of finding for their sons.

Judy spoke her mind and some people, unable perhaps to keep up with her incisive intellect, found her abrasive and dogmatic. But I loved her for her intelligence, her honesty and her sense of fun. Judy was a superb organiser, a great leader and she had natural class. She was utterly brilliant with the staff at Brocket, who all loved her. Now I wanted my family to appreciate her, and welcome her, too. My father had fought his parents over his choice of an 'unsuitable' partner. The last thing I wanted was to do the same thing all over again.

At least the trustees were beginning to understand

what I was trying to do at Brocket, if only because money had started to come in. The family couldn't help approving, even if they worried about the informal relationship I had with my staff, and the generosity with which I paid them. Personally, I thought that these loyal, incredibly hard-working people were worth every penny: happy, well-motivated staff are always a worthwhile investment.

The time eventually came for the European summit. First, the colonel descended on Brocket with his staff. Then came the politicians, starting with the Foreign Secretary himself, Lord Carrington. None of us could really believe that anyone so important could possibly choose to stay with us. As the foreign ministers of Europe's most powerful countries sipped their cocktails in our Morning Room, discussing affairs of state, the staff had a spring in their step. We were all determined to ensure that nothing whatsoever should go wrong.

Of course, that's easier said than done when you've got a large house filled with egotistical, temperamental, arrogant politicians. Lord Carrington had already warned us that the French Foreign Minister, Claude Cheysson, could be very difficult. He insisted on having the best of everything, including bedrooms. Carrington had therefore ensured that Cheysson had the biggest room on the second floor.

He had, however, overlooked one crucial detail. For hanging above the bed in that room was a five-foot-wide painting of the aftermath of the Battle of Waterloo. It depicted the generals Wellington and

Blücher on horseback shaking hands, surrounded by a carpet of dead Frenchmen.

The German Foreign Minister, Hans-Dietrich Genscher, on the other hand, was quite a different kettle of fish: a really hearty, jovial soul. He also shared his countrymen's thoroughness, and their natural desire to get to the sun-loungers – or in this case the bedrooms – first. Before Cheysson even arrived, Genscher had done a quick recce of the rooms to see who had got what. This included Cheysson's room.

The next morning, at breakfast, Genscher made a point of sitting next to Cheysson and boomed loudly, 'You haf a gut night, ja?'

'Mais oui,' responded Cheysson unenthusiastically. He was not the kind of man who likes a jolly chat first thing in the morning.

'Ja,' chortled Genscher. 'Und I heard zat you slept unter Vellington und Blücher, ja? Ho-ho-ho-ho!' He bellowed with laughter, clutching his sides.

Cheysson went the colour of a beetroot, flung down his napkin and stormed out.

A massive international crisis was now brewing. Cheysson was convinced that the whole thing had been a deliberate Anglo-German plot, intended to slight him and humiliate France. He was reported to be up in his room, trying not to look at the painting, packing his bags and preparing to fly back to Paris. Lord Carrington went to work with a crack team of Foreign Office smarm-merchants, soothed the ruffled Gallic feathers, and Cheysson eventually calmed down and agreed to stay.

All went well for the rest of the day. As the politicians got on with their summit, they were guarded by two defensive rings around Brocket. The outer ring was controlled by special forces, whose positions were completely hidden from view. The visible patrols around the inner grounds were carried out by the police.

Just before dinner I'd wandered into the ground floor of the stables where the police emergency unit were lounging about, with their jackets undone and their hats on hooks, when two loud gunshots rang out in the night. I'd like to say that the police's elite officers leaped into action like cogs in a well-oiled machine. In fact, they ran around like headless chickens – or rather, hatless coppers – as they tried to sort out whose headgear was whose. Having got themselves thoroughly muddled up, they charged outside, piled aboard their transport and disappeared.

A short while later, everyone returned and I learned what had happened. Some unfortunate lorry driver had apparently had the same Friday night routine for years. On his way home at the end of the working week, he'd stop his lorry in the lay-by on a nearby main road, then dive into my woods to shoot a pheasant to take home to the wife for the Sunday roast.

This Friday evening, he'd slipped into the woods, fired his gun . . . and then keeled over with a heart attack as a dozen SAS soldiers with blacked-out faces rose out of the undergrowth, pointing submachineguns at him. Somehow, I doubted that he would be back again.

The summit ended without further mayhem, the Euro-politicos disappeared and Lord and Lady Carrington said their goodbyes. We all collapsed in a heap and I poured stiff drinks all round. We would have our own debriefing the next day to list the many lessons that we had learned, but one thing had not been lost on any of us: Brocket Hall was now well and truly on the map.

Meanwhile, Judy had bought a flat in Albert Square, the real one, near the Oval cricket ground in south London. She had very little money left over to furnish it, so I grabbed a few rolls of carpet from the store at Brocket, found some spare bits of furniture and, most important of all, a large bed.

Judy was now working flat out at Morgan Grenfell, one of the City's top merchant banks, and was obviously doing really well. She was regularly being sent overseas and I would sometimes go with her, particularly to Paris. We'd walk arm-in-arm along the banks of the Seine, or wander round the Latin Quarter. Everything seemed perfect in our lives.

Work was going as well as pleasure. The Euro summit had generated an enormous amount of publicity for Brocket Hall, and the press seemed just as keen to write about me. My head swelled. My ego basked in the attention. Some of my friends thought I was making a big mistake. But I persuaded myself that all this coverage was more to do with my business than my vanity.

After all, I was part of the Brocket Hall package. I greeted the guests, was usually asked to join them at cocktails and dinner and often spoke after dinner. I worked hard to create an atmosphere where people felt that they were my personal house-guests and not face-less customers in an impersonal hotel. And it seemed to work. We were soon hosting everything from two-week courses for the Angolan workers in De Beers' diamond mines to a four-day wedding celebration for a family of ultra-Orthodox Jews.

The wedding party arrived all wearing traditional black clothes, black hats and ringlets. They checked to make sure that we had, as requested, replaced our reg-ular kitchen staff with special kosher caterers. Soon afterwards, Flick and I were summoned to the hallway and told that the guests needed a prayer room. We led a group of husbands and wives into the library, hoping that might suffice.

As we stood in the middle of the room one of the men looked up at the ceiling and admired the painted panels by Cipriani depicting Greek mythological char-acters in various states of undress. Without warning, one of the wives took an almighty swipe at him with her handbag. She knocked him to the ground and yelled, 'That'll teach you to lay your eyes on such debauchery on the Sabbath!'

Before dawn the next morning, the phone by my bed rang. It was Jean, the Hall's maître d'.

'It's Mrs Steiner,' she said. 'I don't think she's very well.'

'It's five in the morning,' I grunted. 'What do you mean she isn't very well?'

'Well, I think she's dead.'

I slipped some clothes on and went up to Mrs Steiner's room on the second floor. I felt the old dear's pulse and there wasn't one. Judging by the temperature of her body, I estimated that she'd died some four to five hours ago.

A doctor and the police were called. By now, the poor unfortunate husband was kneeling in his grief, facing the passage wall and chanting prayers.

The doctor came and confirmed Mrs Steiner's death. The plod arrived, complete with size fifteen boots and helmet under arm. He cast a disapproving look at Mr Steiner, then asked, 'Well, what 'ave we got 'ere now? Looks like the bleedin' Wailing Wall.'

I cringed. We all cringed. But the copper wasn't done yet. 'What's this?' he enquired, looking at Mrs Steiner. 'Another stiff? Yep, stiff as a board. Been gone long ago.' With those words he dismissed himself, pleased with his powers of observation, leaving the distraught Mr Steiner to wail even louder.

The next task would normally be to wait for an ambulance to move the body. But Jean, who was Jewish herself, explained that the removal had to be immediate. One of the kosher caterers would put Mrs Steiner in the back of his van and take her away.

She assured me, 'I promise you that this is quite normal, and Mr Steiner has agreed.'

By now, however, it was time for breakfast and the guests would soon be up and about. We had to get Mrs Steiner to the van without anyone noticing. But how?

A stretcher was produced, Mrs Steiner was strapped on to it and a plan formed in my head. As well as the ceremonial staircase at Brocket, there was also a lift. It was very small, rather old-fashioned and had glass doors on every floor, but it would carry Mrs Steiner down to ground level.

The lift, however, was at the far end of an eighty-foot passage from Mrs Steiner's room, and several other bedroom doors opened on to the passage. I didn't want any guests to emerge just as the corpse passed by, so I posted a chambermaid at each door. When the coast was clear they would give the thumbs up. But if their door was about to be opened, then they should wave their hand in warning.

With me on one end of the stretcher and a waiter on the other, we revved up ready for the dash to the lift. Finally all the maids' thumbs went up, we raced down the passage, made it to the lift and . . . disaster!

The lift was designed for vertical bodies, not horizontal bodies. 'Quick! Pull the straps tight,' I said to the waiter as I pulled the ones at my end. 'Now give me a hand to stand her up.' We held Mrs Steiner upright, with me standing alongside her, keeping her from falling down. I pressed the button and we started to descend.

I mopped the sweat off my brow, grateful for the narrow escape. But then I looked through the glass door of the lift and saw, with mounting horror, two elderly occupants on the floor below obviously waiting for the lift to take them down to breakfast, I did the only thing that I could do. I hooked my right foot around the bottom of the stretcher and started an animated conversation with Mrs Steiner, shaking my leg so that she nodded her head in reply.

Chattering happily, we made it to the ground floor and loaded the old girl into the back of the van. Ever since that day a distinctive lady's perfume has hung in the air of Mrs Steiner's old room and it has never diminished.

Soon, Brocket Hall was doing well enough for me to buy a Rolls-Royce to ferry our guests back and forth. And my trips to the States were paying off as more and more Americans started using Brocket. These included a party of wealthy businessmen and their socialite wives, who had all given donations to the World Wildlife Fund. They had been invited to a private reception in London to meet the Fund's patron, Prince Phillip. And while they were here, they were going to Royal Ascot too.

One of the guests was Zsa-Zsa Gabor, the Hungarian-born actress who married nine times (the first when she was fifteen). When she arrived at Brocket, Zsa-Zsa announced that 'I hate all bloody animals,' which wasn't entirely wise, given the circumstances. Then she regaled us all with stories of her prowess as a polo player. In fact she went on so much about it that Flick couldn't resist offering her a horse to ride, supplied by a local stables.

Faced with such a public offer, Zsa-Zsa had to accept. Having poured her not inconsiderable shape into a pair of jodhpurs, she was ferried off to the stables. There she was presented with a fine thoroughbred of seventeen and a half hands. This was a seriously big animal, and no matter how hard Zsa-

Zsa tried she just couldn't get up into the saddle. In the absence of a trampoline or a rocket, two of the stable lads were co-opted to give her the old heave-ho, which they did with a little too much enthusiasm. Zsa-Zsa sailed straight over the saddle and landed with an almighty thump, and a spluttering of Anglo-Hungarian curses, slap-bang in the manure on the other side of the horse.

Zsa-Zsa's fury now gave way to a loud, high-pitched wail, not dissimilar to an air-raid siren. She was, she told everyone, mortally wounded and required immediate hospital treatment. Flic had her chauffeured off to the nearest A&E department, where they diagnosed a sprained wrist and applied a stretchy bandage – as much for her wounded pride as anything else. Zsa-Zsa arrived back at the Hall soon afterwards, telling anyone who'd listen, 'Now you know why I hate ze bloody animals, darlinks.'

The following night's dinner was a black tie event and various society characters had been invited. One of these was Margaret, Duchess of Argyll, a woman whose sexual appetites made Zsa-Zsa look like a nun.

Many years before, the two ladies had fought for the affections of some dashing young blade, and the duchess had won. Zsa-Zsa had never forgotten this defeat. As dinner-time approached she hissed, 'I gonna get my own back on that beetch. Just you wait.'

Zsa-Zsa had the whole confrontation worked out in her mind. She started pacing up and down the entrance hall, muttering the words that were going to reduce the duchess to a gibbering wreck. By the time the guests were due, I was actually quite worried that there would be an unsightly catfight.

Finally, the limo arrived and the duchess was ushered through the front door. Zsa-Zsa's great moment had come. She stepped forward to deliver her crushing rebuke. But before she could say a word, the duchess slipped her mink coat off her shoulders and placed it in Zsa-Zsa's hands. As an automatic reaction, Zsa-Zsa grasped it. The duchess sailed on past, saying over her shoulder, 'Hang it up, will you?'

The duchess made a triumphal entry into the Morning Room, where pre-dinner cocktails were being served. Meanwhile Zsa-Zsa was still standing, holding the duchess's coat, with smoke coming out of her ears. I thought she was going to explode in some volcanic eruption of rage, but then the room went quiet. I turned round to see a breathtaking sight. It was Judy wearing a very dark blue satin ballgown. Round her neck was the most ravishing sapphire necklace with matching earrings.

In an instant, Zsa-Zsa's fury abated and a huge smile spread across her face. She went up to Judy and gave her a big kiss. 'Darlink, you look absolutely wonderful,' she said, clearly meaning it.

I sidled up to Judy and asked her where she got those fabulous gems.

'Zsa-Zsa lent them to me. Don't tell anyone,' said Judy. So there was a good side to the old battle-axe, too.

The next day we got ready to bus everyone off to the World Wildlife Fund reception. Zsa-Zsa did not intend to go quietly. First, apparently troubled by some detail of her appearance and deciding that the fault could not possibly lie with her, she flung her vanity-table mirror (originally given to my grandparents by the Duke of Gloucester as a wedding present) straight through her bedroom window and sent it crashing on to the lawn below. Delayed by this outburst, she was the last guest to arrive downstairs. When she appeared, she came to a full stop by the front door, rather like a train hitting the buffers, and threw a complete fit at the prospect of travelling in a coach.

'Darlink, I cannot possibly travel in one of those things, I cannot!' she announced and stood rooted to the spot. Not even dynamite would have budged her. I told the coach driver to leave. I would have to take Zsa-Zsa in the Rolls.

Finally, we reached the Portman Hotel, in London, where the reception was being held. As we started to climb the stairs to the reception room we met Prince Philip coming down. Zsa-Zsa held her hand out and gushed, 'Darlink, how are you? It's so nice to see you again.'

Philip did not say a word, nor did he break his stride as he swept past Zsa-Zsa and me with a look of total incomprehension on his face.

Zsa-Zsa wasn't standing for that. As he passed us, she hissed, loud enough for half the hotel to hear, 'Bloody Greek gigolo!'

The next morning, unabashed by her royal snub, Zsa-Zsa decreed that she liked my Rolls so much that she simply had to have one. The Jack Barclay dealership in Mayfair sent one up, immediately. After lunch, the guests started to trickle away. The last to leave was Zsa-Zsa. She had decided to *blitzkrieg* the Savoy, for which she now departed, scattering kisses and 'darlinks' to everyone in the vicinity.

We heard nothing further until several things happened all at once. First, the bailiffs arrived (too late) to repossess Zsa-Zsa's Rolls, as she had failed to pay for it. Second, the general manager of the Savoy rang to warn that she had left and failed to pay, and lastly our bank rang to tell us that she had not paid us either. The general manager of one of London's leading hotels later told me that this was how Zsa-Zsa managed to stay at posh places around the world. When enough bills had caught up with her, she simply rustled up a new husband.

I, however, was more interested in rustling up a wife. By now, I'd got to know Judy's parents pretty well. They were wonderful people: kind and unassuming and always pleased to see me. Her mother was very beautiful, with the same high cheekbones as Judy, and her father had a mischievous sense of humour that was never far from the surface. One weekend in 1982, when I was staying with them in Eastbourne, I did the decent thing at last, and asked Judy to marry me. She said, 'Yes.' As I slipped a diamond and sapphire engagement ring on to her finger I was filled with happiness and excitement. I was thirty years old. I was about to enter the prime of my life, with the woman I loved by my side. Wasn't I?

– 12 –

Viva Las Vegas!

FOR MOST FAMILIES, THE NEWS THAT THEIR ELDEST son had got engaged to a beautiful, intelligent, loving young woman, who was also a successful banker, would count as a reason to celebrate: hugs, kisses and tears of joy from the womenfolk, hearty slaps on the back from the men. My family, however, are made of sterner stuff.

Soon after word of my proposal to Judy got out, I was informed that there would be a family meeting at Brocket Hall. I was ordered to be present. Sensing something serious, I asked my solicitor, Peter Mimpriss, to come with me. I walked into my own dining-room, a grand, formal chamber, with classical columns at one end, to be faced with a line-up that resembled the Spanish Inquisition. The trustees were ranged along one side of the table. Peter and I were told to sit opposite them. My uncle David coughed and cleared his throat before addressing the room.

'Ahem . . . Some matters have come to our attention that are very serious.'

Like a schoolboy in the headmaster's study, I desperately ran through all the things that might have offended the trust or other members of the family. I was often criticised for doing this or that wrong, but this time it looked as if I had strayed over the line of acceptability.

My uncle continued, 'One is the matter of the new brochure. I see that the caption under the picture of the ballroom showing the portrait of the Prince Regent says: "The picture was presented to his mistress, the wife of the first Lord Melbourne."'

The other trustees looked a bit perplexed. One of them asked, 'What actually is the problem with the caption?'

'Well,' replied my uncle, 'you can't possibly say that.'

'Say what?' asked another trustee.

'Mistress,' said my uncle.

'Why not?' I asked. 'That is surely factually correct?'

'That's not the point. You can't say, "mistress".'

'Well, what do you suggest?' I asked.

'You must say, "friend".'

'But,' interjected one of the trustees, 'it's not the same thing. A friend is someone with whom you get on well, and a mistress is—'

'Yes, yes, we all know what a mistress is, but you cannot actually say it,' my uncle insisted. A lively debate ensued. The brochure remained as it was.

'Now the other point,' said my uncle.

I suppose I was expecting a broadside about my custodianship of Brocket and perhaps some effort to oust me from the place. But what he said next took me utterly by surprise.

'It has come to our attention that the woman you are engaged to marry is a porno star.'

For a second I wanted to burst out laughing. I looked quizzically at Peter Mimpriss, who shrugged his shoulders. He obviously had no idea what all this was about. My uncle, however, was about to give another demonstration of the trustees' surprising awareness of the contents of porno magazines.

'I . . . er . . . I have a copy,' he said, fumbling under the table and then passing over a magazine, opened at the relevant pages. 'And this one too,' he added, sliding a different magazine over to me.

I stared down at the pages. There was no denying it. That was Judy's spectacular body, all right. And absolutely none of it was left to the imagination.

'Did you know this, Charles?' asked another family member.

'Er . . . no . . . I had no idea.' I was stunned.

'I mean, one can't have the woodsman or the gardener looking at nude pictures of Lady Brocket, can one?' added another trustee.

'Of course, there is absolutely no way that you can marry her,' one of the elders stated with total finality.

I tried to resist. 'Well, that's ridiculous. Just because—' I got no further before I was interrupted.

'And, just so that you are aware of the position you are in, if you go ahead and marry Judy, the trustees will start immediate legal action to remove you from the trust. And that means from Brocket.'

I was staggered. The family's immediate response to my engagement had been not to congratulate me but to threaten to take away my home, my birthright and my business. What right did they have to impose their views on me? Who were they to say who was or was not 'unsuitable'? And why was none of my family expressing the slightest affection, or sympathy towards me, let alone listening to my side of the story? My opinion was clearly of no interest to them. My feelings for Judy were an irrelevance. It was almost medieval.

I did my best to maintain an impassive façade, but inside I was boiling. I looked at Peter. The rather bemused expression that had been on his face up until now vanished.

Taking his cue he sat upright and said, 'I think that you are slightly overstepping the mark here, gentlemen. Charles is legally the sole beneficiary of the trust and as such can only be removed by his death. Any—'

He was not allowed to finish the sentence. 'That may be your view,' said a trustee. 'Other lawyers will doubtless be prepared to challenge that position. Also, the trustees can arrange matters so that Charles is not able to live here, nor have any income worth speaking of from the trust. He will be on his own and nothing to do with the running of Brocket.'

So that was their answer.

'I see.' I sighed. 'Well, there is not much more to be said.' And with that the meeting ended. Outside I spoke with Peter.

'Are they bluffing or not?' I asked.

'Well, no, I don't think they are. As far as the legal

position is concerned, I doubt that they would succeed in effectively putting you outside the trust. But if they want to try, they can use trust money to fund the action, while you would have to depend on your own money. And you cannot afford a big legal battle. Then there is always the possibility of some loony judge ruling in favour of the trust.'

'So what's your advice?'

'Face up to the fact that if you want to marry Judy you will have the whole family against you and face a very uncertain future. They mean business. It's the way that they think and I don't think they'll ever change,' Peter said.

'Jesus. I knew there was likely to be opposition to Judy and me getting married, but I never dreamed that it would centre around pornography!'

I had to find out exactly what this was all about. I drove down to Judy's flat in Albert Square, feeling physically sick from the shock of what had happened and the fear of what was to come. I was furious that she had not told me about her past, that she had allowed me to be ambushed by my family in this way. And I couldn't help wondering if there were any other dirty secrets, hidden away in her past, that would now emerge to haunt us.

'Darling, I'm sorry,' Judy said. 'I hoped that no one would ever find out . . .'

And then she tried to explain. When she went to Cambridge University, she'd fallen in with a set of rich, aristocratic, high-living students. She'd been asked to stay at stately homes and invited on smart foreign holidays. But, unlike her new friends, Judy had no family money. She could not afford air fares, or fancy dresses. So when a talent scout had spotted her in Cambridge, and offered her £5,000 − more than most British people then earned in a whole year − just to pose for a few pictures, it seemed like her problems were solved.

Her contract had specifically stated that her pictures would not be published in Britain. But pornographers are hardly known for their honesty, or their care for people's feelings. Five years after they'd been taken, the shots had made their way into British top-shelf magazines such as *Knave* and *Mayfair*. Since then, Judy had lived in terror of her secret coming out.

I was in no mood to sympathise with Judy's predicament. I was too busy thinking about my own.

'I'm really amazed that you didn't come clean on this,' I complained. 'Now, if we marry, we won't be living at Brocket. And we won't have any interest in the trust. Not without one God-almighty battle.'

'But surely they can't be serious?' Judy asked.

'Deadly. You should have been there.'

'So what now?' she whispered.

'I'll have to get away from all this for a while. Maybe go to New York. I'm sorry, I think this may be the end of the line.'

I left with tears in my eyes. My family history was repeating itself. Just like my father, I'd been given a straight choice: walk away from the woman you love, or lose everything. It was Judy or Brocket. I loved her desperately, but Brocket was my home. If the title was to mean anything, if I wanted to hand on anything to future generations, how could I possibly choose her? I didn't know what to do, or how to deal with the situation in which I found myself.

Of course, all this begs the question: why should my family want to ruin me? It's not entirely surprising that my elders were shocked when they discovered Judy's secret. These days, no one bats an eyelid at 'toff totties' baring all for men's magazines, but twenty-odd years ago standards were rather different. Even so, we'd had the sexual revolutions of the sixties and seventies, so times were changing. Any family that cared about its members' happiness would have realised that I loved Judy, that she was fundamentally a great girl, and that the important thing to do was to find a way of getting past this temporary embarrassment.

But for the family, personal happiness wasn't the issue. In common with many upper-class dynasties, they cared far, far more about preserving the family name and reputation, and they were willing to be utterly ruthless in doing so. At no point did anyone reach out a hand to me, or offer the slightest support. As one of my relatives said to me recently, 'Of course, you could never have married a stripper. You'll understand that when you get older.'

I felt utterly miserable and utterly powerless. Even so, I could and should have resisted. After all, my father had stood up for his rights when he was barely out of his teens. I was a grown man of thirty. If I had married Judy, any scandal over her past would soon have evaporated when people saw for themselves what a great woman she was. And bad publicity could work both ways. I could have gone to the papers, pouring out my heart about how my family were preventing me from marrying the woman I loved. But I didn't. Instead, I flew to New York and did something far, far crazier.

I planned to stay with some friends, listen to some jazz in my favourite Greenwich Village clubs, look up some girls I knew who might be able to make me feel a bit more cheerful. Along the way, maybe I'd find the time and space to think through things properly, and come to a sensible decision.

But fate intervened. At JKF there was a cab strike and, to make matters worse, the roads into Manhattan were jammed. 'Sure you can get to the city,' said a cop. 'In a helicopter.'

I sat down with a coffee and idly thumbed through my address book. Isa's name caught my eye and I stared at her number. We hadn't talked for some time. The chances of her being in America were slim, but, on the off-chance, I called her parents' house in Merrick, Long Island. Her father, Gus, answered the phone. We'd met before, during one of my weekends with Isa, and he seemed pleased to hear from me again. Sure, he said, Isa was in town. She'd be delighted to see me. Why didn't I head on over to their place? In fact, he'd come to the airport himself to pick me up. It wasn't far. No problem.

The offer was typical of the man. Soon I could see his stocky, balding figure striding towards me as I waited at the exit from the arrivals terminal. In the car, he told me Isa was at her friend Sharon's house, just down the road. When I got to the Lorenzos' home, I dropped off my kit then walked off to find Isa, while Gus phoned to let her know I was coming.

I rang the doorbell and Isa answered. I can see her now, standing on the doorstep, her long blond hair lit up by the early afternoon sun, her eyes set off by her pale blue shirt, her legs in skintight jeans. I could say she looked gorgeous, or even spectacular, but those would just be crass understatements. One of the world's most beautiful women was right in front of me, her face lit up with a smile that suggested she was thrilled to see me. We looked at each other, neither of us saying a word, for what must have been a minute, at least. And as I stood there, a thought suddenly came into my head: This is the answer to all my problems.

Here was the girl of my family's dreams. She was ravishing to look at. She came from a respectable background. She wasn't aggressive, or rude, or opinionated. She was kind, she was harmless. She'd produce beautiful children. She'd look marvellous greeting guests at Brocket Hall. She . . . well, I could go on. But you'll already have noticed the flaw in my argument, which was that Isa wasn't actually the woman I loved. Nor was it fair to ask her to take on the burden of helping me run Brocket Hall – not if she didn't like mucking in.

Perhaps Prince Charles felt like this when his family – which has a similar disregard for personal happiness – told him, 'You can't have Camilla. But do meet the lovely, doe-eyed, virginal Diana Spencer . . .' And just look what happened to them.

Anyhow, I finally managed to say, 'You look utterly beautiful.'

Isa put her arms around me and gave me a hug, pressing her body against mine. She shut the door behind her and then I said, 'Do you think we should get married?'

And she said, 'Yes,' without a moment's hesitation.

You see, I was solving Isa's problems, too. Her relationship with Carlo Cabassi had continued, on and off, over the past three years. He'd presented her with an enormous diamond engagement ring, worth £25,000, and was expecting her to marry him. But she'd always had her doubts about Carlo, and her parents were convinced he was a Mafioso, who'd ruin her life. So when a proper English lord turned up on the doorstep, offering to make her a lady and the mistress of a grand country house . . . well, it was like the fairy-godmother telling Cinderella, 'You shall go to the ball.' Of course, she had the same tiny problem I did: she had someone else's engagement ring on her finger. But no one was thinking about that.

Isa banged on the door behind her. It opened to reveal Sharon's entire family, mysteriously gathered in the hall. Sharon was a big, dumpy brunette with a raucous Noo Yawk accent: Isa's plain friend. She gave a shriek of excitement and suddenly the whole family were yakking away nineteen to the dozen, and Sharon's mother was dashing off to the kitchen to make huge piles of food that no one wanted to eat. It was as if a great tidal wave of excitement was gathering force, picking me up and carrying me away.

Suddenly, we weren't just getting married. We were getting married right now. Sharon knew a place in Maryland where you could get a quickie wedding. Movie stars went there the whole time, she said.

Isa called her parents, who were as thrilled as everyone else by the news.

Now Isa's mother was offering to loan us her Mercedes sports car, and Sharon was volunteering to be the witness at our ceremony and squeezing into the back seat. Before I knew it, I was behind the wheel, hitting the freeway and belting south, on the 150-mile journey to Maryland.

We got there to find that the registry office that was famous for its instant weddings had closed six months earlier. I asked a local policeman where the nearest place was that would let us get married today.

He shrugged his shoulders and said, 'Vegas.'

Okay, where was the nearest airport with flights to Las Vegas?

He shrugged again: 'Philly.'

'Fuck it,' I muttered. 'Let's go.' So we drove to Philadelphia, doing 120 miles per hour all the way, dumped the car in the terminal car park, ran to the ticket counter (with Sharon shrieking at top volume, every step of the way) and finally collapsed in a breathless heap on the first plane out to Vegas.

We gulped down a couple of glasses of champagne, still giddy with excitement, and settled down for the remainder of the five-and-a-half-hour flight. And now, at last, I started thinking. Remembering Judy. Knowing, deep in my heart, that I was doing the wrong thing.

'If only . . .' The two most useless words in the English language. If only I'd had the courage to take a deep breath, hold Isa's hand, look her in the eye and say,

'You know what? This isn't the right time to get married. Why don't we just go to Vegas, have a great time, then slow down and think about this properly?'

I could have flown back home a few days later, talked to my friends and they'd have said, 'Your family are being outrageous. Tell them to fuck off.' I'd have had the moral support I needed to face down the trustees and marry Judy. If only . . .

Trouble was, I didn't have the guts even to start the conversation. I'd been the one who'd suggested all this. How could I back down now? Besides, Isa seemed so happy, and every time I looked at her I found myself changing my mind and thinking, Maybe this could work. It is such a perfect solution . . .

The real clincher was Sharon. She was sitting on the far side of Isa, yakking away about how this was the most exciting thing she'd ever heard in her entire life, and how she couldn't wait to visit us at Brocket Hall. I'd rather have faced down a herd of charging rhino than told Sharon she wasn't going to get the wedding she'd been promised.

So we landed in Vegas, grabbed a cab and set off down the Strip, past endless neon-lit chapels, blaring Elvis music, filled with horny old men and gold-digging bimbos. The cab-driver was obviously used to couples who needed a licence, fast. He drove to a shop where I picked up a wedding ring. And then, when I announced, 'I'm damned if I'm going to get married in one of those Elvis parlours!' he took us to the registry office.

We signed the papers. We made our vows. The

whole thing took ten minutes flat. Every time we said, 'I do . . . I do . . . I do,' I was thinking, I shouldn't . . . I shouldn't . . . I shouldn't. But I did.

The cab had waited for us outside and the driver took us right back to the airport. Las Vegas is three hours behind New York and Philadelphia, so it was still only the early evening in Vegas. We had time to catch another flight back to Philadelphia. First, though, I had to call my mother and tell her what had happened.

'Hello, Mummy, I just got married.'

'Who to?' she replied.

'Isa.'

My mother hardly said another word. She cried, partly, I suppose, from the sheer emotion of her son getting married; partly out of disappointment, because it hadn't been the proper, grand wedding of an eldest son, and she hadn't even been there to see it, and partly from relief. At least Judy was out of the picture. My mother had met Isa and liked her. Why not? There was nothing about her to dislike.

The only available flight to Philly went via Chicago. When we finally touched down, the Mercedes ran on autopilot back to Merrick. We grabbed a few hours' sleep, then flew back to England. Lord and Lady Brocket were back to reclaim their estate.

– 12 –

Loadsamoney!

I DON'T THINK I WAS OBVIOUSLY A TOSSER. BUT if you'd met me in the eighties, I'd probably have come across as being pretty pleased with myself. And why not? Isa and I were treated like the next best thing to Charles and Diana, fawned over by glossy magazines, who presented us to their readers as the ultimate example of a glamorous young couple, living in a dream home, surrounded by luxury and style. The publicity just added to the booming reputation of Brocket Hall, and the profits it made. By 1989 it was Europe's top conference venue, taking £25,000 . . . a day. And over a third of that was pure profit.

We never missed an opportunity to make a few extra bob. We sold framed prints of an old engraving of the Hall. They cost us £12 each to produce, but sold for £45. When we discovered that guests often pocketed their heavy, nickel-plated key fobs, each engraved with the name of their suite, we started selling those, too.

The same applied to our heavy, white cotton bathrobes bearing the Brocket crest, and the silver teaspoons, both of which people were happy to buy, once they knew that they'd be spotted trying to pinch them.

I wasn't too proud to do my own bit to boost sales. When companies came to the Hall for a gala dinner, our head butler, Alan Davidson-Lamb, would line up a discreet arrangement of unframed prints on a table in the entrance hall. Guests would invariably ask him if Lord Brocket would consider signing a picture, at which point, with a sharp intake of breath, he'd say that, 'His Lordship might, if I can persuade him. Please wait one minute, sir.'

I would be round the corner, waiting, and would then appear to autograph the picture as conspicuously as possible. Other guests would notice and there would then be a rush as they all scurried to have their pictures signed, until the scrum looked like the china department on the opening day of the Harrods sale. This little operation alone raked in between £800 and £1,200 a night.

The more money I spent, the more money Brocket made. The family couldn't believe it when I installed floodlights to illuminate the building, grounds and lake at night. The cables alone cost £27,000. But the sight was so spectacular that we immediately received even more bookings for grand dinners and corporate events. A new conference room for top-level meetings cost £320,000 – virtually the same as the bill for the renovation of the whole house, just a few years earlier. The men's lavatories, next to the meeting-room, had glass cisterns with goldfish swimming inside. Guests at the Hall, men and women alike, would rush to the gents' just to see the fish float up and down as the loos were flushed and refilled.

We built a suite of underground offices for the staff, painted with murals of the park so that no one would feel claustrophobic. We converted a stable-block to provide yet more rooms to satisfy the ever-increasing number of customers. To pay for the conversion, which cost £750,000, we borrowed money from the bank. Naturally they needed security. In order to give me a means of providing it, the trustees – this time acting precisely as I wished – very kindly allowed me to take personal ownership of the Hall and its immediate surroundings, a decision that would later (through no fault whatever of theirs) turn out to have drastic consequences. The trustees also insisted on retaining all the land around the Hall. That would prove to be the smartest move they ever made.

For now, though, everything seemed to be going splendidly. Our cigar suppliers told us that Brocket had the highest consumption of Monte Cristo As, the world's largest cigars, in the entire country. City financiers, made rich by the mid-eighties stock-market boom, competed to see who could throw the most spectacular parties.

The head of one well-known UK merchant bank decided to have his birthday bash at the Hall. He requested a fireworks display by the lake, with the explosions synchronised to music. In the house itself, walking round our giant basement conference-room, he declared, 'I visualise a Japanese water garden. I want a bridge over the water to a dance-floor with lanterns glowing around it.' We lined the entire room in waterproof plastic sheeting and installed a river, crossed by a Japanese bridge, and flanked by fountains. It looked amazing, and cost a fortune, but the banker was soon outdone by another client. When this chap ordered his fireworks display, he didn't stick to taped music. He hired the London Philharmonic Orchestra to sit by the water's edge, giving him and his guests a private performance.

One of our guests was August Busch, who owned the giant Anheuser-Busch brewing company, the makers of Budweiser. Naturally, we made sure that we had plenty of Budweiser in stock when he arrived. But there was a problem: we had bought the original Czechoslovakian Budweiser, not the American version. Mr Busch was horrified. He got on the phone to the States, and ordered a jet to take off right away with six cases on board. Probably the most expensive lager in the world . . . as another brewer might have said.

Everyone came to Brocket. Mrs Thatcher once gave a private address to the directors of a massive American corporation. They wanted to know how she saw the future development of Europe. She told them she believed the Germans would try to use the single currency to dominate Europe's finances – a point that did not go down well with two of the corporation's directors, who were German.

Denis Thatcher attended one event, organised by a firm of which he was a director. For a laugh, one of the other directors brought along a life-size cardboard cut-out of Maggie, and sat her in the entrance hall. After dinner, Denis was found squaring up to the lady and giving her a lecture. Caught in the act he cheerily admitted, 'Couldn't resist telling her a thing or two. 'Bout the only time she doesn't answer back!' We snapped a picture of him next to her, and added it to the ever-growing collection of celebrities hanging in the hall.

Of course, we still had plenty of *Fawlty Towers* moments. In fact, as if to prove that John Cleese's legendary show was more of a documentary than a sitcom, we virtually compiled a complete set of episodes. As well as our dead body, and our 'Don't mention the (Napoleonic) War' moment, we had a gang of Irish builders who did almost £50,000 worth of damage, trying to repair a cracked beam with a chainsaw: they sawed through one of the main hot-water pipes, too. We had a gourmet night when all the ovens broke down and we had to cook the whole meal on my old camping-gas stove. We had a rat in the kitchen, and we had a worrying visit from a health inspector who turned up shortly after several hundred ducks had wandered up from the lake, walked through the open front door and left a carpet of droppings all over the ground floor. And then, to top it all, we had Manuel.

When a big American media company came to stay for a pre-Christmas jolly, listed for tax purposes as a business conference, thanks to about five minutes' worth of board meetings a day, the organiser asked us to liven up the main celebratory dinner. So, unknown to our American guests, we hired Andrew Sachs, who acted the part of Manuel.

Dressed in his waiter's costume, he lurked behind the double doors of the ballroom as Alan, the head butler, who was the epitome of decorum, gave him his cue.

'Ahem . . . Ladies and gentlemen, may I have your attention just for a second? The chairman has requested that I enlighten you on the gala dinner that awaits you. For the first course His Lordship has arranged a little warm foie gras and—'

The doors behind Alan burst open and Manuel, clearly agitated, whined, 'No, no, señor! No foie gras! Foie gras eaten by cat. Pâté instead.' And with that Manuel disappeared as quickly as he had arrived.

Taking it in his stride, Alan continued: 'As I was saying, ladies and gentlemen, for the first course, chef's own pâté followed by the most delicious special pheasant dish that—'

The doors burst open again and Manuel spluttered, 'Señor, beeg problem! Beeg fight een kitchen! Chef, he very angry. Gamekeeper he say men shooting bloody bad shots. No pheasant. Chicken tonight.' And with that he vanished again.

Alan continued, 'As I was saying, the chicken tonight has been specially prepared with the chef's own sauce, then finished over a charcoal grill. For the sweet the chef has created his own famous version of baked Alaska that—'

In crashed Manuel for a third time. 'Señor, beeg problem! Fire een kitchen! No sweet! No Alaska! More like Espagne. Very hot. Chef he run outside.' And Manuel dived back out of the door.

Alan looked at the assembled guests, then back at the door. He murmured, 'If you will forgive me, ladies and gentlemen,' then left the room.

Soon afterwards, terrified screams of 'Don' heet me! Don' heet me!' could be heard from behind the green baize door.

Only after dinner were the Americans told that this was not an example of appalling British inefficiency. This was our famous — and, they decided, completely baffling — sense of humour.

Still, they could baffle us too. There was the boss of a gigantic US insurance company, who insisted on being given a room with a giant Jacuzzi. He and his wife kept most of the top floor awake with the noises from the bathroom and, whatever he was doing, she kept telling him over and over not to stop. When the maid went to clean their room the following morning, she found a diving-mask and snorkel. It was still wet and covered in soap-suds. What had he been doing with it? No, on second thoughts, I really didn't want to know.

By now, Brocket Hall was generating so much trans-Atlantic traffic for major airlines, almost all of it in first or business class (which is where the airlines make their profits), that I never, ever had to pay for a plane ticket myself. I could go anywhere in the world, first class, and it never cost a penny. And whenever, and wherever, I went, I always carried a briefcase full of Brocket Hall brochures, because every other first-class passenger was a potential Brocket client.

I even took my sales-pitch to the White House when Isa and I, in common with many other owners of stately homes, were invited to Washington for the opening of a unique exhibition called 'The Grand Tour'. Priceless objects, collected by eighteenth-century English aristocrats on their European tours, or specially commissioned for their houses, were taken out of their surroundings for the first time and put on display in Washington. The week was packed with a constant round of receptions, lunches, dinners and exhibitions.

Towards the end of the stay we were all asked to the White House to meet President Ronald Reagan and his wife, Nancy. The First Lady was very chatty and had clearly done some research on our houses.

'I hear Brocket Hall has some interesting political connections,' she said.

'Yes,' I agreed. 'Prime Minister Melbourne and Prime Minister Palmerston both lived and died at the Hall.'

'Two? That's a bit unfortunate, isn't it?' she asked.

'Nothing in the water supply, I assure you. In fact Palmerston had rather a reputation with the girls and actually died on the billiards table with a chambermaid.'

'That could be awkward,' Nancy replied.

'Not half as awkward as one banquet at Brocket for Melbourne. A huge silver tureen was carried aloft by four footmen and placed in the middle of the table. When the lid was lifted off, his wife, Lady Caroline, stepped out stark naked. Bit of a conversation stopper. Perhaps you should try the same thing here to liven up some of the duller state occasions?'

She opened her mouth as if to speak and then thought better of it. The guest next to me tried to change the subject to something a little more bland. Nancy was definitely not amused.

She would have been even more upset if she had known about some of the other, less respectable folk who hung around Brocket Hall. One night we hosted an event for the UK board members of General Motors and their wives. I was chatting to the chairman, over pre-dinner cocktails, when Alan, the butler, came up to me and whispered in my ear, 'There's a burglar in one of the bedrooms.'

I turned with as much composure as I could muster and gave the chairman an unconcerned smile: 'Will you excuse me for a moment?'

I sauntered out of the room. As soon as I had turned the corner I ran like a lunatic to the back of the house, where I collided with a group of staff.

They told me what the man looked like and in which direction he had gone. He was only three or four minutes in front of me. If I was quick I should get ahead of him.

Grabbing my ammo belt, my double-barrelled shotgun and a pair of handcuffs, I jumped into my car, having told the staff to ring the police and tell them to make for a lay-by on the main road. The burglar must have got to Brocket somehow, and that was the nearest place, outside the estate, to park a car. I hurtled out of the gates, down the drive and on to the main road. I floored it until I was within a hundred yards of the lay-by. Then I abandoned the car and crept up on foot.

There were two vehicles in the lay-by. One was a Volkswagen camper. A light was on inside and it was rocking violently from side to side. That definitely wasn't the one! The other was a Fiat four-door coupé. I crept up to it and felt the bonnet. It was still warm, but no one was in it. This must be the burglar's motor.

Fifteen yards from the car was a ditch. I jumped into it with a loud splash. Shit! There was a couple of feet of water in the bottom: so much for my smart shoes and Valentino suit. With gun at the ready and two cartridges up the spout, I waited in the pitch blackness. I would easily be able to hear the man approaching through the woods, so I would get ample warning.

In my own mind what would follow was quite simple. I would cuff him to the door-frame of his car and wait for the police to arrive. I must have been crazy. I was no longer the fit, hardened soldier that I'd been a decade earlier. And if the army had taught me anything it was that you never carry a gun unless you absolutely intend to use it. Even the tiniest moment of hesitation can be fatal. As I was about to discover.

After a couple of minutes I heard the unmistakable sounds of someone coming through the woods. But what if it wasn't the right man? I would have to allow him to open the door of the car so that the light shone on his face. If I could identify him, I would stop him and cuff him. Yes, that seemed a good plan.

He climbed over the fence and went to the Fiat. With the light shining on him there was absolutely no doubt that this was the man. I jumped out of the ditch and told him to put his hands on top of his head. He did so. I walked up to him and stopped four feet from him. In the blink of an eye he jumped at me.

This was the moment when I had to make the decision to shoot. I bottled it. At the last moment, I swung the butt of the gun diagonally across the thief's chest. It ripped his shirt and produced a long gash in his chest. We both landed on the tarmac surface of the lay-by, my head taking most of the impact.

Semi-concussed by the fall, I wrestled with the thief as blood poured from his chest. Suddenly, I realised the extent of my stupidity. I had not hit anyone since my boxing days at prep school. Now I was struggling for my life against a strong, ruthless opponent. Uprooting one of the white wood stakes that marked the lay-by, he hit me over the head with it. I fell on to the tarmac, dropping the gun. As I struggled to remain conscious, he pressed the barrels against my chest and said, 'Now it's your turn.'

At the moment I was expecting to hear the detonation of the gun, the entire lay-by was bathed in light as a police dog-van raced into it and came to a screeching halt, about six feet from my semi-conscious body. When the driver's door opened and a policeman got out, the burglar dropped the gun and ran off across the road.

I got shakily to my feet and said to the constable, 'Christ, talk about the cavalry getting there in the nick of time! He's over there. The dogs will get him easily.' I could hear the Alsatians in the back, eager to prove their worth.

To my disbelief the officer wouldn't continue the

chase. 'I'm afraid I must take you back, sir. You're badly hurt. You need attention.'

I tried to explain that it was the other man's blood all over my suit, but it was no good. I could see by the expression on the officer's face that he thought I was in shock and didn't realise the extent of my injuries.

The policeman helped me into his van and we drove back to the Hall. The couple who'd been staying in the room that had been burgled were waiting for me. A few items of costume jewellery were missing together with several pairs of the wife's knickers. She was much more upset by the theft of her undies than her baubles.

The next day a search of the woods was made and a trail of pants and jewels was uncovered. The police caught up with the burglar a few days later. He fought like a man possessed. Apparently he was an ex-SAS soldier and had burgled many stately homes. His abandoned car had his prints all over it. He was caught bang to rights.

When the case came to the trial I was called as a witness. At the end, the man was convicted. When he went down he shouted that he would 'hit me' as soon as he got out. It seemed like an idle threat at the time. As I was later to discover, he meant every word. But for now that was the last thing I was worried about. What bothered me more was the truth about my life at Brocket, the bitter secret hidden beneath the glossy façade: the desperate, almost terminal state of my marriage.

– 13 –

Little Brown Bottles

BRITNEY SPEARS ISN'T THAT DUMB. SHE MAY HAVE got married one wild night in Las Vegas. But at least she had the good sense to annul the whole thing fifty-five hours later. It took Isa and me twelve years to undo the knot we'd tied, by which time both of us were on the brink of self-destruction, with consequences that linger, painfully, to this day.

It all began to go wrong within minutes of us arriving at Brocket Hall. I'd called the long-suffering Flick from Heathrow, warning her that 'I'm bringing a wife home with me.'

Flick's response was immediate. 'What's going to happen to Judy?'

'I've already spoken to her,' I said. 'I'll deal with it all when I get back home.'

But there was one thing I hadn't dealt with. There were still pictures of Judy on the table beside my bed. So the first thing Isa saw when she walked into her new bridal home were photographs of another woman.

Understandably, she was furious. To this day, she cites that as evidence of my callousness and treachery. But neither of us was really in any position to complain about the other. Isa knew about Judy and me. And she was engaged to another man when she agreed to marry me. All the same, it was hardly an ideal start to a marriage, and things soon got even worse.

Isa naturally expected that her wedding would be followed by a honeymoon, or, at the very least, a few days when she would be the absolute centre of her new husband's attention. The tiniest scintilla of romance would have been nice. But I failed to provide it.

I was obsessed by Brocket Hall and my business. Isa was perfectly happy for me to show her round her new home within minutes of unpacking our bags. She even seemed enthusiastic when I told her of the dreams I had for the place. The problem came when I plunged straight into work, without devoting much time to her at all.

If you'd asked me then, I'd have said I had no choice. We had some important conferences coming up and I felt that my presence, at all times, was essential. But if I'd really loved my wife, I'd have known that she was essential, too. I'd have made her my immediate priority. Everyone would have understood if I'd hung a 'Just Married' sign outside my bedroom door. Staff and clients alike would have basked in the reflected glow of our newly wedded bliss.

But there was no bliss. Within days, Isa was on the

phone to Carlo and I was having long, anguished conversations with Judy, who was absolutely devastated by the way things had worked out. She already knew, before I spoke to her, what had happened in Las Vegas. My mother had called to let her know.

Mother was delighted by Judy's removal from the scene. But she was horrified when I admitted to her, and the rest of the family, that I feared my marriage had been a ghastly mistake and was contemplating an immediate divorce. Their responses were immediate and unanimous. Divorce was completely unthinkable, particularly after just two or three weeks of marriage. I had made my bed. Now I must lie in it. And Isa must damn well lie next to me.

Actually, Isa liked lying in bed. As a model, she'd been used to early starts. But when she wasn't working, she'd been able to stay in bed all morning. That was not how we did things at Brocket, however, and matters were made worse when my mother arrived for lunch at the Hall one day. Told that Isa was still in bed, Mother simply marched up to our bedroom, flung open the curtains and told Isa in no uncertain terms that it was time to get up. It's hardly the way to treat a grown woman. But then, in my mother's eyes, I'm not sure Isa was much more than a child. Nor was I, come to that.

Confronted with my indifference and my mother's interference, Isa retreated into her shell. She is not an assertive person and has never been one for saying what is on her mind, so I never really knew what she was thinking. Nor did I take the time or trouble to find out. I continued in my single-minded way, working all the

hours God gave, until Isa simply upped and left. She
went back to Italy to meet Carlo, her ex-fiancé. Before
she left, she announced that she was pregnant.

While Isa was in Milan, I went to meet Judy in her
flat in Albert Square. It was gut-wrenching to see her so
obviously heart-broken. Amazingly, she was still willing
to give me another chance, if I could find a way out of
my marriage. If not she'd find a man she could rely on.
She had someone in mind, a nice, dependable man at
work, who'd never made any secret of his feelings for
her.

'Well, there is one further complication for me,' I
said. 'Isa's pregnant.'

'Oh, great,' muttered Judy.

I ended up staying the night, sharing a brief, sad
echo of the passion that had once burned between us.
As I left the next morning, Judy kissed me, and with
tears in her eyes, said, 'Look, it just hurts too much to
talk to you or see you. Please don't contact me again.
Not unless you decide to divorce Isa. Then ring me,
but not unless.'

So that was how we left things. I drove back to
Brocket. I can't describe the pain. And it was all my
doing. Judy later married her colleague. He's turned out
to be a loving husband and an extremely successful
man. However unhappy she might once have been,
Judy probably counts herself lucky to have ended up
with him, and not a wrong 'un like me.

Once I got home, I called Isa several times at
Carlo's flat in Milan. Eventually she decided to come
back and try and make a go of it. Things seemed to be

better for a while but then I went back to my relent-
less work schedule and Isa's unhappiness returned. To
cap it all, she revealed that she had never been pregnant, after all. I thought of contacting Judy to tell her,
but what good would that do? I was committed to
seeing this marriage through to the end, whatever that
was going to be.

So there we were, living in a comfortable, spacious
flat, in one of Britain's most lovely houses. I was forever
popping downstairs to repaint this, mend that or check
on yet another business detail. Meanwhile, Isa was
retreating more and more into her shell. And, as her
pain increased, she tried to find some other means of
getting the comfort that I would not provide.

Isa told me she suffered from migraines and backache. I felt sorry for her. I didn't think twice about the
high-powered pain-killers that arrived with ever greater
frequency from pharmacists in the States. I didn't pay
much attention when the cleaner, Mrs Summers,
started calling our bathroom 'The Drugstore' because
of the line of little brown pill bottles stretched the full
length of the bath.

We had a brief few days of happiness over Christmas
1982. Isa and I prepared the hampers that we gave to all
the permanent staff and took them round to the cottages, receiving a warm welcome and a drink. By
Christmas Day some of the old warmth had resurfaced
and some sort of dialogue passed between us.

But it was short-lived. Come the New Year, business
rolled in at an even faster rate than before. Late one
spring afternoon, I went upstairs to find that Isa had

simply disappeared. There was no note, and only a few clothes had been packed in a suitcase.

I rang around her friends abroad and at home, but no one had seen anything of her. I even called Carlo Cabassi in Milan. He insisted he had no idea where Isa was, and I believed him. Now my mind started working overtime and I began to wonder about her safety.

Because of all the high-security government business we had had at the Hall, I had got to know some people with access to information and manpower on a worldwide basis. That afternoon I got in my car and went to see my contact, Bob.

'Probably perfectly safe,' Bob said, standing behind his computer. 'Now tell me the names of her principal contacts in Milan.'

I reeled off the names of the four most likely people as Bob tapped the keyboard. It was a time when Italy was going through one of its periodic spasms of murder and mayhem. A financier called Roberto Calvi, known as 'God's banker' because of his work with the Catholic Church, had just been despatched in a very public way, swinging from Blackfriars Bridge. The Mafia killed him as a punishment for losing huge amounts of their money. A mysterious Masonic lodge called P2 was also involved in the killing. Meanwhile, a prominent female member of a British banking family – and her girlfriend – had been found murdered in their car high up in the Italian Alps, hidden under the snow.

Bob suddenly sat upright. 'Take a look at this. Jesus, this is heavy-duty.' On the screen there was information about people Isa knew in Italy that cannot be made public, even now. She was potentially in very serious danger. Bob's whole demeanour changed as he shifted into operational mode. 'We'll start in Rome. Tell no one. Carry out all the normal security drills. I'll meet you at the Grand Hotel at midday tomorrow.'

Early next morning, I left for Heathrow with a bundle of cash in my pocket, telling the staff that I was seeing a client in London. I started using techniques I'd first learned as a young army officer stationed in Northern Ireland, when we were trained to throw IRA terrorists off our trail.

On the way to Heathrow, I checked for signs of a tail, but could see none. But you never take that for granted. I drove into the multi-storey car park at Terminal Three, drove straight back out again, and left the car in the Terminal One parking area. I bought a standby ticket with cash and went direct to the departure gate for the Rome flight. There I waited until the flight was just about to close. Then I made a call to Brocket from the payphone. I said that I'd get back from lunch at four that afternoon. I boarded the plane, making sure I was the last passenger on.

At Rome airport I checked again to see if I was being followed but all seemed clear. At the taxi-rank, I ignored the taxi at the front of the line and slipped into one in the middle. I gave the driver no destination but told him to drive towards the centre of Rome. About a mile from the centre I told him to stop and I got out. I started walking in one direction until the taxi was out of sight, then I doubled back the way I'd come until I saw a small *pensione*, one chosen completely at random. I asked the receptionist for a room. I made one phone call to the Grand, mentioning no names, to confirm that I would be there in half an hour.

I had a quick shower and set off on foot. I saw Bob in the foyer at the Grand Hotel and shook his hand.

'Charles,' he said, 'this is the chief of police. He will assist us in extracting Isa from whatever situation she is caught up in.'

I shook hands and we sat down. 'I don't think that I was tailed, anyway,' I said, somewhat relieved.

The chief looked at me coolly, reached into his pocket, pulled out a micro-cassette and slipped it into a pocket player. He held it up so that I could clearly hear a playback of my one call to the Grand just half an hour before.

'In case you think that we recorded this, we did not,' the chief said.

'The Mafia have informers at every level, and the hotels are covered all the time. They want to know who all visitors are, and shady ones always stay at the smaller places like the one you have checked into.'

Hell, I would never make a secret agent.

Bob had a list of Isa's contacts, which we went through one by one. The chief had his men check all the hotels in the city. When I mentioned that Isa had a cousin in Perth, Australia, he had a Qantas 747 stopped and boarded on the runway at Rome airport, ordering the control-tower to abort the plane's take-off.

'Don't worry,' he said. 'This happens all the time.' Isa was not on the plane.

Later that afternoon, news came through that Isa had been spotted in a private house in Portofino, a seaside resort on the Italian Riviera. That night I spoke to her on the phone. She couldn't believe that I had managed to find her, and was clearly in distress.

We agreed to meet in Milan the next morning. I didn't tell her what some of the people she knew were up to. I couldn't see that it would do any good. Isa was so vulnerable. All I wanted to do was hug her and protect her. Who knows what makes one person love another? But at that moment I really did love Isa more than I had ever done before. After a long, heartfelt chat we both returned to Brocket.

Back in England, Isa rightly pointed out that we had still not had a honeymoon, so off we went to Barbados, to stay with friends who had a wonderful old plantation house called Laughing Waters next to the Sandy Lane Hotel. For a fortnight, we were able to relax, lie in the sun and be waited on hand and foot by Sobers, the local butler, and his staff. We had a great time together, but then we got home and all the same old destructive cycles started repeating themselves.

Part of the problem was that we couldn't just be together, having a chat, or curling up in front of the telly. We were never cosy together, never really relaxed in one another's company – something which our friends certainly noticed, even if they were too polite to comment on it.

I began to realise that I was actually happier spending the evenings downstairs with the guests than upstairs with my wife. And she, poor thing, must have realised that, and felt terribly lonely. Isa did not particularly want to be the mistress of a stately home. Life on a big estate can be very isolating. Isa couldn't pop down the road to see her girlfriends, as she might have done if we'd had a normal house in town.

On the other hand, if you live in an ordinary house, you can't have sixty friends to stay for the weekend, which is what we did for the first time in the summer of 1983 (or even one hundred friends as we would have in the year to come). We simply set aside a weekend when the Hall wasn't occupied by a business client and applied all our professional skills, and facilities, to entertaining people we liked.

We laid on clay pigeon shooting, archery, croquet, buggy racing and hovercraft racing for the grown-ups. The whole third floor of the Hall was turned over to the children, and two nannies took charge of them. They had their own dining-room next to ours and Werner produced all sorts of goodies, which always included baked beans, ice cream and plenty of treacle pud. Outside there was a bouncy castle and a mini go-kart track to keep them busy.

The dining-table at Brocket seats sixty comfortably. It was wonderful to see so many people I cared for there, with all the candles glittering in the mirrors, and this was the sort of occasion when Isa looked simply magnificent, every inch the fairy-tale princess. As I leaned back with a glass of fine claret in my hand, I thought of all the times when these same friends had been forced to spend weekends hacking away at undergrowth or smashing down walls, and you could see from the entrance hall up through four floors into the roof. Whatever problems there may have been in my personal life, we had at least achieved something.

And there was still one respect in which Isa and I were behaving like a proper married couple. Early in 1984 she told me that she was pregnant – for real this time. I should have been thrilled. But, given the still unsteady state of our relationship, I asked Isa if it wouldn't be a better idea to leave starting a family for a while. Surely it wouldn't be fair to bring a child into the world with parents who were not communicating properly or might even get divorced?

Isa did not reply. That was not her way. But the next day I found her cupboard door open and her suitcase gone. There was no note. I soon got a call from her parents to say that she was with them. For once, Gus was not his usual cheery self. He wanted to know how I could be so cruel to his little girl. I tried to explain the situation to them, but every word I said just got me deeper into the mire. For a good Catholic like Gus, abortion and divorce were simply not acceptable options.

My mother agreed with Gus, and wrote him a letter saying so. Her line with me was the same as always: I had made my bed, so I should lie in it. When Isa revealed that the baby was a boy, and therefore the heir to the estate, the die was cast. It was inconceivable for the next Lord Brocket to be brought up abroad and be a total stranger to British ways, so I agreed to give fatherhood my total commitment. Isa returned a few days later. I was glad to see her back. And I never once, from that day on, regretted becoming a father.

At the end of September Isa went into the Wellington Hospital in London to have Alexander, our first child. He arrived without a hitch, a bouncing baby boy, with a shock of platinum-blond hair.

Like so many fathers, I was overwhelmed by the emotions I felt when I first held my miraculous, perfect child. I prayed that I could do the little fellow justice and that his world would be a happy one. If we were successful with Brocket it would all be his. We commandeered one of the guest suites at the Hall for the new addition to the family and Alex became the centre of attention for the staff. All the girls clucked around him like a bunch of mother hens.

Isa's mother, Brigitte, was particularly taken with the new addition to the family. Isa seemed less than pleased by her mother's enthusiasm. Her reaction reflected something that explained a lot, I think, about her deep unhappiness, her inner pain, and her need to dull her pain with drugs. I had long known that she and her mother had a stormy relationship. All her life they had argued with one another.

Isa told me and many of her friends that her mother had always wanted a son. She had taken out her frustration on her daughter, who was constantly made aware that she was fundamentally flawed and inadequate, on the grounds of being a girl. Isa's father indulged her materially – in her teens, she had an Alfa Romeo Spider sportscar and a motorboat – but these gifts could not compensate for the knowledge that her mother regarded her as a huge disappointment. Looking back, I wonder if her crushed self-esteem wasn't the cause of all her problems. And my inability to give her the love she needed must only have made things worse.

Christmas 1984 was spent at Brocket. The Hall had been hired for the holiday by a rich, outrageous gay man, who filled it with forty or so equally wealthy, equally wild chums. Isa and I plunged into the party atmosphere, invited a few extra friends of our own, and had a wonderful time. But this was a brief upswing and soon Isa was on the way back down.

By April 1985 Isa's depression seemed to be permanent, and I was at a loss as to what to do. One day I returned to the flat at Brocket to find that Isa had left yet again. This time so had Alex and the nanny. In a panic I rang round everyone I could think of, and found that she had rented a flat in Chelsea.

I visited the flat regularly to see that Alex was all right and it soon became clear that Isa had a boyfriend. Jealousy was my first instinct but I immediately realised I was being unfair. I was not a good husband and things were anything but ideal between us. Who could blame her for being tempted? And who could blame anyone for being interested in her? She was, after all, very beautiful.

Isa's new man was called Nick. Like me, he worked in the hotel business. In fact, I knew Nick very well and liked him. He was clearly feeling very awkward and uncomfortable. No point in beating about the bush. I said, 'Nick, I don't blame you. Don't feel embarrassed. I don't resent you for it.' But the affair didn't last long.

You can sum up the next five years pretty simply. We had occasional good times, often when we could get away from Brocket and relax on holiday together. But the happy days were interrupted by long periods of depression, and ever-increasing drug-taking. When she was on form, Isa was a magnificent hostess. At grand Euro summits, she would dazzle the continent's top politicians as she slipped effortlessly from English into fluent Spanish, Italian and German. The media simply adored her: a supermodel married to a lord, with a beautiful son in a stately home – it doesn't get much better than that.

But with every passing month, it became more common for Isa to cry off our dinner engagements with guests at the Hall, sometimes only minutes before dinner. Alan, the butler, would go ballistic, as he had to rearrange sixty place settings, all of which had to be as immaculately lined up as guardsmen on parade. I'd always make a standard excuse: Isa wasn't feeling very well. That was, in fact, true. I just didn't understand how.

Flick and other members of staff were seriously worried about Isa and suggested that I should encourage her to seek help. But I'm the sort of man who only takes pills as a last resort. I simply didn't realise that a person could become addicted to pain-killers. If I had appreciated what was really happening to Isa, and tried to help her tackle her problems, things might have turned out very differently.

Some people did try to help. One of our neighbours was the romantic novelist Barbara Cartland, who lived at Camfield Place, only ten minutes from Brocket. Camfield is a very friendly place with a sort of magic about it, perhaps because Beatrice Potter wrote *The Tale of Peter Rabbit* there. The blue door in the wall to Mr MacGregor's kitchen garden is still there, complete with the gap at the bottom of the door that Peter Rabbit scampered under when he was being chased.

Like Beatrix Potter, Barbara had a very sharp eye. She'd seen for some time that all was not well on the home front — she'd also seen Isa taking pain-killers — and regularly used to ask us to dinner parties and Sunday lunches in an attempt to cheer us up.

People used to mock Barbara for her pink dresses, her inch-thick mascara and her endless pronouncements about the need for true romance. And it's true, she really did dress all in pink — as someone once said, she looked like an animated meringue. But I thought she was a magnificent woman. She was wonderfully gung-ho, terribly outspoken and unflinchingly loyal. She was also very down-to-earth and not remotely pompous.

In 1987 Isa announced that she was pregnant again and it was a girl. I was delighted by the news. We spent our summer holiday on a beautiful sixty-foot yacht, sailing round the coast of Turkey. On one lazy afternoon the boat stopped. She had run aground. Isa and I had disagreed about the name of our daughter she was expecting. Isa liked the name Natalie and I liked Natalya. We got the chart out and found that we had run aground at a place called Antalya. That settled it. Antalya it was.

On 1 November Isa went into a long, hard labour, and another perfect little being was delivered. Antalya had masses of black hair and huge dark eyes.

With the arrival of a second child, we moved into a house by the lake called Watershipps, after the original, medieval name of the Brocket estate. It was one of the finest buildings on the estate, but Isa was going through another depressive, increasingly angry period. We had just converted the stable-block into bedroom suites for the Hall and Isa had done a superb job overseeing the interior decorations. But no matter how often I complimented her, or how publicly, she still insisted that I didn't appreciate her efforts.

By now, Isa was telling anyone she met that I was a terrible husband: a habit she maintained for years afterwards. Two of the staff, out shopping in the local department store, even heard her listing my faults to a shop assistant. Yet she would never, ever say anything directly to me, so we could never have a conversation to try and clear the air, or put matters right.

By 1988 the gulf between our public image and private reality was yawning wider than ever. We were constantly presented as a golden couple in glossy magazines. Yet behind the scenes, the seriousness of Isa's drug-taking was becoming all too apparent. Guests were starting to comment that her speech was often slurred, her reactions sluggish, her behaviour irrational.

I found her decline more wearing and upsetting than anything I had ever encountered. I would far rather have faced hordes of Turkish troops or Irish terrorists than the situation that existed now.

Perhaps because of the drugs, she seemed unable to control her rage, or limit the damage she was causing. One night, I was lying in the bath while Isa was trying on some new creation that a trendy designer had asked her to wear. I made some light-hearted remark about the dress. Now, I know it's always risky for a man to attempt any form of humour about an item of clothing his wife plans to wear. And Isa was half German, which meant she could sometimes take things a tiny bit too seriously. But even so, it was a bit extreme of her to stalk out of the bathroom, slam the door and then, as an afterthought, punch her fist clean through one of the panels.

What was really worrying, however, was the effect on our children. They picked up all the anger and frustration she felt towards me, something that was noticed by everyone on the estate. There was worse, much worse to come. Isa would betray me and all but kill herself. But I can't tell that part of the tale without re-winding a while and saying one word that would come to haunt me: Ferrari.

– 14 –

Blowing It

WHEN IS A CAR NOT A CAR?

No, that's not the first line from a Christmas-cracker joke. It's an extremely serious question that would come to have a huge bearing on my life. My obsession with classic cars would cost me everything I had worked so hard to achieve. I would be sent to prison for one car-related crime that I had committed, then forced to plead guilty to another that I most certainly had not.

But it's impossible to understand what happened without having a rough knowledge of the bizarre way that the classic car world works. So I'll do my best to explain. I hope it makes sense on the page, even if it often did not in real life.

Now, that question again: when is a car not a car?

This is the key issue in classic cars. The top car marques, be they Bentleys, Bugattis, Ferraris, Maseratis – any of the great names – are almost as rare and as valuable as classic works of art. Just as in art, it's absolutely vital to know which apparent masterpieces are real, and which are forgeries. So, how do you do that?

A £1 million second-hand Ferrari, just like a £1,000 second-hand Ford, should have documentation that establishes its provenance: when it was made, who was the original owner, who bought it after that, and so on. But there are complications. Many classic cars were built to be raced. Their engines blew, or they crashed. Others were altered over time, as parts or body panels were replaced. Or they simply rotted and rusted into shadows of their former selves. After fifty years or more, a once-proud car can be little more than vintage scrap.

But there is one sure-fire way of establishing a car's identity: its chassis number. In any Ferrari, for example, there are three points at which the manufacturer identifies that individual car. First, there is a black and silver aluminium plate, riveted to the bulkhead between the engine compartment and the passenger-bay. This plate is decorated with the Ferrari prancing horse and carries the number of the car's chassis, and the number of its original engine.

Since the plate has only been riveted to the bulkhead, it can be detached, and put on another bulkhead, in another car. As a result, it does not constitute proof of a car's identity.

The engine number is engraved directly into the solid metal of the engine block. This means that an engine can be definitively identified. But racing engines frequently blow up and are then replaced. So a car may get through several different engines. Therefore an engine number by itself cannot identify a car.

The only definite proof of a car's identity is a small steel plate, about two inches long by one inch wide, welded to the chassis just by the front axle. On this is engraved the chassis number. This plate is like an artist's signature. It's the only reliable way of identifying a car.

It's also the only thing you need to have in order to make a car genuine. Anyone who has seen *Jurassic Park* will know that the dinosaurs were supposedly recreated from tiny specks of DNA found in prehistoric mosquitoes. From that tiny scrap of dino-DNA, whole beasts were grown. Well, that's how the classic car business works, too.

Old cars are frequently given total restorations in which all the missing, rusted, burned or bashed-up parts are replaced by brand-new ones. But the law is clear: so long as you've got the original chassis plate, every other bit of a car can be made yesterday, and it's still considered to be the original car, for purposes of authenticity and, most importantly, valuation.

One American lost his entire car collection in the early 1960s, when the barn in which he stored it burned down. He buried the wreckage of the barn and his cars in a great big hole in the ground. Twenty-plus years went by, then an English car-buff who'd heard the story dug the junk back out of the hole, found a single rusted chassis plate that had belonged to a 1959/60 Ferrari Testarossa and built a completely new car around that plate. Now it's worth more than £3 million.

Of course, when there's that kind of money at stake, corruption isn't far behind. Numbers can be forged. Bogus cars and parts are sold as real. The people who are doing it tend to look a bit classier than Arthur Dale, but the principle's just the same.

To sort out the confusion, the classic car world depends on a few supreme experts, who specialise in one particular manufacturer and whose word is law. These men are like Roman emperors, sitting in judgement in the Colosseum. Depending on whether their thumbs go up, or down, you can find yourself with an officially genuine car worth a fortune, or an officially fake one worth peanuts.

So now, bearing in mind that second-hand cars are still second-hand cars, even if they're called Ferrari, follow my journey into the motor-trade jungle. And watch as I come a total and utter cropper . . .

From the moment I first drove round Maisemore, on the back of a tractor, I was always mad about motors. When I first made a bit of money, hiring Brocket as a film location, it was only natural that I wanted to spend some of it on flashy cars.

My first Ferrari was the rusty, eleven-year-old 365GT that I bought in Bristol on the advice of Jim Bosisto, back in 1979. Jim had been recommended to me as an expert on classic Ferraris and Maseratis. He claimed to have been a racing driver himself, and even to have founded his own Formula 500 racing class. By 1979 he was just a sweet, silver-haired old boy in his sixties, who knew the car business back to front and was also a good enough engineer to look after maintenance, servicing and repairs.

That first Ferarri was just bought for fun. The idea that I could actually make money buying cars seemed too good to be true. And of course it was too good to be true. Though it would be many years before that became apparent.

Anyway, Jim Bosisto found a Ferrari chassis plate, No. 3565, which belonged to a 250 SWB (which stands for 'short wheel-base') Ferrari. It cost me £5,500, which was a lot of money for a small chunk of metal with a number on it. But, of course, I was really paying for the right to rebuild the 250 SWB and call it an original car. If I had the original plate, it didn't matter if everything else was new.

I bought the plate and Jim then spent the next decade or so collecting the correct parts for my 250 SWB, as they became available. Meanwhile, as Brocket Hall started making decent money through the early and mid 1980s, I kept on buying more cars. First came a horribly flashy and phallic Maserati Indy that cost £3,500. Then I added two old Maseratis that cost very little but needed to be rebuilt. Jim Bosisto set to work on them, convincing me that they were a sure-fire investment.

Jim had been spending quite a lot of time at Brocket. But until 1985, he actually lived in Wales: he'd come up to the Hall, work on the cars for a day or two, then head back home again. Then his wife died. Soon afterwards he asked if he could come and live on the

Brocket estate. If I could give him somewhere to live and pay him a small retainer, he said, he'd devote himself to my cars.

This sounded like an excellent idea. Jim was a lovely chap to have about the place, with his cheery smile, his flat caps and his dashing silk cravats. So we installed him in a mobile home at the edge of the woods. We connected mains electricity and drainage, and fitted out the inside with a bedroom, bathroom, kitchen and living-room. I made sure that Jim was sent at least one hot meal a day from the Hall kitchen, and I often popped in to see him. It was often easier having a gentle chat about cars with him than facing the tension that enveloped me as soon as I walked through my own front door.

Thanks to Jim's attentions, the random assortment of cars I'd acquired over the years soon began to look like an actual collection. I still had a couple of Mercs from my army days. There was my Ferrari (now looking a lot less rusty) and the three Maseratis. And then Jim bought another Ferrari, a 365 Boxer.

None of these cars had cost very much money. But I began to realise that I might have something worth while on my hands when the Aston Martin boss, Victor Gauntlet, hired Brocket for a weekend to reward his best clients. After Victor and his guests had inspected the full range of Astons, arrayed in front of the house, they asked for a guided tour of my garage. I was amazed by the time everyone took, examining the cars. It made me think that a car collection could be a powerful attraction that would raise the profile of the Hall.

Over the next few months, Jim added three more Ferraris, spending £12,000 – which seemed like a huge amount at the time – on a 1956 250 Europa. He promised me, however, that it would double in value in a year. He was wrong – but only because it increased by even more than that. By now, the press were beginning to take an interest. We painted the garage white and installed floodlights, to show the cars off to their best advantage. And because Jim couldn't manage to do the heavy work involved in maintaining so many cars, I took on another mechanic to help him.

Mark Caswell was a tough Londoner, who ran an auto-repair business. In his spare time, he worked as a nightclub bouncer and a special policeman. He was stockily built, with a neck as thick as his head. He had a growling, Cockney accent, and a tough-guy disposition. He agreed to do a set number of hours' work per week on our cars, in return for the use of our workshop for his business, and the loan of a cottage on the estate. Mark's intimidating manner upset many of the staff, as well as local people who bumped into him while walking on the footpath through the estate. On the other hand, he soon scared away any potential troublemakers, which made him a valuable asset.

Meanwhile, the bank had called Jim Bosisto into their office. They'd noticed that the four Ferraris had trebled in value, thanks to the growing market for classic cars. This sounded like an investment opportunity. If we could put together a proper business plan, they'd be willing to invest in future car purchases.

Jim promptly drew up a list of Ferraris that he

thought would be good investments. The bank then loaned us £1 million, on condition that the car collection was traded as a limited company and that Jim Bosisto, now seventy-two years of age, became managing director of that company.

To celebrate our coup, Jim, Isa and I went out to Italy to visit the Ferrari factory at Maranello. It merely consisted of a few unimposing buildings, with modest offices attached. A small showroom had perhaps half a dozen cars on display. But the really impressive thing about Maranello was the man who had created it all: Enzo Ferrari himself.

Enzo was the Godfather of fast cars. He was quite tall, grey-haired and invariably wore heavy dark glasses, even indoors. Being every inch an Italian, he immediately focused all his attention on Isa, gallantly presenting her with a silk scarf decorated with prancing horses. Though he could speak English, he chose to speak Italian, if only for the pleasure of being able to address every word to Isa, who acted as our interpreter. He told us he'd seen our collection on television and seemed genuinely pleased that we should be so interested in his cars. Jim sat there with an awed expression on his face. He almost got on his knees to pay homage.

In those days, Ferrari was still a small, family company. Enzo's personal assistant was an Englishwoman called Brenda. Not only did she help set up our meeting, but she was always willing to take a phone call, answer a question, or help out in any way she could. I think she realised that I was a fish out of water in the car trade. She warned me that there were very few people

I could trust. I was too thrilled by my surroundings to pay much attention.

After our meeting with Signor Ferrari, we were whisked off to Monza to see his cars perform in the Italian Grand Prix. Isa loved it. There were wall-to-wall good-looking guys, and they were matched – for my benefit – by the stunning women draped over anything red, hot or breathing. We returned on the Orient Express with old Jim looking like the cat that had got the cream. I was pleased to be able to make him so happy. It was a thank-you for everything he'd done.

Isa and I had a private compartment. She was not, however, quite as thrilled by the trip as I'd hoped. For years afterwards, I'd hear her tell people, 'He even brought his mechanic on the Orient Express.' This was her proof that I had always put my cars before her. And the cars were about to become our latest battleground.

When we got home, Isa started asking to be paid for the personal appearances she made at the Hall, talking to guests, taking part in events, hosting dinners and so on. From her point of view, Isa was one of the attractions at Brocket. People liked to come and gawp at her, close up. She had been an extremely successful model, who'd been paid a lot of money to lend her beauty to magazines and advertising campaigns. Why was this any different?

I saw things another way. To me, Brocket Hall was the means by which I would restore my family fortunes, make my name, and prove my sceptical elders wrong. I didn't expect to be paid a huge salary: why should she? Brocket already provided Isa and me with a staggering lifestyle. We had a wonderful home, with cooks, butlers, servants and grounds-keepers all paid for by the business. We never had to buy a meal, or a bottle of wine. We had free first-class tickets whenever we wanted them. Why did she need paying, on top of that? Because, of course, she wanted to be valued as an important person in her own right. But I didn't understand that.

My argument might have washed if I hadn't been spending quite so much money on cars. As far as Isa was concerned, they were my toys. So why couldn't she have money to spend on toys of her own, like jewellery, for example?

I explained, in full pompous-husband mode, that the cars weren't toys. They were a serious business. I even got our accountants to explain to Isa that gems were not a commercial proposition. Instead of listening to my wife, I went to great lengths to persuade her she was being foolish.

Just to make the gulf between us even wider, Isa was deeply suspicious of Jim Bosisto. Something about him made all her alarm-bells ring. She had no evidence, of course. It was her intuition. I told her not to be so silly and, ignoring all her warnings, set off for America with Jim to find lots more cars on which to spend the bank's money.

We spent ten days in the States and parted with most of the £1 million loan. In fact, we bought so many cars that we didn't have anywhere to put them. As soon as we got back, work began on a huge new showroom. The press got wind of this invasion of Ferraris and soon it was all over the papers. The legend of the Brocket collection had begun.

This frenzied expenditure on cars and garages only deepened Isa's anger, and sent her running to her brown bottles even more often. But I was convinced that I'd been right all along. By the end of 1988, the £1 million worth of Ferraris that Jim and I had bought in the US were valued at £3 million. I was thrilled. The bank was ecstatic.

My cars were becoming wheeled celebrities. Guests to the Hall invariably insisted on being shown the collection, before or after dinner. Jim or I would give them a half-hour tour, complete with amusing anecdotes about wacky races and madcap drivers. People absolutely lapped it up, and they were happy to fork out for the special model Ferraris we'd put on sale at the Brocket gift shop, too.

My reputation extended to the very top of the motor trade. Every year, Brocket hosted the annual meeting of all the heads of the car industry. In 1988 Umberto Agnelli, brother of the Fiat boss, Gianni Agnelli, and his wife came to stay. By now, Fiat owned Ferrari. At the end of the conference, Umberto came up to me and said, 'I hear that you want an F40?' This was the new limited-production supercar that Ferrari were shortly to release.

'Yes, but the order book was filled up three years ago. I think I've missed the boat,' I said.

Agnelli smiled. 'I'll get my man to get in touch and give you a confirmed order.'

This was quite a gift. Three months later I was

offered £750,000 by several dealers for the order form alone, or £1 million for the order and car. Quite a price just for a piece of paper! I told them that I was not interested in the money. It was the car I wanted. At that time money simply wasn't a worry. Arrogance, however, was. So was pride. And we all know what comes before a fall.

The bubble was about to burst. All it needed was one last, gigantic puff. And we were about to provide it.

The bank called Jim and me in for another meeting. It was March 1989, the absolute height of the Thatcher–Lawson boom. Property prices were rocketing. Japanese collectors were paying £50 million for Van Gogh paintings. Restaurants were packed. City boys were pocketing massive bonuses. Everyone was rolling in loot.

So now the bank said, 'You've done so well with the first £1 million we lent you, we'd like to give you another £5 mill on top.' No one seemed to notice or care that we hadn't seen a single penny of the 'profits' the cars had made, because they were all still sitting in our showroom. We just pocketed the bank's new money and went off to buy more cars.

Old Jim spent the next few months on the phone while yet more motors arrived from all parts of the globe. I, meanwhile, had decided that the time had finally come to indulge Isa. I took time off from the business, leaving Flick and Alan to run the Hall, which was having the best year in its history (unmatched to this day, I believe). I bought Isa a Mercedes sports car, and a special, long-wheel-base Bentley Turbo for myself, identical to the one that belonged to the Prince of Wales.

We used to use it to drive up to film premières. Since it looked identical to the Waleses' car, the crowds would expect Charles and Di to step out. When Isa emerged from the back seat, there would be a double-take. She was certainly a tall, gorgeous blonde, just not the right one. But she was certainly the next best thing to Di. And the two women had something else in common: for all their public smiles, they were both desperately unhappy in private.

Isa's backache became so severe she checked herself into a local private hospital. Soon afterwards, her surgeon asked me round to his home for supper and a chat. He told me that he had not operated on Isa. There was nothing wrong with her back: her real problem was her craving for pain-killers. We sat next to the fire until late into the night and talked about addiction and how to treat it. The toughest part, he said, was for the sufferer to admit that they were addicted. As long as there was denial, there would never be a cure.

The next evening I went to visit Isa again in the hospital. When I returned home to Watershipps, I went upstairs to find one of our bedroom windows open and the curtains blowing in the breeze. There were footprints clearly marked on the window sill.

I went through my cupboard, but nothing had been touched. Nor was there any sign of anything missing from Isa's cupboard. I called the police, who found a ladder, propped against the wall of the house.

Footprints on the ground showed that it had been carried from a farm building 400 yards away.

When Isa came out of hospital a few days later, she went through her things more thoroughly than I had done, and found that some of her jewellery had been stolen, including a wonderful pair of antique sapphire and diamond Cartier earrings. A little while later, the police got an anonymous message, left on an answering machine. It just said, 'That'll teach him.' They came to the same conclusion that I immediately did: the robber I had tangled with years before, on the night of the General Motors meeting, had done exactly what he promised. He'd come back and got his revenge.

Back at the showroom, the Brocket Ferraris were now so famous they were featured on a special edition of *Jim'll Fix It*. What a pity Jim couldn't fix the car trade. As the cars began to generate a massive amount of restoration work, all of which required specialist parts-suppliers and contractors, I started to realise just how crooked the whole business was.

People saw the Brocket collection coming a mile off. They knew we had money to burn. They knew I was naïve about what went on in their world. They must have thought all their Christmases had come at once. We were ripped off left, right and centre.

We lost $300,000 (then roughly £200,000) when we bought a 1966 Ferrari from an American dealer, only to find before the necessary restoration was completed that he had re-sold it to someone else for twice the price. We bought a rare Maserati 450S engine for $120,000. The dealer said the engine was complete. It was actually a pile of scrap-metal. There went another £80,000. Customs and Excise hit us for £300,000 in VAT bills, fines and interest payments that they claimed were owing on cars imported from the States.

What with these and a few other minor disasters, we'd blown roughly £700,000. But that was nothing. The real scams were yet to come . . .

Back in 1979, I'd bought the chassis plate and some parts from a short-wheel-base (SWB) Ferrari, car No. 3565. A decade later, Jim Bosisto had almost assembled enough additional parts to start rebuilding the car in earnest.

Meanwhile, in 1986, Jim had bought another Ferrari 250 SWB on my behalf, with the chassis number 3539. By then, prices had started to rocket and it cost £150,000. He bought it from a top Ferrari dealer called Massimo Colombo, who was based in Monte Carlo. Naturally, Jim and I had checked out the car's provenance. It was listed as genuine in the definitive book on Ferrari 250s, written by the acknowledged expert in the field, Jess Pourret. He described 3539 as a 'very potent, left-hand-drive, Le Mans-prepared' car.

In the Ferrari 250 market, Pourret's word was law. If he said my car was genuine, it was. By 1989, its value had zoomed up to more than £1 million. So just imagine my horror when Pourret published a new edition of his book, in which my car was now described as a fake. 'The real 3539 doesn't exist any more,' wrote Pourret. With one stroke of his pen, I'd lost a million quid.

I rang Massimo Colombo at his business in Monte

Carlo and asked for an explanation. He swore that he and Pourret had fallen out over a business dispute and Pourret had threatened to get his own back by rubbishing the SWB. 'Then the new edition of the book came out saying that the car is a fake. Typical Pourret,' huffed Colombo.

This typified the absurdities of the car business. Even Colombo agreed that there were barely any parts of the original car No. 3539 in the machine now sitting in my showroom. But, he insisted, it did have the all-important plate, with the genuine chassis number. He also claimed to have a letter from Pourret confirming that fact.

Pourret disagreed. He wrote me a long and tortuous account of why he no longer believed that car was genuine. In fact, he claimed, his discovery that the car was fake and his determination to publish the truth had been the real reasons he and Colombo had fallen out.

Caught in the middle of this extremely expensive argument, and unable to work out who was telling the truth, I tried to get some independent advice. I contacted Enzo Ferrari at Maranello and received a written reply that I still have, stating that Jess Pourret, the world expert on Ferrari 250s, was not trusted by Ferrari themselves.

I had the chassis examined by an ex-Scotland Yard forensic scientist who reported, 'I am entirely satisfied that the number [3539] is the original Ferrari chassis number.'

None of this made any difference. Pourret was

unmoved. He refused to change his book and restore the car's genuine status. It remains, officially, a fake to this day.

By now, the cars were becoming more of a burden to me than a pleasure. In March 1990 I had my first real disagreement with Jim. Some of the deals he'd done had been superb. Ferrari Daytonas that we'd bought for £80,000 were going for £250,000. Another car was under offer for £250,000 that had only cost us fourteen grand. All told, we had generated around £1 million of actual cash profit on car transactions.

Set against that, however, we'd lost a fortune thanks to dishonesty in the trade, tax disputes and the downgrading of the SWB. And with interest rates heading towards 15 per cent, our bank loans were becoming ruinously expensive. The net effect was that borrowings had risen to £7.5 million. We had a lot of fancy cars in our showroom, but we were massively in debt.

Worse still, Jim had bought three more Maseratis at quite absurd prices. When I queried these purchases, Jim stalked out of his office, saying that if his decisions were to be questioned he would return to Wales. The bank would discontinue the operation without him, he said. He would not even discuss the matter further.

Isa suggested that I should slip a written note through Jim's door, which I did. He eventually talked to me after a week. The deals were done, he said. He would not renege on them. He was a gentleman and his word was his bond. Nothing could have been further from the truth.

When the Maseratis arrived from the States, Steve

Gwyther, one of our mechanics, rang me and said, 'You'd better come down to the showroom, LB.'

I couldn't believe my eyes. The cars were total wrecks – three piles of junk. And there was worse to come. A few days later, Steve called me again, asking me to join him as soon as possible. As I emerged from my basement office, I met Don Bennett, the estate manager, getting out of his Range Rover.

'Hop in,' he said, opening the door. I jumped in and Don drove off at top speed. 'It's Jim,' he said. 'We think he's dead. There's no answer to his door. John, the woodsman, is forcing it right now.'

We got to Jim's mobile home just as John was opening the door. Jim's dead body was sprawled across the hallway, lying on the floor like a bunch of discarded rags.

The police arrived and inspected the scene. Gradually, John, Don, Steve and I all became aware that some of what we saw did not tally up. For example, Jim kept a pistol for his protection. But it was always kept in the right-hand-side drawer next to his bed. Now it was on top of the unit, ready to be used. It was clear that he was expecting trouble.

His big bunch of keys, which he must have used to unlock his front door, was nowhere to be seen. Someone must have removed it, but who?

There was £3,000 in notes in Jim's jacket pocket. Later that morning an Italian man rang the showroom, asking if Jim had left for London. He said he was expecting a payment of £30,000 in cash. But for what? And was Jim's money a deposit on that payment?

I was sure that Jim had died under suspicious circumstances. Don and Steve both agreed, but the police weren't interested at all. They were convinced that there was no reason to suspect foul play. So Jim was laid to rest in a cemetery near the lovely Pembrokeshire coast. Isa stood by me at his graveside as I cried unashamedly for the strange old man who'd been so much part of our lives for the past eight years.

A short while later, I received a call from the executor of Jim's will. When he'd heard of Jim's death, he'd asked Jim's bank how much money there was in his account. The answer was astounding: £120,000. This made no sense. Jim always told Isa, Steve and me that he had no money. He'd even just asked me to pay the £80 road tax for his Citroën.

Jim's only surviving relative came to collect his belongings. As he was going through his possessions, he found some papers that unravelled everything. They indicated that the prices that Jim had agreed to pay for cars that he had purchased for the Brocket collection were much lower than the prices the collection had paid. He'd obviously pocketed the difference.

Several of Jim's deals had been conducted through a German agent called Herr Daub, an eighty-year-old man based in Hamburg. I went to meet him, taking Isa as my interpreter. Daub told us that, when Jim agreed to purchase a car, sums that varied between 100 and 300 per cent were added to the price. When the extra money came in, Daub returned it to Jim. Isa asked why he did this and Daub said that Jim had explained that the tax laws in the UK for old-age pensioners were very strict and that I had arranged this with him to enable him to get some income.

We had also discovered that Jim had been signing money out of the company account and putting it in his own. The £120,000 found in his bank account was just the tip of the iceberg. He must have had other accounts elsewhere. But the truth about them had gone with him to the grave. Jim's betrayal devastated me.

I had to admit that Isa's feminine intuition had been right all along. Now I was beginning to wonder whether she wasn't right about the cars as well.

Isa's father, Gus, whose business sense was very sharp indeed, was urging me to sell my entire collection. He was convinced that the eighties bubble would soon burst, that recession was on the way, and I should get out while the going was good. At the time, I had just received an offer of £15 million for ten of my cars from a Japanese consortium: enough to wipe out all my debts and still leave me with a thirty-car collection. But all my advisers in England insisted that the economy was in splendid shape.

So I didn't listen to Gus Lorenzo, and I looked that Japanese gift-horse squarely in the mouth. Then I found another man to take Jim Bosisto's place. His name was Rick Furtado. He was a smooth operator, with immaculate, slicked-back black hair, a wardrobe filled with expensively casual Ralph Lauren gear, and a cool, calm manner. I thought he seemed like a decent enough chap. Isa took one look at Furtado and said she didn't trust him an inch, an opinion she repeated to anyone who'd listen.

Only later did I discover that Rick Furtado had more than a dozen American convictions acquired between 1971–89, for larceny of controlled substances, breaking and entering, cheque fraud and falsifying car number-plates. But by then it was too late. My business was going belly-up. The bank was getting ready to repossess my house. And I was halfway to a conviction for fraud myself.

– 15 –

The Insurance Scam

I'D JUST GOT BACK FROM A BUSINESS TRIP TO THE States, drumming up corporate business for Brocket Hall, when I first heard from Rick Furtado. He said that he was an agent specialising in the sale of classic cars, particularly in the Far East, and said that he had a purchaser in Japan for one of my Maseratis. He offered me $440,000 (roughly £300,000 at that time), which I thought was an astronomic price, far more than the car was worth. I was only too happy to sell.

Rick insisted that the car had to be in 'Japanese condition', which meant that it was so immaculately clean and shining that you could eat a meal off any part of it. As a Brit, I rather disapproved. We tend to think that a car has been properly restored if it is in full working order. The only way to prove that is to drive it regularly. And that means accepting the odd speck of dust and dirt. But who was I to argue?

The car was cleaned so thoroughly that the engine

was actually removed and every tube and wire polished – twice. When it was perfect, we shipped it out to the Far East. We got our money without any problem. Later I found out that Rick had in fact sold the car to another agent for over £500,000, and it had then been sold for the third and final time to the actual Japanese client, who paid $1 million (roughly £700,000).

Still, I'd got what I'd been promised and I'd made a massive profit, so I had no complaints. When Rick bought a Ferrari from me for £120,000, I began to think I'd struck lucky. And then Rick came in with his biggest offer of all. He said that one of his Japanese clients was interested in buying a ten-car package.

By now, several months had passed since Gus's first warning of recession and I was beginning to see warning signs that the good times might be coming to an end. We were still doing decent business up at the Hall, but the cash wasn't flowing quite as freely as it had before. So I was now much more open to offers. I gave Rick the go-ahead.

He flew over and spent a complete week at Brocket photographing all the cars in detail and building up a thorough documentary file for each machine. Then he came down to see me at Watershipps, to talk me through his conclusions.

Rick had selected the ten cars he wanted for the sale. The auctioneers Phillips had valued them. The total price came to £7.9 million. We had to take out insurance to cover that amount. But, as usual, there was a minor snag.

One of the cars on the list was a Maserati 'Birdcage' (so called because its tubular construction looks like a birdcage, underneath the body panels), bought by Jim Bosisto. Or, to be precise, it was the semi-restored re-build of a car, number 2456, that had been burned in a garage fire more than twenty years earlier.

The original birdcage frame was so melted and twisted in the fire that it was junked. All that remained of the car was bought by a Maserati collector in New York called Joel Finn, who planned to restore it. Finn, though, was not just a collector. He, along with an Englishman called Richard Crump, was one of the two recognised world experts on Maserati Birdcages, and his book on the subject was the absolute authority on which cars were or were not genuine – just like Pourret's book on Ferrari 250s. So Joel Finn could set the rules for a market in which he himself was trading.

After a few years, Finn decided he couldn't be bothered to rebuild the car and sold the bits to another American, Bob Rubin. Richard Crump, who was the agent in the sale, confirmed the car was genuine, and was paid for his services.

As part of the sale, Finn listed all the existing parts, including the engine of car number 2456 in his own handwriting. Rubin commissioned the top restorers in the business to get to work on the car. They built a new body and a new birdcage frame and then Rubin, too, decided he'd had enough. That's when Jim Bosisto bought it for our collection.

By 1990, the price of a complete Maserati Birdcage had risen to £1.2 million. Rick Furtado was saying his

Japanese client would pay this amount, so I was quids in, even allowing for the £100,000 it would cost to complete the final bits of restoration.

Then I got a call from Joel Finn. He said, 'I don't know what you think you have bought but all I sold Rubin were some parts from No. 2456. I did not sell him the car. If you want the title, you'll have to buy it from me.'

Rubin and Crump both insisted that Finn had already sold the title to the car and sent me sworn affidavits to that effect. But none of that mattered. If Joel Finn told the world that my Maserati was a fake, I'd never be able to sell it and I'd lose £1.2 million. So now I'd have to pay for his co-operation.

Finn and I met at a Silverstone race meet. I wore a wire to record our conversation. He told me that he would 'sell' me the title to my own car for $100,000. He kindly agreed to take $10,000 up front and then the balance when I needed the title to complete my sale to the Japanese. Assuming, of course, that I ever did complete the sale. (I still have the invoice confirming the transaction.)

In August 1990, Saddam Hussein invaded Kuwait. The rise in international tension had an immediate dampening effect on the economy, particularly the travel industry. Americans don't like to get on planes if they think someone might be trying to blow them up.

By September, we were all working away, preparing the ten cars to Japanese standards. We hadn't actually met the Japanese client, or received a single yen, but Rick was entirely confident that the deal would go

through. The bank were so impressed with his performance that they insisted on giving him Jim's old role
as the collection's exclusive agent. Oddly enough, the
CV he sent them made no reference to his convictions.

Then, in October, as the car debts mounted and the
economy worsened, I had another communication
from the bank, concerning the car collection. I was
informed that there would be 'absolutely no further
increase in the borrowings'. If I wanted any more
money, I'd have to raise it by selling cars. Oh, and one
other thing: could I please provide a formal valuation
for Brocket Hall? My loan agreement made me personally responsible for the money, and the Hall was
pledged as my security for the loan. So if I couldn't pay
back the loan, the bank were taking my house.

They were wha-a-a-at?

No one had told me anything about personal guarantees, let alone any guarantees based on Brocket Hall.
I'd spent the past twenty years fighting for my right to
live at the Hall, and working to make it a success. There
was no way I would ever risk giving it away to a bank.
Except that I had. And none of my expensive lawyers or
accountants, on whose advice I'd relied when signing
the contract, had highlighted the clause that gave
Brocket as the collateral for the money I'd borrowed to
buy cars.

I went to see another lawyer. He gave me the obvious advice: sue your solicitors and accountants. Just one
problem: my family were all agreed that it was fearfully
ungentlemanly to do anything as vulgar as suing one's
advisers. 'Made bed . . . lie in it . . . see it through . . .

family name, etc.' I dare say you know the patter by now.

Still, there was no need to panic. The Japanese deal would solve our debt problems at a stroke. The business at Brocket continued to perform reasonably well, although there were signs of companies drawing in their horns. But even if that suffered a dip, we were building a golf course on the estate. It wasn't making money yet. But in the long run, it looked like a sure-fire success.

In November, Isa announced that she was pregnant again. She didn't seem especially happy about having another child. At home she spent so long in bed, blaming it on her back, that Alex and Antalya often asked the nanny and me, 'Will Mummy be paralysed for life?' I'd reassure them that she was really quite all right, so then they'd ask, 'Why isn't she up, then?'

It wasn't easy trying to find a way through my business problems knowing that things were going so badly at home. And now, to make my stomach really lurch with fear, Rick Furtado had gone quiet about the Japanese deal. Rick had kept assuring us that his clients would be flying over 'at any time', but there was no sign of them.

By Christmas I was seriously worried. There were indications in the car market that prices were about to start falling. If the Japanese got wind of this, they would surely back out, the bank might pull the rug out from under me and I'd lose Brocket. God, how I'd wished that I'd never met Jim Bosisto, never cared about those damn cars. I'd become as addicted to Ferraris as Isa was to her pain-killers. I'd wallowed in the attention and prestige they'd brought me. As if that really mattered, compared to my home, or my children.

Then one day in early 1991 the phone rang. It was Rick. 'I'm afraid the deal has gone cold,' he said flatly. 'The Japanese see the market dropping and they want out. Listen, I gotta go.'

That was that. Our lifeline was gone. We'd spent months fixating on a deal that was going sour. Meanwhile, we'd not sold anything to anyone else. And now it was too late.

On 17 January 1991 bombing raids on Baghdad signalled the start of Desert Storm – the first war against Iraq. And with that, the car market froze. It wasn't a matter of prices plummeting. People simply stopped trading. No one wanted to buy, at any price.

Interest rates on our borrowings had risen to 17.5 per cent. So my debts were rising, and I had no way to pay them off. I thought of all the possible deals I'd ignored when the market was still going up. I'd even turned down £750,000 just for a piece of paper – the F40 order form. It wasn't worth anything now.

The gloom around Brocket Hall was suffocating. One company after another was ringing up to cancel its booking. None of the Americans wanted to cross the Atlantic with a war going on, but they weren't the only ones. A merchant bank in the City of London scrapped its event when its Europe-based director refused to fly the Channel.

The shame I felt was overpowering. All my family's criticisms seemed to be coming true. I really had been just as reckless and foolhardy as they'd said. The maximum value of my property and business was about £9 million, almost exactly the amount I now owed to the bank. To clear the debts, I would have to sell the whole thing, lock, stock and barrel. Seventy years after my great-grandfather had bought Brocket Hall, I'd have pissed it away.

One morning, after yet another sleepless night, I went down to the showroom and talked to Steve Gwyther about the bind we were in. Steve was a thoroughly nice guy and a superb mechanic. He loved working on the Ferraris and attending the events where they were displayed. He had a good salary and cottage to go with it. I had just built a double garage for him so that he could have his own workshop facility at home. Brocket Hall and its cars were his life.

''Course, the cars are insured for far more than they are now worth,' Steve commented, raising a subject that would soon take on enormous significance. Then he said, 'This is a real fucker. Perhaps we ought to talk things through with Mark. Whatever the answer, we'll need Mark's input.'

I agreed and convened a meeting that evening at Watershipps. I can recall it virtually word for word. But then, you do tend to remember an event when you and everyone else involved in it are interrogated by the police, and when you've got thirty months of enforced leisure, courtesy of Her Majesty, in which to sit and think about it . . . again, and again, and again.

Anyway, Steve Gwyther, Mark Caswell, Isa and I then had what the police always referred to in their documents as 'The Kitchen Meeting', so called because we all sat round the modern, pine table in our kitchen. It was designed as a conservatory, with a glass roof and plain white units. If you ever play golf at Brocket Hall, Watershipps is now the clubhouse, rather than my private home. And what happened next explains why.

There was a real atmosphere of fear in the air. Mark and Steve were shocked by the apparent suddenness and size of the financial problems. I explained that the conference business was solid, whatever its immediate problems, ditto the golf club. The problem was the cars.

'Well,' said Mark, 'if the bank want the loan reduced and it's not possible, why not just close the company and let the bank take the stock?'

'Because,' Isa interjected, 'Charles gave them a personal guarantee. That means that they can sell Brocket. So all our homes and livelihoods go down the pan.'

There was a profound silence as this sank in.

'Bastards!' exclaimed Mark.

'Fuckers!' added Steve.

'Quite, but that doesn't get us any further,' I said.

'Well, how much would get us out of the shit?' asked Mark.

'I reckon that £4.5 million would do it,' I said. 'That would reduce the debt and the interest payments for long enough for the market to recover, which it almost certainly will do.'

'That's four cars at about a million quid each,' said Steve thoughtfully.

Ever the practical one, Mark said, 'Seems simple to me. I know this bloke who has a crusher. Just drop some of the cars into that. They'll never be found again and there'll be no evidence. Then claim for them. Insurance company will never find them.'

'But I couldn't do that!' I protested. 'That would be sacrilege. The cars are all pretty rare, and two are unique.'

'Yeah,' agreed Mark. 'And you're always saying that one of 'em is an old dog.'

'True, but a crusher is still out of the question.'

We spent a while longer trying to work out how we could make an insurance claim without destroying the cars. The conversation then revolved around how a claim could be made, but ended without conclusion. We agreed to meet the next evening for supper.

That night Isa and I talked about it some more, our ideas getting more and more outrageous.

'Why don't you blow the cars up?' Isa suggested.

'Don't be daft,' I replied tetchily. 'No, there's got to be an answer. We just don't know what it is.'

The next evening, Isa prepared steaks for the four of us and we all sat around the kitchen table once again. The police – imaginative boys – called this 'The Steak Supper'.

Steve suggested which cars he thought we should dispose of, if this was to be the answer. Two of the Ferraris that Phillips had put high values on were poor cars, both technically and on the road. The other two should be relatively easy to dispose of as they were just bare shells at this time. One of them was the Maserati Birdcage.

Once again, we went over the whole crusher

business, with Mark pointing out that this was the simplest, safest solution, while I went on about how the cars were precious works of art that mustn't be destroyed. (As if most of them hadn't been crashed, burned or otherwise obliterated once already.)

'There's another slight problem,' muttered Steve. 'What if the insurance company don't pay up, due to some small print in the contract? We're fucked bigtime! We should do something that is not irreversible.'

And so our plot was born. We'd dismantle the chosen cars, take them away from Brocket, then report them as stolen and collect on the insurance. We reckoned we'd be covered, even if the insurance didn't pay up. As Steve pointed out: 'If the claim goes ahead the cars can be disposed of. If the claim is rejected then they could be found after a "tip-off" and be rebuilt. We wouldn't lose everything.'

There was silence.

'Well, where do we go from here?' Isa asked.

We talked for a while about how car parts could be made to disappear, then magically reappear again without anyone noticing. Then Steve said, 'Dismantling the cars would only take a day or two, especially with Mark's help. He's got all the equipment for it. But where would we store the stuff?'

'No problem,' said Mark. 'I know several places in London. I could probably find a lock-up, or, better still, a container.'

'Well, shall we do it, then?' I asked.

There was a silence. All we could hear were the ducks on the lake and the distant traffic of late commuters.

Isa sat next to Mark, with tears in her eyes, begging him. 'Please, Mark, help us. Just think of our children, think of our families.'

There was a long silence, then Mark said, 'Okay, it's a deal, but what's in it for us? Steve, what do you want out of this?'

'All I really want is my dream car, a Porsche 911 Targa,' said Steve. 'Twenty-five thousand pounds will buy a good second-hand one, so I'll help for that.'

Mark shook his head. 'If I'm going to risk my neck, I need more than that. I think we should get £40,000 each.'

He looked at Steve for approval. Steve nodded and so the deal was struck. But even then Mark added, 'I still say we're mad to do it this way. The crusher is final and we could never get caught if anything goes wrong. But if you won't do that, we'll do it this way. And I want a cash advance now.'

'Well, if we're skating on thin ice, we might as well tap dance,' I said. I gave Mark £3,000 to tide him over, and with that the meeting was over and the guys went home.

That evening Isa and I talked about what had been suggested. The thing that seemed to bother her most was Steve getting a Porsche.

'You know that's the one car I have always wanted,' she moaned. 'We've been married eight years. You buy yourself God knows how many Ferraris that threaten to sink the ship and now we're talking about bloody well giving one to one of the employees! It's always the same story. The staff come first and me last.'

I pointed out that Steve wasn't getting a Porsche. He was getting cash. If he chose to spend it on a car, that was his business. I didn't admit, or even recognise, that Isa had a point. But she did, and it was better than she knew. Because Mark soon came back and said he'd been thinking. The price for his and Steve's co-operation had just gone up. It was now £100,000.

Just to add to my problems, Isa's condition was becoming serious. On a good day, she could function. She'd set up a little pre-school for local children that had attracted eighty pupils. Despite being pregnant with our third child, she still modelled for glossy magazines, promoting the myth of the glamorous Brockets, Lord and Lady of Brocket Hall. But, as always, the reality and the myth were two very different things.

Isa's mood seemed to be made worse by her pregnancy. She'd smash things around the house, either in anger or drug-induced clumsiness. Our new housekeeper, Fran, kept finding little hoards of pills around the house in the strangest of places. And as Isa went to pieces, so did four of my Ferraris.

It took three nights of hard work in the evenings to dismantle the four 'stolen' cars and grind any incriminating chassis or engine numbers off their various parts – for once, the last thing we wanted was for any bits to be identifiable. But where were we going to put everything? And how would we get it there?

Mark Caswell found a place in Greenford, just off the A40 on the western edge of London, where we could rent a container for £1,500 a year. And he had the transport problem solved, too. 'I've gotta move some of me sister's furniture this week so I'll hire a van,' he said. 'That way if police ever investigate there will be a legitimate reason for hiring it.'

It took about thirty minutes to unload a van filled with car parts into the large metal box that was to be their new home. Mark had bought two special padlocks that couldn't be cut; he locked the container and we set off for home. We said very little on the way back. We each had our own thoughts about what we had done. The die was cast. But how would it roll? Only the future would tell.

We waited a few weeks, while the conference business weakened even further, before 'discovering' the theft. Steve let everyone know he was going to the garage where all the cars that were intended for sale in Japan were being stored, to change a set of wheels. He asked John, the woodsman, to help him transport the wheels and . . . Oops! Four of the cars were missing.

Meanwhile, Rick Furtado had come in on the deal. He would back up our story, in return for which we would 'compensate' him for the commission he had lost on the stolen cars that he could not now sell. The fact that he had not been able to sell them before they were stolen was conveniently forgotten.

So, Rick flew into the UK to inspect the cars on behalf of his Japanese clients. When Rick arrived, he put on a fine show of indignant fury, saying that the Japanese would sue him for non-performance. And then we waited for the insurance money to roll in . . .

Which it didn't. The loss adjusters inspected the scene and announced that the claim would be settled by the end of the month. The solicitors who had put the policy in place to begin with said that they were ready to issue a writ if the claim wasn't settled soon. Then came the bombshell. The insurers had voided the claim.

This turned out to be standard practice. Insurers often refuse to pay out big claims so as to delay payment for as long as possible. So the solicitors issued their writ. And the lawyers – the only people, naturally, to make a bean from this whole ghastly farce – got to work.

Rick Furtado was asked to produce an affidavit from the original purchasers of the ten-car package to demonstrate to the insurers that the deal was genuine and the valuations therefore reasonable. I did not see the necessity of this as the valuations had been done independently by Phillips, but he was asked to provide it nevertheless. On the other hand, I was as interested as anyone in finding out the identity of Rick's Far Eastern clients.

He had only ever referred to them as 'the Japanese', claiming that he could not disclose their identity as he was prevented from doing so as part of his client confidentiality agreement. This may have been the case but I had always suspected the real reason was that, as with the record price for the Maserati 5000, he was selling the cars on for far greater prices than we were receiving, and he didn't want me calling up the purchaser to check on him.

Eventually a sworn and notarised affidavit arrived, showing that the name of the client was one Warren Liu from California and Hong Kong. Well, that seemed genuine enough.

– 16 –

Falling Apart

BY THE EARLY MONTHS OF 1991, I POSSESSED A VAST collection of Ferraris and Maseratis that were costing me a fortune in interest payments, and that nobody wanted to buy.

My conference business had been hit by the joint efforts of Saddam Hussein and George Bush, Snr.

I was threatened with the loss of my family home.

I had entered into a conspiracy to defraud an insurance company and dismantled four of my own cars.

Two of my co-conspirators were trying to screw me for more money . . .

. . . and the third, my wife, was off her face on drugs.

Meanwhile, as if we were not already in enough trouble, Rick proceeded to drop me even further in it. He said that his cousin, Barry Flynn, was doing some PR work for a man called Khun Sa, a Burmese tribal leader, who was trying to achieve independence for his people, the Shan. Rick said that the Shan were doomed to poverty unless they were allowed to export their minerals and natural resources.

I asked Meg, my PA, to get the House of Lords library to send us all they had on the Shan state and Khun Sa and it did indeed appear to show that what Rick said was correct.

Rick explained that he wanted to set up a gem business with Barry, who now lived with his Thai wife in Chiang Mai, in northern Thailand. This, he said, would be a lot easier if he had the prestige and credibility that he would gain from association with a proper English lord. So he wanted me and Isa to go with him to Thailand to help him impress the local representative of the Shan state, who was called Mook, and thus set up a deal with Khun Sa to buy gems from the Shan mines at good prices. This, he assured us, would all be quite legal, and we would get a terrific holiday into the bargain.

Neither Rick nor the House of Lords library, however, gave me the one vital fact that I needed to know about Khun Sa. He was one of the world's largest producers and sellers of opium, the raw material for heroin. He was, in fact, a drug-lord and, as a general with 20,000 troops under his personal command, a warlord too.

In July 1991 Isa gave birth to our third child, William. He was born six weeks prematurely, by Caesarean section. After the birth, Isa stayed in hospital. Alex and I often went to visit her but these visits became more and more difficult. So Alex would just play quietly for a few minutes and then ask to go home.

Isa finally came home, and life, on the surface, continued almost exactly as it had before, though there was one development the significance of which I did not understand at the time. No sooner had William been born than Isa's mother, Brigitte, seemed to lose her passionate interest in Alex. Suddenly, the new baby was her favourite. Little did I know what effect this favouritism would have on William's life, and mine, over the years to come.

Back at Brocket, we hosted the annual meeting of a car manufacturer, as we had long done. I was asked to travel all over the world to judge cars at concours d'élégance (beauty contests for fancy motors). And suddenly, it looked as though the good life would continue for real.

For months my brother Richard, who'd been helping me as a consultant at Brocket, had been promising me that the bank would have to change its mind and put together some form of refinancing for our loans. Brocket Hall was too high-profile to be allowed to go bust. There was even a picture of the house on the front cover of the bank's brochure. Also, the millions of pounds we owed was too big a sum simply to write off.

So we started talks with the bank, whose first demand was that we should appoint a professional manager to run the business. I was effectively fired, and when the new man, William Pound, brought in a new team, it meant Flick had to leave as well.

Pound was an excellent administrator, but his self-professed weakness was marketing. So a new marketing director was appointed. She proved to be far less successful at attracting business than we supposed amateurs had been. Unfortunately, her dictatorial manner, either overriding suggestions made by members of staff or claiming them as her own, alienated the people who worked for her.

In no time at all, the 'professionals' were massively increasing the cost of running Brocket, while driving sales down to record lows. Even worse, the place lost its unique selling point: the feeling that you were coming to stay not in a faceless hotel but in a real person's home – a person who'd greet you at the door, have a drink with you in the evening and stay for dinner, too.

In the midst of this confusion, Mrs Thatcher arrived to take over the Hall for a week to write her diaries. There were writers stationed in various rooms while she would circulate from one to the other, correcting, adding and cajoling. Maggie and I had always got on well. I had attended her farewell drinks party at the Cavalry Club, in Piccadilly, after she resigned as Prime Minister. After the rest of the guests had left, I sat with her and another Tory peer, Anthony Colwyn, in the empty club and, in a sad, exhausted voice, she wistfully sighed, 'Where did it all go wrong?' Anthony and I glanced at each other, and after a moment's silence I said, 'Too many yes-men.'

By the end of 1991, with the bank obviously open to renegotiating the loan, it became obvious that the phoney insurance claim had been not only illegal but unnecessary. I met the mechanics. 'I think we should withdraw the claim,' I said.

'Well, if you had taken my advice in the first place and stuffed them in a fuckin' crusher we wouldn't have a problem, as there'd be no evidence,' snapped Mark. 'No body, no case.'

And then, ever the practical one, he added, 'So you withdraw the claim, how are you going to pay us?'

'I'll just have to do it by instalments,' I said.

'Oh yeah? Over how much time? I need money now. If the police ever find out what's happened, you'll be ruined and the bank will pull the plug. Then we'd get nothing.'

'Why should the police find out?' I asked.

'Because Lady B is in another world, that's bloody well why!' said Mark. 'If ever things go pear-shaped that will be the reason. And if they do, I'm not taking any flak for you. We'll say we was forced, threatened with eviction. That would land you right in it.'

I started trying to work out a deal, giving them equipment and cars from the estate that they could either keep or sell.

Then Steve pointed out a minor flaw in my plan: 'How the fuck are you going to withdraw the claim without it looking like you're guilty? If it's a genuine claim you'd fight to the finish.'

It was a good point, one that would require a lot of legal cunning to resolve. Meanwhile, the bank was making it clear that one condition of refinancing our loan would be that they would have first call on the proceeds of our insurance claim. They wouldn't be too thrilled if the claim suddenly disappeared – not when £4.5 million's worth of assets had vanished from the company books.

But there was one more car disaster to come as those bloody short-wheel-base Ferrari 250s came back to haunt me once again. Quick recap: there were two cars. One was bought from Massimo Colombo on the basis of being genuine, but was then – for reasons already given – described as a fake by the world's top Ferrari 250 expert. But there was the other 250, the one that had been built around the chassis plate, No. 3565, that I'd bought on Jim Bosisto's advice, back in 1979.

By the end of 1991, I'd already spent some £50,000 on restoration work, with about £75,000 more still needing to be spent. That would be fine if the car was genuine. With Desert Storm done and dusted, the car market was beginning to warm up again, and a genuine 250 could go for as much as £1 million, so we'd make a massive profit. But was it genuine? Now that I knew the extent of Jim's treachery, I began to wonder whether he hadn't been cheating me from the start. I was already involved in one fraud. I certainly didn't want to be up to my neck in another.

So I did everything I could to establish the truth of the situation. I faxed and spoke to the ever-helpful Brenda at Ferrari HQ. I corresponded with another Ferrari expert, Antoine Prunet. I tried to see if there was another car with the same number anywhere: by now I had my own huge database of information on Ferraris, which was as exhaustive as any in the world.

There was no factual evidence to dispute the authenticity of my car, just my lingering suspicion of Jim Bosisto and my absolute determination not to take any risk whatsoever. So, to be on the safe side, I sold the car to Rick Furtado for £80,000, which was the price of a semi-built replica. He could then finish off the restoration and sell it on, with a mark-up for his profit. The bank were very unhappy about all this, because the car was on the books at £1 million. But Rick met them, talked them round, and the deal was eventually authorised.

Right, I thought. That's one less problem to worry about. Well, so it was . . . for now.

Back at Watershipps, Rick formally introduced us to his cousin Barry Flynn. With him was an American ex-Green Beret colonel who was in command of the bodyguard for Prince Sihanouk of Cambodia. The colonel said that the prince wanted to hold a conference in Britain and would like to use Brocket. Barry then added that Khun Sa, the mysterious Burmese warlord, was prepared to present me with a legendary, massive, 48,000-carat rough-cut ruby for display at Brocket, so long as it was then presented to the Queen to be donated to charity.

All Isa and I had to do in return was to write a letter, in ridiculously flowery language, extending our good wishes to Khun Sa and agreeing to meet his representative, a man called Mook, in Thailand. And there was one last thing: could Rick please have a pair of Isa's shoes? As a gesture of goodwill, Khun Sa wanted to cover them in jewels, and then present them back to her in Thailand.

Aside from Isa's continuing pain-killer abuse, everything was looking up. Officials from the bank

Myself as a young boy

Robert O'Cahan, my great-great-
grandfather, who started the
family brewery

My great-grandfather in typical
jovial stance

First World War ambulances and crews for which my great-grandfather
raised money

The second Lord Brocket holding my father, *c.* 1941

My father lends his support to his father's election campaign at Wavertree, Liverpool

My grandfather (left)
with David Lyon
(centre), and King
George VI

The second Lord Brocket
in coronation robes

Bramshill, bought by my grandfather, is now a police training college

My mother and father in Cannes, *c.* 1951

My father with one of his prize bulls, 1958

Revisiting my childhood home, Maisemore

Carton in County Kildare was one of the estates acquired by my grandfather

As inspecting officer at a police passing-out parade, 1973

With Princess Anne, as her ADC, and (left) Commanding Officer Colonel Bill Stockton in Germany, 1974

Spandau prison in Berlin where I helped guard the sole occupant, Rudolf Hess, in 1974

Renovation at Brocket Hall: building work gets underway, 1979

Hard at work in a bathroom

A mucky business: tracking the sewer system

Katharine Hepburn and Bill Fraser filming *The Corn is Green* at Brocket

Judy

Isa and Alex help with prizegiving

Our final holiday with the children before I went to prison

Isa and I in 1983

With Foreign Secretary Sir Geoffrey Howe and Lady Howe
during the FCO Summit in 1986

With Baroness
Thatcher, who
was a frequent
visitor and who
wrote her
memoirs at
Brocket Hall

Isa with Jim Bosisto on the Orient Express on the way to visit Enzo Ferrari

On holiday in America, 1993

My last outing at Silverstone in 1995,
in Lauda's Formula 1 Ferrari

The 1957 Maserati 300S, driven by
Sterling Moss and Fangio

The lake at Brocket
Hall at night

The Time Lords, with Dave Mumford far left and Eddie King fourth from left

With team-mates on *I'm a Celebrity*

A changed man

called a meeting at Watershipps with the bank, trustees and me. They took responsibility for having lent us £5 million at the height of the market, leaving us stranded when it collapsed. In recognition of this they agreed to lend the combined car and conference business £15 million, interest-free over ten years. In return, they would take a 25 per cent stake in the business that could be bought back in the first five years on extremely favourable terms.

All we had to do was meet the capital repayments on the existing debt. To do that, we just needed to maintain a 15 per cent occupancy rate at Brocket Hall. If we were full on one day a week, we'd be fine, even if we were completely empty for the other six. By way of comparison, our occupancy rate in 1989 had been close to 90 per cent: all we had to do was be one-sixth as successful. If we couldn't do that, I thought, we all ought to be shot.

Of course, it was one thing to agree a deal. It was quite another to draw up the huge contracts on which the bank insisted. Meanwhile, Mark was bitching about not getting his £100,000 from the insurance pay-out, but until the deal was done I didn't have the money. And there was still the worry that the car parts might be discovered. I was walking a very narrow tightrope over a very deep drop. Still, at least the end was in sight.

We spent Christmas 1992 with Isa's parents at the holiday home in Puerto Rico. When we got back, we faced one of the saddest moments in an upper-class parent's or child's life: the first day at prep school. We were sending Alex to Ludgrove, the same school Charles and Diana had chosen for William and Harry, which explained why the front gates were surrounded by packs of press photographers and TV cameramen.

As we settled Alex into his dormitory and looked around his new classroom, I remembered my first days at Spyway, left alone on that cold bleak driveway. We said goodbye to Alex at the front entrance and gave him a big hug and a kiss. He was being so brave and would not show his emotions or cry. He stood there on the doorstep like a little statue, abandoned but resolute. My heart went out to him and the lump in my throat threatened to overwhelm me if I said one more word.

For the next few weeks we thought about little else but Alex and how he was coping. In fact, he had a difficult start, not because he was lonely but because the turmoil at home was acted out in his behaviour as anger, which he took out on other boys. The poor boy had had a bad time, and the love that he should have been able to count on had not been there when he needed it. I was working all the time. His mother was constantly 'unwell'. And – just like I had been when my mother was prostrate with grief – he'd been terrified that Isa might be paralysed at any moment because of the endless days spent in bed with her 'back problems'.

As the time passed, Alex began to work out his anger and had a better relationship with the other boys. He liked the school atmosphere and was probably better off away from the poisonous atmosphere of his parents' home. I was almost always the one who went to see

Alex, or took him to and from school. I always reassured him that his mother did love him, regardless of anything, even if she could not show it.

In February 1993 Isa and I went on our mission to Thailand. We met local generals and government officials, whose presence reassured us that Rick's connection with Khun Sa was both genuine and aboveboard. Rick never did produce the fabled 48,000-carat ruby, but there were compensations. Away from all the pressures of life at Brocket, Isa and I were able to relax and enjoy ourselves. A little sparkle returned to our relationship – all too briefly, alas. We returned home bronzed and happy, but as soon as Isa walked through the front door she relapsed into her old lethargy and took refuge in her pills. Her headaches and backaches returned and she was seldom out of bed before midday, if at all. One weekend we had a mutual friend to stay with his fiancée. The pills kept Isa in bed all weekend and so they never saw her.

Soon after we had returned from the Far East, I received a telephone call from an American called Peter Shirley, one of the founders of Microsoft. He told me that he had bought the short- wheel-base Ferrari 250 that I had sold to Rick Furtado for £80,000, the price of a replica, rather than a genuine car. He had paid around £300,000. It was an odd price: too much for a replica, but too little for the real thing.

'I understand you were a former owner of this car?' said Shirley (who was, though I did not know it, taping the conversation).

'Yes.'

'Is this a genuine car?'

'As far as I'm concerned, yes. And all the components are correct.' I said, entirely truthfully.

'Do you think the plate is genuine?' asked Shirley.

Now I was in a tricky position. Obviously, I had once suspected that there might be something wrong with the plate, given Jim Bosisto's record of deceit. On the other hand, none of my research had turned up any actual evidence to suggest that it was fake. I had simply sold it as a replica to be on the safe side. If I suggested that the plate was not genuine, and it was genuine after all, I could be slandering whoever had sold the car to Peter Shirley. So what should I say?

I tried to come up with one of those non-committal forms of words that lawyers like to use. The best I could manage was 'I have no reason to suspect that the plate is anything other than genuine.' Which was true: I'd researched the subject as thoroughly as possible, and no evidence whatever had suggested the plate was fake.

Phew! Glad I'd got that sorted. Or so I thought . . . More than two years later, this conversation would come back to haunt me.

For now, though, Brocket Hall stayed open, the newly completed golf club flourished and I kept being asked to fulfil public roles as the chairman of this or that worthy organisation. In June 1993 Brocket again played host to a summit of Europe's foreign ministers, and the staff had their customary laugh at the expense of the French, who always seemed to be grumbling about England and the English.

One breakfast, Alan, the butler, and the waitresses

had to make a hasty retreat from the breakfast-room as they fought to hold back their giggles. One of the more pompous French aides had been heard to mutter, 'Zees English croissants are 'orrible,' as he munched his way through a Weetabix on which he'd tried to spread his butter.

By now, though, Isa could no longer play the role of the beautiful, multilingual hostess. Her drug-dependence was painfully obvious to anyone who saw her. Rick had found her in cupboards talking to herself. Her car had dents all over it, as she was regularly misjudging manoeuvres. She was often found in shops talking to assistants she didn't know, saying things that were totally off the wall. The bedspread and furniture were covered in burn marks, as she kept passing out with a cigarette in her hand. The cigarettes would burn right down, but she'd never feel a thing. It was only a matter of time before she started a serious fire.

Our close friends Michael and Rory Campbell-Bowling begged me to get Isa into a clinic for her dependence before she accidentally killed either herself or the children. Rory's own doctor, Robert Le Fevre, was well known for treating drug problems and ran Promise, a unit near Maidstone that was used by many celebrities with similar problems. Rory even managed to do something that had always been beyond me: she spoke to Isa and made her admit that she had a problem and needed help.

Isa went through terrible withdrawal symptoms at Promise. But during her eight-week stay, the drugs worked their way out of her system and her old, sweet nature – the charm that had first drawn me to her all those years ago when she came to model at Brocket – began to surface again. She got a bit of colour back in her face, and her figure lost some of the bloated look that drugs seemed to inflict. Towards the end of her stay, I took Alex and Antalya to visit her, telling them that Mummy was having a rest and getting better. Isa played with the children, but sadly, distractedly, as if she could not quite believe they were real.

For a week after she returned home, I really thought Isa might recover. But then the anger returned, the explosions of rage became worse and her behaviour finally reached a point where it could no longer be ignored. One evening, Alex was at home with his friend Jack, the son of our estate manager. Sick of yet another row with Isa, I joined them in Alex's room and we were playing a game when Isa stormed in and yelled, 'Tell Alex what you wanted to do before he was born. Go on. Tell him!'

I could not believe what she was doing. Surely not even the drugs could make her stoop so low. I begged her to stop, but Isa wasn't having any of it. 'Go on!' she screamed again. 'Tell him you wanted to kill him when he was little.'

I knew at once what she was referring to: my long-forgotten concern that Isa and I were in no fit state to start a family. Alex looked stunned. 'What, Mummy?'

Isa's face was contorted with rage. Then she hissed, 'Your daddy's going to tell you how he wanted to kill you. That's how much he loved you!' Then she left the room, slamming the door so hard that chunks of plaster fell from the ceiling and crashed down to the floor.

Alex was sitting on the edge of his bunk. His little face slowly crumpled up and huge tears rolled down his cheek. I sat next to him and held him tight. For a while nothing was said. Jack got off his chair, stood in front of Alex and, planting his hands firmly on his hips to reinforce the importance of his words, said, 'Don't worry, Alex. Everyone on the estate knows that your mummy is addicted to pills and doesn't really mean what she says. It's only the pills speaking.'

Alex stopped crying and said, 'Is that true?'

'Yes, everyone knows it,' said Jack.

Alex looked a little relieved. 'Oh, that's all right then,' he said. But his mother had wounded him to the heart.

Unable to accept responsibility for her condition, Isa kept blaming me. Finally, she did what Mark had always feared. In the middle of yet another argument, she screamed at me that she was going to tell the police about the cars. If she did, I said, we would all lose everything. She said she didn't care, and I could see that in her condition she meant it.

I rang Michael Campbell-Bowling and told him what Isa was threatening to do. Michael knew absolutely nothing about what we had done but certainly understood that the mere hint of police involvement would decimate our bookings at the Hall and cause the bank to withdraw their rescue package.

Rory then came on the line: 'Look, I know Isa better than most people. I'll drive up now and talk some sense into her. I don't know what happened and I don't want to know, but she can't be that suicidal towards her own family.'

Just after lunch Rory arrived. She and Isa walked down to the lake to talk. Fifteen minutes later she returned, her face flushed with fury. 'Charles, come with me' was all she could bark. We got in her car and she drove to the golf club car park.

She reached into her pocket for a miniature tape recorder and, with hands still shaking with rage, she rewound the tape pressed 'Play', and left the recorder on top of the dashboard as the following conversation unwound:

> *Rory:*   I have no idea what the hell is going on and don't tell me because it's none of my business and I don't want to know, but I gather that you are going to tell the police that Charles has put in a false claim about the cars?
>
> *Isa:*   Yes, that's right.
>
> *Rory:*   Are you out of your mind?
>
> *Isa:*   No, it's what he deserves.
>
> *Rory:*   You can't be that stupid. You will be damaging yourself and the children.
>
> *Isa:*   I don't care.
>
> *Rory:*   Isa, you will ruin your whole family. And think of the wider family.
>
> *Isa:*   Well, Charles should have thought of that.
>
> *Rory:*   So that gives you the justification to do

	the very same damage that you say he broke the law to avoid?
Isa:	Yes. It's what he deserves.
Rory:	Christ. I give up. I just hope you can live with yourself. One day, some time in your life, you will have the children to answer to.

'I'm sorry, I lost my temper after that,' said Rory.

We sat there for some time taking all this in. I thanked her for trying to help and before she drove back to London, she said she would keep the tape.

In the morning I met with the mechanics again. We decided that, if she did indeed go to the police we would all deny it, especially as the claim was being withdrawn. There was no evidence. There was nothing they could do.

Amazingly, Isa and I still carried on as if nothing had changed. We had trips arranged to California, Paris and Berlin, where we planned to meet some old army friends and go with them around the newly liberated countries that had once lain behind the Iron Curtain. Isa wasn't really in a fit state to travel, but so many people had arranged so much for us and she wanted to come, so that was that. I thought the travelling might even help her.

We spent a couple of days in San Francisco and I showed her all the tourist sites: the trams, Fisherman's Wharf, the view of the city at night from the top of the Coit Tower. She was oblivious to it all. Her only interest, wherever we were, was finding a chemist to give her pills, or a hospital which she could pay for a pain-killing injection. At public events, old friends would try to talk to her, but then give up, unable to penetrate her chemical haze.

Finally, one morning, I was forced to act and – whatever lies you may have heard to the contrary – laid a finger on a woman for the first and last time in my life. The breakfast tray was brought into our hotel room. Isa went to pick it up. I could see she was going to throw it at me, and trash the room. I needed to bring her to her senses.

I slapped Isa once with my open hand. She sat back on the bed. Then she started screaming. She just sat and screamed. Rick Furtado was staying in the same hotel. I rang his room and asked if his wife, Pam, could come and try to calm Isa down while I packed up our things for the return to San Francisco and our flight home.

We hardly spoke a word driving back up the coast road, but as we boarded the plane the effect of the medication was slowly dissipating and things improved. On the flight back I dozed off and when I awoke I found that Isa had placed a present on my lap. I opened it and it was a gold Cartier table clock that she had bought on the plane.

When we got back she had it inscribed: 'To Charles. I will always love you.'

Somewhere deep inside, Isa was desperately crying for help. But she was now also spreading the word about the insurance scam.

Grassed Up

ONE EVENING I GOT A CALL FROM MY MOTHER. ISA had told her that I had committed an insurance fraud. What Isa did not say, though she knew it full well, was that I had already arranged to withdraw the claim. Mother was horrified. She wanted a family meeting in my uncle David's house on the estate to discuss the whole subject. My heart stopped beating for some time as I collected my wits.

I entered the room and they all stared at me. I had already thought through what I was to say. Any admission could only be destructive and would serve no good purpose. There was no evidence for an attempted fraud as long as the others said nothing. In any case, the claim was to be withdrawn as soon as the bank agreement was signed. Lastly, Isa was addicted to drugs and was known to have said many things that were pure fiction.

So when I was asked outright if I had organised a

fraud on the cars, I said no, Isa had invented the whole story. I hated lying to my family but there was no other choice under the circumstances.

Then in December 1993, after legal negotiations that had cost £400,000 (on our account, of course), the deal with the bank was done. We got the £15 million, interest-free. I set off for the Christmas holidays in Puerto Rico in a light-hearted mood, an enormous weight lifted from my shoulders. But the reaction from Isa's family was all doom and gloom.

'Ja, it is finished,' moaned Isa's mother, Brigitte, mired in Teutonic angst. 'There is no way that you can repay this amount. You are ruined! Kaput!'

Then Isa chipped in. 'Mum's right. You can't repay this much. It's all over.'

Exasperated by their obtuseness, I tried to walk them through the deal. The chances of having to pay back the whole amount in ten years' time were minimal. By then, the business would have grown, the value of the company would be much higher, inflation would have eaten away at the value of the loan, and we'd certainly be able to refinance the deal if we needed to. In the meantime, we had an interest-free loan that any other company would kill for. It was a fantastic deal, by any standards.

They didn't want to know. Mother and daughter had decided that the ship was sinking. So Isa should abandon ship now, while there was still a bit of money in the kitty.

I, meanwhile, had to abandon something else: the fraudulent insurance claim. To cut a long, tortuous, fiendishly complicated legal manoeuvre short, we took advantage of the fact that the claim was wrapped up in a series of legal actions. My lawyer, David Sarch, was as aggressive as possible towards the insurance company, making it clear that I intended to take them to court in order to get my money.

Sarch had predicted what would happen next. The insurance company applied to the court, asking it to order me to lodge my share of the costs – some £700,000 – with the court, so as to prove that I could afford the proposed action. That money could only come from the bank, because I certainly didn't have it. And they weren't going to stump up that kind of cash, up front, on a lawsuit they might lose. So I couldn't provide the money. So, regretfully, I was forced to inform the insurance company that I was dropping my case against them. They'd won.

The insurers must have been thrilled. I know I was. The claim had been dropped. No suspicion attached to me. It was now mid 1994. I had the cash in the bank and the claim off my back. I was almost home free. The only problem was Isa. She was heading down to rock bottom.

She spent most of the time in bed, and when she did get up she would bump into things as if she were drunk. I tried, we all tried, to talk to her but there was no will to listen or perhaps not the physical ability to take it in. The nanny, the housekeeper or Isa's secretary would often find her talking to herself, slumped at her desk or on the sofa in the sitting-room. I regularly found her sitting on the loo asleep.

You'd see her in the coat cupboard talking to the wall, or passed out in the linen cupboard. She would come round and tell you an amazing story about what she had just done or where she had just been.

Then one evening I came back to Watershipps to find Isa unconscious on the sofa. Her head was right back so that the light from the table lamp spilled on to her face, which was covered with a blanket of little midges.

I brushed off the midges, sat her up, still unconscious, held her and cried tears of desperation and pity. She was such a beautiful creature but so fragile. I just had no idea of where to go from here. Isa wouldn't listen. And there was no way of making her have treatment against her will. I was terrified that she'd kill herself if this went on much longer.

By now, Isa's parents had long since stopped listening to me. But Fran, our housekeeper, agreed to call Gus Lorenzo and tell him what was going on. She warned him, 'Mr Lorenzo. It's very simple. If you do not get Lady Brocket into a clinic right away you will not have a daughter for much longer.'

Gus came over on the next plane. He warned Isa that she was in real danger and she finally believed him. It was as if she had been waiting all this time for someone to tell her this, or perhaps it was just that she was now ready to hear it. But even so, nothing really changed.

We made a rare visit to Ludgrove to see Alex in his school play. It was a murder mystery, and he played the part of a convict, complete with a uniform covered in arrows. I remember watching him with a huge sense of relief, thinking about how close I, too, had come to wearing prison gear. Thank God it would soon be over.

Isa did not sit with me. She was across the aisle of the hall, sitting next to Princess Diana, both comparing notes on how utterly beastly their husbands were being. (Funnily enough, I'd known Diana years beforehand when I went out with one of her flatmates at Coleherne Court, in West London. Diana's relationship with Prince Charles had yet to become public knowledge. She struck me as very sweet, rather tragic and naïve. Why did no one warn her about the huge royal elephant-trap that was opening up in front of her?)

Soon afterwards, Isa moved out, borrowing a friend's house nearby, and taking our youngest child, William, with her. At the end of the first week, Fran went down to deliver some things that Isa wanted and got no answer from the door. She forced her way in and found Isa lying unconscious with her eyes rolled back in her skull. William was wandering about, having had no food. The back door was open to the garden, which had a running stream. Fran rang me in a panic. I told her to get Isa to the hospital as quickly as possible: I'd meet her there. We established what she had been taking, and she was injected with the antidote.

Within ten minutes Isa came round. I hugged her. I knew I would have to take her home but I also knew, as sure as night follows day, that she would be in the same state again very soon.

Isa's mother flew over and we sat in the kitchen to discuss her daughter's condition. She simply refused to believe Isa was a drug-addict. Fran, who is a shy person and does not like to meddle in other people's affairs, finally lost her cool with Brigitte one morning. 'Go up to Isa's bedroom, right now, and then look me in the eye and tell me that she is not drugged out of her mind,' Fran snapped. 'You'll find her slumped on the loo.'

Brigitte went up with Fran but when she saw Isa she simply said, 'Oh, she's just tired.'

'What are these pills, then?' Fran demanded angrily, holding out a fistful of assorted pain-killers. 'She's taking a vast amount each day. She gets duplicate prescriptions from a pharmacy in Welwyn Garden. She calls taxis to go to other chemist shops. She goes to hotels just to call the hotel doctor to get more pills. It's not her fault. She can't help it. She must get help before she accidentally kills herself and the children.'

Fran strode over to the bed. 'Look!' she said, pointing at the duvet cover. 'These are burn holes. It's only a matter of time before the whole place goes up.' She walked out of the room in disgust, lost for further words to express her frustration.

Brigitte refused to see what was staring her in the face.

Isa and I had agreed that a divorce was inevitable as she was determined not to have treatment. We all met round a table at the solicitors. After a calm, sad meeting we agreed that the divorce would be done quietly. Isa and I agreed a settlement that would buy her the house she wanted and enable her to live comfortably.

I left, expecting the whole process to be completed in a matter of weeks. But merely drafting the agreement is too simple for some lawyers. Her solicitor told Isa that she could do a much better deal for her and that the matter should, if necessary, be taken to court. It was the declaration of a legal war. And the first weapons of personal destruction were just about to be deployed.

One day in September 1994 I got a call on my mobile phone from the Brocket manager, William Pound. He told me that Isa had been arrested for forging prescriptions. I returned home to find Brigitte in a panic. She said that Isa had resorted to forging the prescription because I had hidden her pills the night before.

I took her up to our room and pointed to the bedside table. 'What are those?' I asked. 'They are the two Prozac that she should have taken.'

There was one more piece of news, given to me by Fran. Isa had finally carried out her threat. She'd told the police about the car fraud. Her words hit me like a knife in the gut.

Isa had been taken to the St Albans police station. I went straight there but she refused to see me. I couldn't believe that she'd really done it. But then again, would it matter, now that I had withdrawn the claim?

As I desperately tried to work out where I stood, the inspector in charge of Isa's case – a detective I knew well from the many times when I had been invited to drinks at police headquarters – asked me to step outside the building for a private chat.

He said, 'I regret to say that your wife has made some serious allegations concerning some classic cars. I thought you ought to know.'

I thought I was going to throw up. So now it was certain. Isa really had pressed the self-destruct button. I returned home and sat in the kitchen, unable to think coherently, just staring vacantly into the night.

Later I ran through the evidence. It came down to the mechanics. No body, no case, as Mark had always said. The next morning I went to see them. Mark was very calm, as if he had nothing to fear, but Steve was a bag of nerves. We agreed that, as long as nothing was said by them, there was no case to answer. The withdrawal of the claim would be the end of the matter.

Isa was charged but received just a caution. At the beginning of September the decree nisi came through. We were due to move out of Watershipps anyway, as it was being turned into the golf clubhouse. So Isa moved a few hundred yards down the road to Palmerston House, which we had been given as part of the deal for us quitting Watershipps. I stayed behind in Watershipps for the weeks before the conversion was due to begin, trying to get used to the horrible silence that follows once your children have all been taken away.

Meanwhile, all my cars were up for sale, any offer considered. My favourite one was Niki Lauda's 1975 Formula 1 Ferrari. It was due to be auctioned at a classic car sale in Laguna Seca, California, but I wanted one last blast behind the wheel. So I called up Silverstone and asked if I could have the track to myself – and Niki's Ferrari – for a morning. It tells you something about the height from which I was about to fall that they said, 'Yes,' without any hesitation.

Steve Gwyther and I loaded the car on to the trailer and set off for Silverstone. The car was readied for the track, I put on some fireproof racing overalls and shoehorned myself into the cockpit. Steve passed me my helmet. I pulled out the padded lining to squeeze it over my head and suddenly a freak hailstorm broke out around me as hundreds of little green and cream capsules clattered all over the cockpit, splattering on the metal floor. They were Prozac. I remembered the words of one of Isa's doctors: 'They hide their pills in the most unexpected places.' The pit crew doubled up with laughter at the sight of me surrounded by drugs. How were they to know it was no laughing matter?

A short while later, in California for the car sale, I had to watch the Ferarri 250 that Pourret had trashed as a fake go for a knock-down £250,000. The Lauda Ferrari had to be sold to a friend of Rick Furtado as incomplete, thereby costing me a further £250,000, when a vital box of parts mysteriously 'went missing'. The parts magically reappeared soon afterwards and the car was sold on by Furtado's chum for its full £700,000 price.

But there was better news to come. While I was out in California, I got a message from England. The final settlement had been reached on the insurance claim. It was now formally withdrawn.

I went out and celebrated in style. All the rounds were on me and I was happy to pay, because we'd unscrambled the mess. I was sure I was in the clear.

I'd not received a single penny of insurance money. Whatever happened, or whatever Isa said, I could not now be accused of committing a fraud.

Well, yes, I could, actually. To my amazement, I got home to find that the police were stepping up their enquiries. One day Rick came into the office looking white. He had just returned from his home town, Boston. While he was there, he'd had a meeting with his cousin, Barry Flynn. Two British detectives had walked into his office, informed him that Lord Brocket was an international drug-dealer, and asked for help in catching me.

I couldn't believe what I was hearing. Why would two British policemen fly thousands of miles to spread a bare-faced lie? Little did I know that the campaign against me was only now beginning.

Isa, meanwhile, was denying that she had ever said anything to the police at all. I rang the deputy chief of the Hertfordshire police and asked for a meeting. Politely, but firmly, he confirmed that my wife had made detailed criminal allegations against me.

I drove back to my office in the old stable-block at Brocket (I'd moved out of the main offices since being removed from my executive role at the Hall). After a while, Isa rang from Palmerston. She said she was going out to the chemist for some pills. I asked her if she could drop by the office. Isa has already given her account of what happened next to the media, accusing me of attacking her. My recollection is very different.

When she arrived, Isa stood in front of my desk as I pleaded with her: 'I've just talked to almost the top man in the force and he has stated that you did give a detailed statement after all. How could you? You knew the claim was being withdrawn, and Rory spelled out to you what the result would be. We will lose every-thing. Literally everything.'

Isa exploded with fury. 'If he says that he's a liar. I never talked to anyone. Get him on the phone. Now! Go on!'

She completely lost her temper and started smashing her fists down on the desk. I was suddenly really frightened. In her current state, she was capable of anything. As she became more frenzied I hit the emergency number on the phone next to me. It rang a mobile that was always with Mark. He picked it up right away. 'Mark, Isa is hysterical. Could you come?'

'I'm coming through the front gates,' he replied. 'I'll be with you in one min—' But before he could finish Isa hit the phone out of my hand on to the floor. I got up from my side of the desk and made towards the door as she rained down blows on my chest in an uncontrolled, hysterical frenzy.

I made it into the main reception area while Isa started punching the glass panes of the office door. I was terrified that she'd smash through the panes and cut her wrists. It was obvious that physical restraint would be necessary, but in her frame of mind she might allege that any restrainer had assaulted her. So I dialled 999 on the reception phone. I'd just managed to ask for the police when Isa dived at the phone and cut it off.

I had to get out of the office. Isa was hell-bent on destroying herself, and taking me with her. I simply couldn't take any more. Something in me had burned out. The tension of the last three years had somehow finally melted down into nothingness.

I started towards the main exit door but Isa raced in front of me. As she went, she picked up a flowerpot with a Bonsai plant in it. I was waiting for her to fling it at me. Then, as she reached the main door, she turned round and yelled, 'You're not leaving! Oh, no way, we're not finished yet!' She stepped back to block my way out, but she didn't notice a piece of wood that had been screwed across the bottom of the doorway, to prevent rain getting in. As I approached she tripped over it and fell backwards on to the paving outside. At exactly the same time Mark drew up in his car.

The plant pot had landed on Isa's left foot and shattered. She sat on the ground and screamed at the top of her voice, thumping the ground with her fists.

I knew that if I stayed she'd allege that I had tried to murder her, or worse. I had to get away. Ignoring Mark, I drove down to the Hall, walked past Sally, the receptionist, sat at William Pound's desk and sobbed. I just couldn't take any more.

I called my mother to tell her what had happened. As I put the phone down, Sally came in to tell me that the police had arrived, following up the emergency call. Isa, meanwhile, had gone back to Palmerston House, and called the police herself. She alleged that I had called her into the office and beaten her up and that her leg was broken.

The following day I was arrested, put in a cell for several hours and then interrogated for another two hours. Finally I was released on bail but the papers, tipped off by the police, were full of it the next day: 'Peer arrested for assault on wife'. Suddenly I was a wife-batterer, an allegation that has lived with me ever since.

No one, though, ever mentions how the case actually ended. After our divorce proceedings had begun, Isa had threatened to leave Britain and move to Puerto Rico, taking the children with her. I could not make legal moves to stop her unless I had evidence she intended to act on the threat. As a result – and this is not pleasant, but we had gone way, way beyond pleasantness by then – I had, on legal advice, tapped Isa's phones.

I ran through the tapes and eventually found one of her talking to a friend saying, 'It was an accident. I fell over the bloody step as he tried to get out but he deserves all he gets.'

Just as I had played it for the second time, the tap light flashed as it monitored a new outgoing call. It was Isa calling her father.

'I'm okay, Dad. I fell over the step,' she reassured him. The rest of the conversation was irrelevant. I'd heard all I needed to.

I went into the kitchen to make some coffee and the phone rang. It was Gus. I put the tape on. 'I've just had a call from Isa,' he said. 'What happened?' I told him and at the end he said, 'Well, she told me it was an accident and that she fell backwards as you brushed past her.'

I now had both Isa and her father on tape, confirming that it wasn't assault. I drove down to the police station, put the tapes on the desk and said, 'Let's see the end of all this stupidity.' The charge was withdrawn, but a decade later some of the mud still sticks to my reputation.

– 18 –

You're Nicked, M'Lord!

YOU KNOW THOSE FAIRGROUND GAMES WHERE LITTLE furry gophers keep popping out of holes and you have to bang them on the head? That's what my life was like. As soon as I'd smashed down one crisis, another blew up.

Next on the list was the pressing matter of clearing away the car evidence, speaking of which, anyone familiar with my story, as told by Fleet Street, may be wondering when they're going to get to the bit where the cars are found with their backsides poking out of the lake at Brocket Hall. Or when we bury them under the golf-course bunkers. Answer: they aren't. Neither of those myths is true. What we actually wanted to do was to take the bits, into which they'd now been dismantled, and dump them deep in the Bristol Channel.

Steve had an old friend down in Wales, a man he'd known since birth and trusted absolutely, who had his own fishing boat. If we could get the parts on to his boat, tipping them over the side would be no problem. We didn't want to use a trucker to take the stuff down to the Welsh coast, because that would mean bringing one more person in on the deal and, in any case, trucks are notorious for getting bogged down. The last thing we needed was to get the stuff down to Wales and then get stuck on the bloody beach.

The best idea was to get a powerful four-wheel-drive and a trailer. I bought an old silver Range Rover. Then I spent four and a half grand getting a firm in Devon to fit a seven-litre diesel engine that had come from a US army armoured personnel carrier. With that inside it, the Range Rover could have towed the *Titanic*.

The trailer had to be specially made. It needed to be small enough to back up to the container for easy loading. It also needed some kind of canvas cover, like an old Wild West wagon, to stretch over the parts, to keep them hidden on the journey to Wales. I put in an order with a firm, Up North, and waited for them to deliver the finished trailer.

Bang! Down went that gopher . . . for now.

Pop! Pop! Up sprang two more.

By December 1994 it was clear that the Hall was doing appalling business. Somehow, the management upon whom the bank had insisted had managed to get occupancy levels below the critical 15 per cent return that we needed to keep afloat. It hardly seemed possible, particularly since the economy was slowly beginning to bounce back. But, amazingly, they'd managed it.

Meanwhile, Isa was spiralling out of control. After my supposed 'assault' she had obtained a court order forbidding me to contact her in any way except by fax. I was supposed to see the children every Tuesday, Wednesday and Thursday afternoon for two hours. They were also meant to stay with me at Watershipps every other weekend. The two houses were only 300 yards apart, but even so, the simplest message about the kids' arrangements had to be faxed back and forth.

The absurdity, however, didn't last long. At the hearing for Isa's prescription forgery case, she was told to seek treatment or face the possibility of a prison sentence. She was also told that she might have trouble obtaining any access to the children, as a court could say that she was an unfit mother. She accepted that she had to go to a clinic.

Now I had the children full-time, which was magical. We went to plays, saw all the Disney films they'd missed, went ice-skating and ogled the dinosaurs at the Natural History Museum. But what was happening to Isa? Whenever anyone called the clinic they'd be told she was not there. The nurses revealed that she regularly spent the night away. The patients had the freedom to come and go at will.

Gus rang me, sounding angry and concerned. He, too, had been told that Isa had been spending nights out of the clinic. Both her American Express and Harrods cards showed recent use.

Then a developed film arrived in the post.

Presumably Isa had put Palmerston on the return address instead of the clinic. The pictures showed her with a new boyfriend: I later discovered his name was Martin. In many of the shots was a huge, bulky blonde called Sarah Dale, a travel agent with whom Isa had made several trips to Italy.

Martin was a known hard drugs user and I feared for Isa. Gus was furious. He rang the clinic (as did I) and threatened all sorts of mayhem if they didn't rectify the position. The management simply said the clinic was voluntary, so there was nothing they could do. I tried to visit Isa but the clinic discouraged it and after my first visit she told me not to come again. An iron wall seemed to have risen between us.

With Isa still supposedly in the clinic, I was asked to join the parliamentary ski team to compete against the Swiss parliament. This is a long-standing tradition between the British and Swiss governments. The competitors go with their families, and the evenings involve a lot of singing and drinking.

I took Alex, who loved skiing. We were invited to travel out with a party including the Environment Minister, Marion Roe. The minister's daughter, Philippa, who had her own successful public relations business and had strong political connections, came too. She was very beautiful and yet was rather a tomboy. She always spoke her mind and had a strong sense of right and wrong. After the hell I'd been through with Isa, it was wonderful to be with someone so bright and full of life.

We began a lovely, friendly relationship. She was like

a bandage round my battered heart. After our holiday in Switzerland, Philippa came with me when I flew to America to be the keynote speaker at a series of events in Washington and Chicago, organised by the British Tourist Authority. My mind, though, wasn't on tourism, or the blues clubs of Chicago that I usually loved, or even the gorgeous girl by my side. I was thinking of that container, and the trailer that would soon remove its contents for good. We were only days away from getting the finished trailer. But it was too late.

On 9 February 1995 I was lying in bed next to Philippa, at her London flat, when the phone rang. It was Val, one of the girls in the offices at Brocket. The first words that penetrated my semi-conscious daze were '. . . and they want to arrest you . . .'

Philippa, suddenly awake, sat up beside me. 'What is it? What's wrong?'

'Nothing. The girls are having a laugh.'

'Don't be daft,' I said to my PA. 'Next time let me have a bit more sleep, okay?'

'No, seriously,' Val insisted, trying to instil some sense of urgency into me. 'They're all over the place. They really would like to arrest you.'

Later, I found out what had happened. After Isa's original allegations, the local police started investigating and got absolutely nowhere. She had a conviction for forging prescriptions and had an obvious grudge against me, so her testimony was worthless without corroborating evidence. But she didn't know where the car parts were, which meant she couldn't tell the police the one thing they really needed to know.

Under normal circumstances, the investigation would probably have petered out without any great drama. I was one of Hertfordshire's most prominent citizens, a member of the House of Lords and the owner of a house that was frequently used for major political gatherings, guarded by Hertfordshire police. Crucially, I had also withdrawn the insurance claim that my wife was alleging had been fraudulent, so I hadn't profited from the deal and the insurers had not lost out.

That being the case, the police would probably have decided they had better things to do with their resources than pursue me over a fraud that had not, in the end, taken place. I'd have been called in for a gin and tonic with the Chief Constable and been told that I was damn lucky I'd come to my senses and withdrawn the claim, and I'd better not even contemplate anything like that in the future, or I'd be in trouble.

But there was a catch. At the time of Isa's arrest, a police officer had leaked details of her allegations to the media. Until such time as I was charged, the papers had to be very careful indeed about repeating her story, since they would clearly be risking a massive libel action. But by 1994–5, the subject of 'Tory sleaze' had become a national obsession. If a prominent Conservative peer was involved in an insurance fraud, it was bound to become a massive story and constitute yet another problem for John Major's embattled government. That meant two things. First, the media were buzzing round my story like flies round a pile of manure. And second, the government had an obvious incentive to make an example of me, if I should ever be charged, tried and convicted.

That put the Chief Constable of Hertfordshire in a very tricky position. He had a high-profile case without any evidence. A Scotland Yard inspector called Ives had been brought in to keep an eye on the local officer in charge of the case, Inspector Kerlin, and the whole thing was becoming a major potential embarrassment. So he told his team: 'Get some proper evidence or we're dropping the case.'

The police decided that the best way to get their evidence was to mount a huge raid on Brocket Hall. They chose the morning of 9 February 1995. Because the raid was supposed to be top-secret, they were unable to call the Hall to check what was going on that day. So it was just too bad that a fleet of police cars should come roaring down the drive, lights flashing and sirens blaring, carrying fifty officers and several dogs . . . just as Michael Heseltine and a gathering of European trade ministers, who were all staying at Brocket Hall, were preparing to get up for another day's hard summiteering.

It was also a rather amusing irony that they should barge in on Heseltine – a Conservative minister whose daughter I'd once slept with – when I was actually in bed with the daughter of another Conservative minister. But anyway . . .

The cops charged in at full pelt. They raided the administrative offices in the Hall and my own office complex in the old stables. They raided my house and the mechanics' cottages. They sealed off the Ferrari showroom and Mark's own workshop. As the police dogs, which were trained on the estate, barked in excitement, the staff went about their business not knowing whether to treat it as a joke or not.

I, meanwhile, was beginning to grasp the seriousness of the situation. I called my solicitor, who said he'd drive me up to St Albans police station, so that I could be arrested: there was no sense in failing to co-operate. Then I explained to Philippa that Isa had told the police that I'd filed a fraudulent insurance claim. I also admitted that she had been telling the truth. In fact, I told Philippa the whole story.

Philippa's response was amazing. She approached the problem like a commanding officer would, faced with an attack of marauding natives. She gathered bits of paper and started making lists of things to do and deciding on the order of priorities.

'I have half a mind to have a word with the Prime Minister,' she said. 'It's bloody ridiculous! The claim has been withdrawn. You haven't taken anything and look at the way they have raided you, when the government itself is in residence. It's a bloody farce.'

With some difficulty, I dissuaded Philippa from picking up the phone to Number 10 there and then. Downing Street would certainly not thank me for dragging them into this. Leaving Philippa unable to go to work or think of anything else, I met up with my solicitor, David Sarch, and set off for St Albans police station.

'Do they have any evidence?' David asked.

'No, I don't think so. I think all they have is Isa's statement.'

David got a call on his mobile to say that the police wanted us to meet them at the estate first, so that I could open all the safes.

'Do you have anything that is incriminating on the estate?' David asked. 'Any documents, anything on computer?'

'Nothing whatsoever. The computer has been fixed.'

'Fixed?'

I explained that I'd had programmes installed that would automatically scramble everything on the hard drive if anyone tried to use the computer without the correct password. Then I added that there wasn't anything important in the files, though Rick Furtado might not be too happy about having all the details of his dealings with his cousin Barry Flynn and Khun Sa open to scrutiny. By this time, I'd been told by my half-brother Rupert what Khun Sa's real business was. David Sarch clearly knew about it, too.

He gasped. 'Khun Sa? *The* Khun Sa? Bloody hell! Government summits, ministers' daughters, world's biggest drug warlord and . . . Well, let's enter the gates of Troy . . .'

We swept in through the main gates and parked at the back of the Hall. Police cars were everywhere. As I went into the Hall I met Alan, the head butler. He drew himself up ramrod straight and said with great dignity: 'My lord, may I express my extreme distaste at the unwelcome presence of so many police officers. I have been asked to express, on behalf of all the staff, our sympathies for you and our assurance that you have our full support at this difficult time.'

Then he added, with a smirk, 'Your lordship may be interested to know that there has been a sudden rush on sales of the miniature Ferrari models that we sell to guests. It seems that the ministers wished to take away with them a keepsake for the occasion.' It was true. I might be having a tough time selling real Ferraris, but the toys were a sell-out.

For the next few hours, the police bagged and filed my possessions, while Inspector Kerlin looked more tense with every passing minute. David Sarch went to have a word with Kerlin and his team, then came back and told me, 'Interesting. It seems that after your wife's statement the inspector was told to put up or shut up. But now there's a problem. There is no evidence that what your wife said happened, actually did happen.'

'So what do we do now?'

'Well, we have to go to St Albans police station, where they will formally arrest and bail you. They will then interview you. The two mechanics and Rick Furtado have been taken to different stations and will all be grilled. I suggest that you say nothing, or deny the charge. Later on, when the dust settles, and we know what we are up against, we will know what to do.'

One thing was puzzling me. 'What will they actually charge me with? No money was taken and we with-drew the claim a long time ago.'

'Makes no difference,' said David. 'Under most European and American law you have only committed a misdemeanour and you would probably just receive a ticking-off. But under UK law you have conspired to commit a fraud and the conspiracy applies whether or not you actually committed fraud itself. In theory, you could get up to twelve years in prison – and that's five years more than you would get for actually stealing the money.'

At the station, the press were waiting, having been alerted by the police themselves, so David got me in the back door. I stood at the desk while the charge was read out and I was arrested on suspicion of conspiring to defraud the General Accident insurance company out of £4.5 million, the value that the auctioneers had put on the four cars we had dismantled.

I was then asked to take off my watch and belt, which nearly made my trousers fall down, and I was put in a cell. David was not allowed in the cell and so we had a farcical situation where we discussed the impending interview through the flap in the cell door. Then he passed his cellphone through the flap and I called Philippa. I advised her to stay away, if only to save herself the embarrassment of being linked in public with me. But she was determined to come up, so I asked her to bring my washbag and a pair of earplugs: I knew from my army days, when troopers were always ending up in one cell or another, how noisy jails can be at night.

Two hours later, Philippa arrived and sat with me in my cell. She looked around and turned her nose up at the smell and the smears and graffiti on the walls. As I hugged her I feared that this was the end of the line for us. If she was caught up in all this, the press would have a field day. Her parents would certainly not thank her for it either.

We talked about the case for a while.

'What evidence do they have?' Philippa asked.

'None. David says that if the mechanics say nothing the charges will have to be dropped.'

'But surely they will say nothing? They have everything to lose and nothing to gain. They'd have to be barmy. It's not as if it was some heinous crime. I mean, the insurance company paid out nothing, the claim was withdrawn and it actually cost you the value of the dismantled cars. They are lost for ever!' She was getting more and more indignant.

'I know,' I said. 'But I don't think the police see it like that. A conviction means instant promotion. They are not likely to drop it in a hurry.'

'What does David think will happen?'

'He thinks that they'll get nothing out of the others. I'm certainly not going to say anything. If that is the case that will be the end of it. I just have to sit tight and deny everything.'

We kissed goodbye and Philippa left for the night. The bed was a concrete slab and the mattress a slice of foam that stank of urine. So did the tattered blanket. The toilet was in plain sight, with no privacy at all.

A microwaved plastic plate of baked beans was pushed through the hatch in the cell door. They let me out to brush my teeth and then I sat on the mattress. It was eleven in the evening and the cells were already filling up with shouting men trying to kick down the steel doors with their shoes. Thank God for the earplugs. I made a pillow out of my jumper and almost immediately drifted off to sleep. At least that was one old army skill that hadn't deserted me.

The following morning David appeared and we went into the interview-room for a full day of questions. Then, in the afternoon, the police had a major breakthrough. They got to Mark by threatening that they could put him inside, leaving his family without their husband and father. For a tough guy, he cracked easily. So he grassed me up, as we criminals say, and told the police where the dismantled cars were stored, in return for being promised a suspended sentence. The container he'd rented in Greenford was broken open and the parts discovered. And with that, my fate was sealed.

– 19 –

Enter Mr Rocker

THINGS WERE LOOKING BAD AND NOW MORE RATS started scuttling from my sinking ship. Rick's cousin Barry Flynn faxed the police telling them that the claim was a fraud. Since he had no evidence and his claim was based on hearsay, there was little Barry could do to harm me. But he did make sure that Rick, too, was now in this up to his neck.

After the interrogation, the police demanded that I be remanded in custody until the sentencing. I was granted bail, at £32,000, but because my bank accounts were frozen I had no means of paying. By pure chance, an old army friend called Jonathan Baines had seen news of my arrest and called David Sarch to see if there was anything he could do to help. So he guaranteed the bail.

As part of my bail conditions, I was ordered not to contact the mechanics, Rick, Isa or Michael Cambell-Bowling. For some reason Isa had included Michael in her allegations, claiming that he was going to find a garage for us to store the parts in Portland Square. This was totally untrue. Michael was completely innocent, knew nothing whatever about the conspiracy; and the car parts were in Greenford, as the police would soon discover.

But that didn't stop them banging on Michael's door at 5 a.m. and taking him away for questioning. His wife, Rory, who had tried so hard to help Isa overcome her drug-addiction, had to watch Michael be dragged away, while desperately trying to comfort her terrified children. The Campbell-Bowlings' youngest daughter, who suffers from chronic asthma, had a serious attack. She was rushed to hospital and spent a full nine months in an oxygen tent. There were many times when it looked as though she might die.

I felt terrible that such a dear friend and his family should have suffered so much on my account. But there was one lesson that, looking back, I really should have drawn from the way the police treated Michael. They were prepared to mount an early-morning raid to grab a man who was falsely linked with a crime in which not one single penny had been stolen. That could only mean that someone somewhere was taking this case very seriously indeed. They were out to get me, and anyone connected to me. And later events would prove just how far they were prepared to go to achieve that aim.

I was released on bail on my forty-third birthday, 12 February 1995, and went straight to the golf clubhouse to have something to eat. The members were incredibly supportive and offered to help in any way they could. In fact, the reception they gave me brought tears to my eyes. As they shook my hand or patted me on the back I told them that it would all be sorted out and that it was all a big mistake. I hated the deception, the false pretence of total innocence. But for now, at least in public, I could not admit a thing.

Soon it became clear that I had to be extra-careful in private as well. David Sarch was a superb solicitor, but he did not specialise in criminal work. I needed someone who did, so I employed Steven Barker of Barker Gillette. He regularly worked with a top barrister, Desmond da Silva QC.

Steven arrived at my home, Watershipps, the next day. I had been told that it was normal police practice to bug phone lines and so I called some people who did security work for the government. They were busy with their equipment when Steven walked into the room. By the end of the day the security team reported that the airspace was bug-free and so were the lines up to the exchange. Beyond that, they could not comment.

While Steven was at Watershipps, he called his office. A short while later, he took a call from the police. 'We understand that you are acting for Lord Brocket,' they said. 'If there is anything we can do to help you, just call us.'

Steven slowly put the phone back on its cradle. 'Very interesting,' he said. 'I have not told anyone that I am representing you. The only way that the police could have known is from the call I made to my office an hour ago.' So the police did, indeed, have a bug at the exchange.

The next day, Steven tested how far the police were prepared to go. He called a colleague from his office and told him a sensational, but completely fictitious story about supposed criminal activity. Within an hour, the police were calling up to ask about a small detail of the story. 'So, now I know that my office phones are bugged, too,' Steven told me. 'I will have to watch what I say.'

'But how the hell do you conduct your business?' I asked.

'Oh, Charles, in this country you have to live with such things. It happens often and there is nothing you can do about it.'

While all this was going on, my poor little son William was distressed, confused and crying almost all the time. His mother was in the clinic. His father had just been arrested. His parents were legally forbidden to talk to one another. It was no way for a baby boy to grow up. I suggested to Isa's mother, Brigitte, who adored William, that she should take him to Puerto Rico until the fuss had died down.

But when would that ever happen? One morning Sarah Dale, the mountainous, six-foot-six-inch travel agent, whom I had last seen lurking in the background of the pictures of Isa and her drug-addict boyfriend, rang Palmerston and talked to Fran, the housekeeper.

'If someone doesn't come and collect Isa now, she will die,' Sarah barked.

Isa had discharged herself early from the clinic and had been staying with Sarah in her house in Battersea. Now she was dangerously ill.

Fran immediately told me. But I was in a crazy, impossible position. My bail conditions made it illegal for me to go to the rescue of the mother of my children. None of my family could help: Isa would refuse to listen to them. There was only one person who could always get her attention: her father, Gus.

Fran rang Gus. He arrived the next morning and we drove to Sarah's house. We got there about midday and rang the doorbell. Sarah's huge, jowly face appeared. She looked pleased to see us, if only because we would take Isa off her hands. 'Come this way,' she said.

Sarah led Gus and me upstairs. We walked into one of the bedrooms and saw a sight that will stay with me till the day I die. Isa was lying on a sofa bed, wearing a grubby pair of pyjamas, with her pills and the contents of her handbag scattered around her. She looked dreadful. It was enough to make anyone cry with pity and shame. All I wanted to do was hug her and comfort her.

Isa was barely conscious. Gus and I lifted her up and dragged her to the bathroom, where we splashed cold water on her face. Then we got her dressed. We carried her downstairs and tried to get a cup of coffee down her, while Sarah stood and watched, like a huge, predatory vulture in the corners of our eyes.

By now, Isa was able to mumble a few words. We wrapped her in her coat, carried her into the car and laid her across the back seat. She lay with her eyes shut, unaware of what was happening as we headed home.

At Palmerston we put her to bed and fed her as much as she would eat. Gus rang the airlines but they wouldn't take her until she was fit enough to travel.

Over the next few weeks Isa regained some strength and the colour started to come back to her cheeks. Her sores began to clear up and she gained some weight, although she could only take in soups and easily digestible food. In the privacy of Palmerston we agreed that the bail conditions could go out of the window. What mattered was looking after Isa.

Once Isa was well enough to be up and about, she and Gus went house-hunting for a place of her own. The amount she would get in her divorce settlement would cover the purchase of a decent property, and Val, my secretary, set up countless viewings. And then, just as some degree of normality was returning to our lives, the impossible happened: the police came and arrested me, yet again.

Soon, I was back in the cells at St Albans police station. This was beginning to become a habit. I still had no idea what the hell was going on. But when Steven Barker arrived, he told me what it was all about.

'Charles, you are being charged with violating your bail conditions. The police want to remand you in custody until the trial. It's pure bloody-mindedness. They know full well that you are not a danger to the public or at risk of fleeing the country. Are you interested in what they're alleging you've done?'

'Go on, tell me.'

'Sarah Dale, who professes to be your friend, contacted the police and told them that you violated your bail conditions and talked to Isa when you and Gus collected her from her flat.'

'You're kidding! You have to be! You mean that she

has deliberately tried to jail me? And she knows that I am the only one able to look after the children.'

Steven showed me Sarah's statement. It was a deliberate attempt to jail me. By now, I was past trying to work out the motivations behind other people's malevolence. I had long suspected that Sarah, who was bisexual, had harboured some sort of crush on Isa. Perhaps she wanted me out of the way. Or maybe Isa had poisoned her mind. It really made no difference. I was up the creek either way.

But then Steven gave me some good news. 'I've seen Gus Lorenzo. He could not believe that anyone could be capable of this. As he was with you when you went to collect Isa, he has given a statement that you did not talk to Isa. He would have heard it if you had.'

An hour later I was standing behind the glass screen in the prisoner's box at the magistrates' court, looking around at the smirking faces in the press gallery and on the police benches. It was clear straight away that the police thought that they'd got me fair and square. They expected me to be jailed at the end of the hearing.

A police inspector appeared in the witness box, read Sarah Dale's statement and then asked for me to be committed forthwith.

'One moment, Officer,' my lawyer intervened. 'May I ask you to read this statement?'

Gus Lorenzo's evidence was passed to the police inspector. As he read it his smirk disappeared. He looked up, saying nothing.

My lawyer spoke again. 'When I asked you to read it, I meant you to read it out loud, please.' While I sat impassively in the box, the inspector read out Gus's evidence, which completely contradicted Sarah Dale's testimony. He was then passed a further statement from Gus, which explained that Isa was under the influence of drugs and in no condition to walk properly, let alone make any statement herself.

The magistrates immediately dismissed the police application and, yet again, I was released from the cells.

Gus finally flew back to New York with a pale, frail, but living Isa. Within two days, however, he rang me to say that Isa had secretly taken a store of pills with her and had tried to take an overdose. 'I only wish that we had believed you and Fran long ago, so that her addiction would not have reached this stage,' he said. 'It is so difficult to understand why one's only child should take drugs.'

Isa was admitted to yet another drug clinic, this time in Florida. Knowing that she had no desire to come back to the estate, I moved into Palmerston House with Alex and Antalya. William, of course, was still in Puerto Rico with Brigitte. Next, I resigned all my chairmanships and directorships. Just one major task remained before I faced my trial and possible imprisonment: I had to sort out the gathering financial disaster confronting Brocket Hall.

Somehow, the Hall's management had failed to achieve even the minimal occupancy rates needed to meet the very generous terms of the bank's £15 million loan. So the bankers had another bright idea. They brought in a man who specialised in resolving tricky situations. His name was David Rocker.

Rocker was a genuinely unpleasant individual. He was the kind of man who wore grey shoes and brown nylon suits: 'Here comes the man in the plastic suit,' the girls in the office would mutter when they saw him approach. He was quite short – at least from my vantage point – with a flabby paunch and thinning, wavy brown hair. He had an appalling temper, which could explode at any moment. But what particularly upset me was the sight of his little pink nipples, clearly visible through his synthetic-fibre shirt.

Rocker attracted complaints the way magnets attract iron filings. Long-standing clients who'd been coming to Brocket Hall for years found that their treatment had changed dramatically. It had long been accepted that guests could bring their own wine, on payment of a small corkage fee. One client who always liked to do that was making arrangements with one of the staff when Rocker grabbed the phone and shouted, 'If you don't like our wines, don't come here!' then slammed the receiver down.

Rocker soon came to regard Brocket and its contents as his personal property. He liked to drive the Ferraris up and down the drive, although 'drive' is perhaps an exaggeration. He was completely unable to handle a serious sports car: you could hear the grinding of gears for hundreds of yards around.

Then again, Rocker wasn't driving the cars because he liked them. He was driving them to prove that he could challenge the old social order. In his mind, those grinding gears were the sound of the hated upper classes collapsing before his one-man revolution. To say that he hated me, and everything I stood for, is an understatement. He'd tell the staff: 'I'll make sure that the aristocracy never have houses like this again.'

By now, I, too, was beginning to wonder how much longer Brocket Hall would exist, come to that. I'd get despairing appeals for help from the staff, outraged at yet another lunacy on the part of their new bosses. Unable to take any direct action, having been sacked from my own business, I'd talk to the trust or the bank, but the response was always the same: the management had their full confidence and must be allowed to do their job.

Then my brother Richard and I had an idea. Sir Ian McLaurin, chairman of Tesco, had brought his board to the hall for many years, shunning the top London hotels. When the golf course was built he and his wife had immediately bought memberships and were among our best ambassadors. Perhaps he could help sort out the mess.

At the end of 1994 I spoke to Sir Ian, a slim, impeccably neat, intense man, who never said a single word more than he had to. He and I agreed that Brocket needed a chairman who had the clout to negotiate with the bank and make the necessary changes to the staff. The golf club membership and committee agreed: they, too, were desperate to see better management.

Once I had been arrested, however, my ability to influence matters was diminished still further. The first response of my family elders was not to rally round and ask how they could help, but to inform me that it would be best for me to end any association with

Brocket Hall and depart the premises. So just when I was down, they decided to make me unemployed and homeless, too.

Luckily, my staff and clients came to my rescue. Through all the crises of the past few years, I had still done my best to meet and greet guests at the Hall, have a chat with them and show them round the cars. The fact that I had just been arrested, far from horrifying all respectable members of society, made guests even more curious to set eyes on me. When they were denied the chance to meet me (and then tell all their friends), they complained bitterly at my absence. Word had got around that I was not attending and future clients had phoned to say that they were thinking of cancelling their booking if I was not going to be there.

The members of the golf committee convened a meeting at which the strong view was expressed that they were not at all happy with the proposal that I should go. Finally, David Sarch, my solicitor, pointed out (as previous lawyers had done before him) that the trustees did not actually have the right to evict me, however much they might wish to do so.

So a compromise was agreed. I would host various functions at the Hall, particularly those which VIPs were attending. I would continue to use my offices and home. And I would continue to draw expenses to enable me to live.

One such event was the launch of the new Piaggio scooter, at which several prominent Italian industrialists turned up. So too did Sarah Dale, whose travel business depended on Italian clients such as Piaggio.

'Hello, Charles,' she said gushingly, only too keen to show the Italians what close friends we were.

I suppose one had to admire her sheer gall in daring to attend, let alone speak to me. But I hardly felt inclined to be generous.

'Good morning, Sarah,' I replied. 'The last time we met you attempted to jail me. I am amazed that you have the gall to turn up here, let alone talk to me. Did you never even think of the children?'

I then ushered the Italians to the cocktail bar, where they told me that her account was to be cancelled.

All the while, I was having to turn up at the magistrates' court for what seemed like an endless series of minor hearings, along with all those accused with me as co-conspirators. These included Michael Campbell-Bowling. As we all stood there like condemned men to have the charges read out, I looked into his eyes to say how sorry I was that our friendship should have come to this. Michael looked haggard and tired. With complete dignity, he accepted it as one of those things that happen in life that you are powerless to do anything about.

It was blatantly obvious that no reason had been given to justify the charge against Michael. His counsel tried to appeal to the magistrate's conscience by pointing this out.

The prosecutor then got up and said, 'My response to the learned gentleman, and to the court, is that Mr Campbell-Bowling's mistake was to be a friend of Lord Brocket in the first place.'

So that was it. They were not concerned about the

evidence. They just wanted to throw their weight around to ensure that at least some people landed up inside. The fact that this process would destroy a few lives here and there was merely a trivial detail.

– 20 –

War at the Hall

BACK AT THE HALL, SIR IAN MCLAURIN WAS LEADING the calls for change. He handwrote me a letter saying that the marketing was so pathetic that he would not even use the marketing director to 'clean the Tesco's toilets'. Meanwhile, the bank were telling the trustees that the company – and therefore the Hall – would have to be put up for sale unless something were done to improve the business.

It wasn't, in theory, a difficult problem. There was nothing wrong with the Brocket Hall product. Glowing letters and companies returning year after year demonstrated that. The 15 per cent occupancy rate we needed to survive was just as achievable as it had always been. We needed a management team that would grip the problem by the scruff of its neck and sort it out.

It didn't take a genius to join the dots. I went to see Sir Ian at his home, just fifteen minutes from Brocket, and asked if he would consent to become chairman of the company and appoint new management.

'I'll take it on, but on condition that you play no part in the company until further notice,' he said. 'I must have free rein to make changes.'

'I guarantee that you will have my full co-operation,' I said, overjoyed that he had agreed and convinced that this would save Brocket for the family.

Sir Ian added 'I will liaise with the present chairman. The first thing I will do is to remove the manager and the marketing director. That's where the rot lies. I have a fair idea who should be their replacements. I have someone particular in mind.'

A few days later Sir Ian dismissed William Pound, the general manager. In his place he appointed David Rocker – who had hitherto been acting as a consultant for the bank – as a temporary replacement until a full-time manager could be found. McLaurin then asked me to assemble the entire company in the conference-room, so that he could speak to them. There was a sort of carnival atmosphere in the main office as the staff all waited for Sir Ian to arrive. Everyone believed that this was the start of something good.

At 11.45 a.m. Sir Ian breezed in. He promised that he would do his best to rediscover the success that we had enjoyed just a few years before. He said that the first task was to appoint a new managing director and mar-keting director and that this should be done very soon. He added that he would stay as chairman for a period of five years, and then review the situation. With that he left.

I addressed the staff with a light heart and said that this heralded the rebirth of Brocket. We would soon return to the occupancy rates that we had only two years before. We should thank our lucky stars that we had someone with real clout to call the tune.

How wrong can you get?

It is easy to find top managers fast for a place like Brocket, but days went by without any attempt to appoint anyone. I went to see Sir Ian.

'I thought you were going to appoint one of the top hotel managers?'

'Rocker will do for the moment,' Sir Ian said. 'He is perfectly capable and has the recommendation of the bank as being a sound person.'

'But he has told the staff that he specialises in the liquidation of companies!' I protested.

'I'm not willing to discuss it,' snapped Sir Ian. And that was that.

So Rocker was left in total command of Brocket Hall. And didn't we just know it.

Both the bank and McLaurin had insisted that the Ferraris should all be sold as fast as possible, without making the disposal so obvious that prices plummeted. Meanwhile, the whole car operation was to be shut down.

This caused one immediate problem. We shared the showroom building with a car bodywork company called Prestige Coachworks. They had spent a small fortune on the building, installing paint ovens and other apparatus, on my promise that they would get a secure lease on their workspace.

One day I went down to Prestige, to be informed by the distraught owner, Shane Willis, that Rocker had told him that he had four weeks to get out. I went up to Rocker's office – which happened to be my old office – and asked why Prestige were being evicted.

At first Rocker said nothing. Suddenly he exploded, 'Because I bloody well say so!' He smashed his fists repeatedly down on the desk. I stood, rooted to the spot, as he turned round and started punching the wall behind him with his fists. At least Isa had the excuse that her rages were chemically induced. This man just seemed to be naturally unhinged. I started to back away as he announced, 'No one crosses me!'

I explained that Prestige had a tenancy in law but Rocker never listened. Instead, although I was still the sole director of the car company, he had the locks changed on the Ferrari showroom complex and barred me from entering. Bizarrely, he gave Rick Furtado a new set of keys and allowed him to continue to operate his car brokerage business, even though Rick had been charged with the same offence as myself and his long list of previous convictions was by now common knowledge.

With great glee, Rocker informed me, 'You have been removed as a director of the car company and so you no longer have access to the company premises.'

I was really beginning to wonder if this man knew anything about the law. 'David,' I said, 'there is actually a legal process that you have to adopt to change the directors of a company. You can't just announce one day that the directors are different.'

'I bloody well can!' he shouted. 'I can do what the hell I like, and you are no longer the director of your company!'

When David Sarch wrote Rocker a formal letter informing him he had no right to act as he had tried to do, Rocker replied by screaming obscenities down the phone. 'Jesus, that man has a serious problem!' Sarch gasped afterwards. 'He's barking mad!'

Back at Brocket I got a call from Prestige. It was Shane: 'You'd better get here quick. People are locked in the workshop and storeroom and are doing something with all the company spares.'

'Christ, the stock is worth a small fortune,' I said. 'I'll come now.'

I arrived to find Shane and four of his staff by the door. 'They're in there making a hell of a noise,' he said. 'God knows what they are doing but if Rocker's involved I'd watch out. He's probably setting you up for something.'

I repeatedly banged on the door but got no response. Then I rang Rocker in the clubhouse.

'Mr Rocker says he's having lunch and won't talk to you,' the waiter told me. So there definitely was something fishy going on.

I rang David Sarch, and he instructed me in no uncertain terms: 'Charles, lever open the door, sit in the office then call me.'

With the help of the Prestige men, we broke the lock and found that the mysterious intruders were Rick and Steve. They were moving everything, obviously in preparation for something, but as my bail conditions forbade me to speak to either of them I went into the small glazed cubicle that formed the office, rang David Sarch again and asked him what to do.

'Right,' he said, 'the first thing to do is carry out a stock check. Knowing Rocker, he will sell the stock to Rick for a pittance and guess who'll be the fall guy? Or it will just disappear. Call the police anyway to ensure that there is no problem.'

I rang the police and just sat there, behind the desk, waiting. Somehow the bush telegraph had been working and in no time Fran, the housekeeper, appeared with a tray of toasted sandwiches and a glass of wine. 'By the sounds of it you may be needing this,' she said with a wink as she left.

The next arrival was an experienced, middle-aged policeman, PC Wardby. I explained that I would like to carry out a stock check but I was afraid that there would be a scene. The words had no sooner left my mouth when the door burst open and Rocker stormed in.

Prodding PC Wardby in the chest with each word to convey his authority, Rocker said, 'Officer, this man is guilty of breaking and entering. He is also guilty of theft as he has stolen a padlock. You will arrest him.'

Wardby stared at Rocker for a moment and then said, very slowly and deliberately, 'Sir, do not poke me in the chest. Do not tell me what to do. It is not possible for a man to break into his own property.'

Wardby went into the office and talked to my solicitor to verify the facts. He then talked to his superior. Finally, he told Rocker, 'I have talked to Lord Brocket's solicitor and to my superior and he must be allowed to carry out a stock check.'

Rocker blew up. 'No, he bloody well won't! I won't allow it!'

He lunged towards the officer and landed on the desk, with me still behind it, smashing the plate of sandwiches and the glass of wine and sending shards all over the little office. He then ripped the phone out of the wall saying, 'If anyone uses the phone I'll report you for theft of company electricity and, Officer, I expect you to charge him for the theft.'

Wardby got hold of Rocker by the shoulders and frog-marched him out of the workshop. At the door he said, 'Sir, I caution you that if you carry on I will arrest you for a breach of the peace. Do you understand?'

Rocker, beside himself with rage, stormed off, with the Prestige men all grinning.

Throughout this I had not uttered a word. I had just sat behind the desk. The officer came back into the office. 'Blimey, I've never met one like that before. No wonder he's called Rocker. He's completely off it.'

I carried out my stock check while the officer waited.

I discussed the situation with Philippa, whose support remained unwavering, and my family. We couldn't understand why Rocker was still at Brocket. He had absolutely no knowledge of the hotel and catering industry. Every minute that he stayed in the post threatened the chance of a quick rectification of the situation.

Unless that was what was supposed to happen.

Soon afterwards, I got a phone call from Sir Ian

McLaurin: 'I'm afraid that I have given instructions to the bank to sell Brocket,' he informed me, with a casual air more suited to the announcement of a new price for baked beans than the selling of a man's business, property and children's inheritance.

I was frozen to the spot. 'Are you serious?'

'Yes.'

'I don't understand. Why this sudden change? Why have you not appointed a new person to take over from Pound, as you said you would?'

'I don't wish to discuss it,' snapped McLaurin.

That was the end of the conversation. After nearly twenty years of hard work, the man we had trusted to save the business was closing it. I could not, must not, accept this.

That evening I drove over to Sir Ian's house. I implored him to tell me what the real reason was for the about-turn. 'Is it anything to do with the showroom incident?' I asked.

'Well, that didn't help.'

'What did Rocker tell you?'

'That you were drunk, that you assaulted him and that you broke in.'

'Ian, you are an intelligent man. Surely you should speak to others who were at the scene before you come to conclusions as to what happened?'

'It's not important, anyway.' Sir Ian looked at me and said nothing more. He sipped his whisky. He could see that I was visibly upset at the prospect of the family home being sold off, but he showed no sign of sympathy.

Then he said, 'The main reason is that the bank have refused to write off the major portion of the £7 million. That was a crucial part of my plan and the fact that they won't means that my plan is unworkable.'

'But that doesn't make any sense,' I said. 'An idiot could run the business if the debt was written off. The reason why we are in this situation is just *because* the bank will not write off the debt. But the existing agreement requires only a 15 per cent bednight occupancy to finance, and any management worth its salt can achieve that. You said that you would make those changes. So why is this now not the case? Or did you never really intend to rescue the company? Was that why you kept Rocker?'

He looked at me but would not answer. Finally he said, 'Charles, that is all I have to say. My decision is final. The place will be sold.'

I left with tears in my eyes. I simply could not believe it had come to this. I rang Richard when I got home and recounted the conversation that I had just had.

'I wonder if what he said about the bank refusing to write off £7 million is true?' he said thoughtfully. 'Perhaps you should ring up first thing tomorrow and find out. Ring one of the directors, Brian Clare. And record it, okay?'

At 8.10 the next morning I phoned Brian Clare, with the tape running. I tried to sound as casual as possible.

'You're in the office early,' I said. After a few pleasantries I broached the subject. 'I was talking with my brother about the various scenarios involving a write-off of debt and—'

'Charles, there has been no suggestion of a debt write-off,' he said.

'But I thought there was a request for the bank to write off £7 million of car debt?'

'I can assure you that no such thing has been requested,' said Clare. 'Not unless there is a written request for such a write-off in today's post, which is sitting unopened on my desk.'

I rang Richard and repeated what Clare had told me. We decided we needed to speak to McLaurin again. At midday Richard and I were facing him in the sitting-room at Palmerston. I asked him again why, just two weeks after taking over as chairman, he was trying to sell the business.

'I told you, Charles,' he said. 'The bank refuse to write off £7 million of car debt and as that was central to my plan I cannot continue.'

Richard then took up the conversation, telling McLaurin that I had phoned Brian Clare and been told that there had been no request to write off the car debt.

There was a silence. Then Ian said, 'Well, Charles has made my business plan unworkable.'

'What do you mean?' I asked. 'What exactly have I done?'

'You have made it unworkable,' McLaurin said.

Richard looked exasperated. 'I don't believe you actually had a business plan as such, did you?'

'Think what you like,' said McLaurin defiantly. 'Brocket will be sold.'

He got up and left.

Richard turned to me. 'This is neither a write-off problem nor a business plan problem. So what is the real agenda?'

From this moment on it was clear that I had to fight like hell and use any means to prevent Brocket being sold. At least I had the bank on my side. They assured me that they'd far prefer to see a successful business at Brocket than make do with the scraps after it had been sold at a rock-bottom price.

I had one further weapon. When I borrowed the first £5 million, I was stuffed by a clause that my lawyers missed. The next time around, I repaid the compliment in spades.

As I have earlier described, the trustees had transferred the Hall and a plot of fifty-six acres, which also included the stables, car showroom and my house, Palmerston, to my personal possession. This had been the security for the first loan and would be sold if the conference and car businesses were closed down, as per the McLaurin plan. But the 1,450-odd acres of park and farmland surrounding this central island still belonged to the trust. And, for once, my trustees had come up trumps.

The brilliant trust solicitor had kept one of the three driveways to the island on a six-month licence. It could be terminated at any moment. The lodges at the two other entrances were owned by the trust, which meant that they also had control of the gates.

All the staff cottages were on a licence arrangement and could be taken away at a moment's notice.

The entire estate water supply, which supplied all the

buildings and the golf course, was on trust land and controlled by the trust.

Fearing the worst as things began to go haywire, I had registered the name 'Brocket Hall' as a trade name and put it in the ownership of the children's trust so any hostile purchaser could not use it.

The furniture in the Hall was owned by the trust and could be removed at any time. It would cost an incoming company a small fortune to refurnish the place to any acceptable standard.

The current golf clubhouse at Warren House was only on a six-month licence and would be denied to a hostile purchaser.

Our old marital home, Watershipps, was also on the island. The business had just spent over £700,000 to convert it to a new golf clubhouse, which was just about to open. The snag was that, in the divorce settlement, Isa had a 50 per cent claim to this property.

The land butting up to the golf course was registered as agricultural land and I, as the trust's beneficiary, had a perfect right to carry out activities such as pig farming. The smell alone would have stopped any golf activity. I also had a right to hold clay pigeon shoots – very loud clay pigeon shoots.

Then there was the delicate problem of the sewer. This had been constructed over trust land without specific permission and was connected to all the main buildings. In a hostile take-over position this could be shut off at a moment's notice. The new owners would, quite literally, find themselves in the shit.

There were many other smaller so-called 'poison

pills' and their net effect was to ensure that any purchaser who bought the Hall without the trust's
approval would find that their life would soon become
intolerable.

There was only one person who did not realise the
importance of the poison pills. That was Rocker. He
openly boasted to me, the staff and even the trustees
that the poison pills were irrelevant. He added that the
trust was irrelevant, too, and that he would sell Brocket
to whoever he wanted. 'The likes of you have no right
to own a place like this,' he declared, like a good little
revolutionary. 'The aristocracy are history!'

Well, maybe they are. But not at the hands of people
like him.

Blindly careering down this cul-de-sac, Rocker glee-
fully prepared a glossy package of pictures and accounts
and started mailing them out to sell Brocket.
Meanwhile, I did my best to fight him.

Having lost my job, I no longer received a salary
from the company and was virtually penniless. But
Philippa, who was as tireless in her support as ever,
found a City deal-maker, Adrian Bradshaw, who was
prepared to help me negotiate with people and companies who might be prepared to take a 49 per cent stake
in the company and leave me living at Palmerston, with
a full salary and 51 per cent of the shares.

A five-minute tour around Brocket and the surrounding park was invariably enough to persuade
potential investors that the hotel, golf club and leisure
facilities added up to a fantastic business proposition.
Accountants had estimated that if Brocket were prop-

erly managed it could generate up to £20 million per annum as a conference centre. If we converted it to a proper country-house hotel, there would be additional costs, but the annual income would be a minimum of £30 million. Not surprisingly, three companies in particular were interested in getting involved, and papers were drawn up.

Meanwhile, Rocker had opened up another front in his war against me, by forming a strange alliance with Isa. He realised that if Palmerston had no heating or services it would be easier to evict me. As a bonus, I would not be able to have the children to stay with me. This would be of great assistance to Isa's lawyers, who were attempting to gain her full custody. He cut off the gas, electricity, water, telephone and even the burglar alarm.

Since my arrest had been transmitted by satellite around the world it was hardly surprising that all my friends knew what had happened. They were without exception absolutely fantastic in their support of me. Many of them offered to have me and the children to stay.

Then a national newspaper wrote that Philippa and I were going to get married. I knew full well that I would probably go to prison. But Philippa was a PR. Her clients would not want to be associated with a criminal's wife. Meanwhile, her heart was set on becoming an MP. I knew that any chances of selection at the next election would be doomed if she associated with me. I liked, fancied, respected and admired Philippa, but I didn't feel that I could give her the kind of love that would justify such a massive sacrifice on her part. With a heavy heart, I said that we should end our affair. I left her with a mixture of anger and sadness in her eyes.

The battle for Brocket continued, with Rocker doing everything he could to frustrate my efforts to save the business, by trying to persuade the bank that nothing short of a total sale would do. As always, he was treating the customers with his own, very special charm.

I received a call from David Morris, the American chief executive of a large financial company that regularly hosted the annual conference of the world's central bankers at Brocket. It was a very prestigious booking.

'Charles, I'm sorry to bother you but I have a bit of a problem with your new general manager, Mr Rocker,' he began. 'As you know we tend to socialise well into the early hours on the final night. I asked Rocker if he could ensure that there were several staff on duty to serve drinks right through the night if necessary. He just said to me that I would have whatever staff he saw fit on the night. If I didn't like it, then I could go elsewhere.'

'He *what*?'

'He said that we could go elsewhere. It was as if our business meant nothing to him. I was so cross that I did make enquiries to book elsewhere but good places were not available. Anyway, we love Brocket. I don't like to complain but that is no way to behave.'

There was no point in saying anything to Rocker, or indeed the board, as the whole thing had reached a total stalemate. The business struggled on, with the debt climbing, the bookings diminishing and the totally de-motivated staff living in fear of instant dismissal for making any contact with me.

Amid the conflict I walked into a bar in Chelsea to have drinks with my half-brother Rupert, and saw a gorgeous girl across the other side of the bar. I was too feeble to dare go up to her and say hello. But with typical City-boy nerve, Rupert simply walked across, introduced himself and got the conversation started. We ended up having dinner and going back to her place for a few drinks afterwards.

A while later Melissa wrote to me at Brocket. It was clear that the attraction was mutual. I told her everything about my arrest and that I was guilty. She said it made no difference to her. We had dinner in the club-house next to the lake and in the warm summer night air we made love.

From that moment on we virtually lived with each other. She was petite, utterly beautiful, gentle and kind. She loved the children.

Naturally, there was a catch. Melissa had a strange arrangement whereby her ex-boyfriend paid for the upkeep of her house in London. With my natural talent for turning a blind eye to uncomfortable facts, I paid no attention to the implications of the deal. I was too busy enjoying myself.

Now that Brocket was hardly ever busy, and Rocker hated me being around when it was, I had plenty of free time. For the first time in years, I was free to do what I wanted without having to check the diary and see that I had to deliver a speech to a bunch of politicians, company directors or computer salesmen.

Melissa and I spent most of our time between her London house and Palmerston. At weekends we stayed with all the friends who had been ignored while I'd been obsessed with Brocket, or wrapped up in my conflict with Isa. Little by little, I realised that I was falling in love with Melissa, and to my delight and her surprise, for she had always kept her emotions well hidden behind the immaculate façade of the perfect mistress: almost as if she treated relationships more like business transactions than passionate commitments – she seemed to be falling for me, too.

Melissa loved organising expeditions for the children whenever they came to stay. We were always so relaxed in each other's company, never, ever, short of anything to say. We could have the quiet, cosy evenings, cuddled up in front of the TV, that had always been impossible for Isa and me. Or we could just be totally spontaneous and uninhibited. Melissa was game for anything. She loved rollerblading and even bought me a pair of skates so that we could hurtle through the streets of London, disrupting the traffic together.

In contrast to my new-found happiness, Isa's lawyers were making our divorce proceedings ever more bitter, and their fees were gobbling up the only remaining capital that Isa possessed. Even if her lawyer had told her, she didn't seem to understand. I, being unemployed, was on legal aid, while she would have to pay for her fees.

As one marriage went through its death-throes,

another seemed to be on the way. Melissa and I both wanted to be together. We didn't know what effect a prison sentence might have. I'd been advised that, in a case like mine, a normal person might get a suspended sentence, or a maximum of three months. We all knew that the court would want to make an example of me, so I'd been told to prepare myself for anything between a six-month sentence and three years. Steven Barker, my criminal solicitor, had been speaking to the police. They were expecting something on the lower end of that range: I should be out on parole within a few months.

Melissa promised to wait for me. One evening, I gave her an engagement ring: nothing spectacular, but the best I could afford at the time. She dissolved into tears and hugged and hugged me. I took her to meet my mother, too. At least she would know in advance this time! We celebrated at a local restaurant and all Melissa did was stare at me across the table all evening with the biggest smile on her face.

Meanwhile, I had to prepare my children for what might soon happen. Alex was getting teased at school that his father was a criminal. I drove down to Ludgrove to tell him that I would not see him for some time. I explained to him what an insurance claim was all about and how, in my blind desire to keep the estate in the family, I had resorted to dishonesty. I explained how we had come to our senses and the tortuous route to the withdrawal of the claim.

'But, Daddy, if you withdrew the claim, surely you didn't actually do anything wrong?' he said. 'That's like me thinking of taking some sweets from a shop and then not actually doing it. Surely they can't put you in prison for that?'

He was trying so hard to be brave, but his eyes were filled with tears. The poor boy never saw much of his mother. Now he was to lose his father too and the worst part was that I couldn't tell him for how long.

As I left him I felt as if I were abandoning him. I turned back and he was standing in the doorway, dressed in his smart school uniform, with his arms by his side. I blew him a kiss and drove off, scarcely able to see with the tears in my eyes.

– 21 –

Guilty

AS ALWAYS, ROCKER HAD BEEN BUSY. FURIOUS THAT I had not been forced out of Palmerston House by his cutting off all the services, he had issued eviction proceedings against me under the Squatters' Act. I rang my solicitor, David Sarch.

'The man's mad!' he said. 'He can't know anything about the law. The court will laugh at him.'

Then one of the accounts girls in the office leaked the fact that Rocker was invoicing the company £1,000 a day and up to £500 a day expenses. The man to whom she gave the information, the estate manager, Jeff Clague, had himself not been paid for several months.

By now, the staff were almost openly rebelling and Rocker was retaliating by firing those he considered to be disloyal, particularly any who communicated with me, and evicting them from their staff housing on the estate.

The only people who were even busier than Rocker were the Hertfordshire police. In late 1995 they rang Steven Barker to say that they had a second charge against me.

'What is it?' Steven asked.

'It's to do with a short-wheel-base Ferrari and a complainant we have,' they said. They revealed that they had been contacted by Peter Shirley, the American to whom I'd spoken on the phone more than two years before. He was claiming that I'd conned him. But they refused to give any further details of the charge against me.

I was baffled. How could I possibly have defrauded Peter Shirley when I hadn't sold a car to him, or profited from any sale to him by anyone else, or even known about the sale until he'd called to tell me he'd bought the car? Clearly, there was no way that I could plead guilty or not guilty if I didn't even know what I was supposed to have done. But by now, in December 1995, the time was approaching when I would have to decide how to plead on the case that everyone understood: the conspiracy to defraud the insurance company.

To fight the case, I would need money. Steven Barker had applied to the judge for legal aid on my behalf, since it is the judge in a case who decides whether aid will be granted.

At the time, legal aid was a political hot potato because defendants who were known to have large amounts of money overseas or hidden away in corporations had managed to get it. Before the trial began, the Lord Chancellor's department rang the clerk of the court to discover whether I had been granted such aid. The clerk refused to say, but was then threatened with disciplinary action if he did not. Unsure of his ground, he admitted that I had.

The next morning the *Telegraph* carried a large article about wealthy people being granted legal aid. The Lord Chancellor's department had told the *Telegraph* that I was a classic example of the unacceptable granting of legal aid. Good to know that the system was ensuring that I received the fairest possible trial!

Steven Barker, Desmond da Silva and I arrived at the court-house with TV and the media fighting to get photos of me. After long deliberations with my family, I had agreed at their request to plead guilty. That way, they reasoned, we would avoid a long trial that would bring enormous bad publicity, hurt my children and – that old chestnut! – damage the family's good name. It was also felt that by pleading guilty, and thus confessing my sin, I might receive some clemency from the court. By law, the judge had to reduce any sentence he gave by one-third in the event of a guilty plea. So if he felt that my crimes merited, say, nine months inside, I would only receive a six-month sentence.

Steven Barker, whose entire profession was based on giving his clients the best possible defence, was strongly opposed to a guilty plea, since it is always possible to make a case on a defendant's behalf, and one never knows how a jury will react.

At least my trial was short, if not sweet. The whole thing was over in minutes. And my guilt was all over the evening news.

The judge set a date for sentencing, 9 February 1996. That gave me just over two months to sort everything out. Now I knew I was to go to prison, my sole duty was to do as much as I could to ensure that Brocket was not sold and that the children saw their inheritance. At least I had Melissa's love and the knowledge that we were planning a life together.

For now, we decided just to jump in the car and became tourists for a while. In the Lake District we walked miles over the hills and mountains and lost ourselves in each other's company, far from the reality of the prison cell that awaited me. Late one afternoon we reached the grassy summit of a mountain. With the glitter of the fading light on the lake below us and the darkening winter sky above, we undressed and lay naked, entwined, on the sweet-smelling grass. For that one moment, nothing else mattered. We held each other tight, looking up at the charcoal-coloured storm clouds racing over us. 'Jump on our backs and ride into the unknown,' they seemed to be saying.

We returned to London a week later. Christmas was approaching. Isa and I had agreed that the children would spend it with her but I was allowed to go over and give the children their presents on Christmas Day. I had told them that I was going to go away for some time and I could see that they were scared that they were going to lose their daddy for ever. I could not tell them how long my sentence would be. I would only find out in court, and then I would be led away to jail, without a word of farewell to my family.

Later that week a call came out of the blue. It was

Gilbert Rowberry, my father's solicitor, who was now almost ninety years old.

'Charles,' he said, 'I may not be around when you come out of prison and I think I ought to tell you a few things about the past that I don't believe you are aware of. I wonder if you could pop in and see me for a glass of sherry?'

It was then that Gilbert told me, for the first time, about the 1925 Trust that my grandfather had emptied. 'Charles, you would never have even considered what you did if the 1925 Trust was in existence. Only your grandfather knows where the money went. That's something no one in the family wants to talk about. There . . . now I've told you.' He sat back as if a great weight had been lifted from his mind.

'But you can't just spend that amount of money without leaving some sort of trace,' I said. 'I mean, it's just too big a sum.'

Gilbert explained that it was almost certainly the trust money that had enabled my grandfather to buy all his properties and companies in the UK and Ireland. 'He never intended to leave anything to your father – or you,' said Gilbert. 'Must have left it to the rest of his children.'

As I drove away I realised for the first time the lengths to which my grandfather had gone. I'd long known what he'd tried to do with the 1921 Trust, the one that contained the entire Brocket Hall estate. But I'd never until then understood the full extent of his actions. He'd deliberately left the family seat devoid of its means of support and its lifeline in times of trouble. He'd been clean, efficient and quite merciless.

So now I knew, not that the knowledge would do me much good.

In January I spent my last precious week with the children, but the days went all too fast and suddenly it was time to return them to Isa. I promised to come and see them before I went for sentencing and I returned to London to Melissa.

All week, the question preyed on my mind: would Melissa be strong enough to survive the impending storm? One night, as she was immersed in a sea of bubbles in her bath, she looked up at me and said, 'Darling, I've never been so happy. I don't want this moment to go away.' But it would and then what would she do?

As my sentencing at Luton County Court beckoned, Melissa said she had to go to New York on business. I was due in court on a Wednesday. She promised to return for lunch on Tuesday, then we'd spend my last night of freedom together. But at lunchtime my cellphone rang. It was Melissa.

'Darling, I have crashed my car on the way back from the airport. I pulled off as the oil light came on and, with all this ice about, I skidded and ran into a village pond. The car is a write-off but I am all right.'

She said that she was coming back to her house and I was to meet her there. I drove round just as all her soaked belongings were being unloaded from the taxi. I had never been possessive about Melissa but I felt in my bones that there was something wrong with this trip to New York. The clothes in her suitcase weren't the ones she'd taken with her when she flew to America.

Melissa dodged the issue and started shouting. Then she burst into tears. She promised that there was nothing going on. Perhaps the fact that I was to be separated from her for so long was making me paranoid. We hugged and forgot the whole thing, with me feeling guilty that I had questioned her at all.

That night, Melissa had organised an early birthday dinner for me, as I was to be sentenced three days before my birthday. Afterwards, we returned to her house, only to find it besieged by paparazzi. Melissa was terrified by the blaze of flashing lights and the shouts of the photographers. We split up, agreeing to meet at the Baines' house nearby. Having given me bail on the day I was arrested, Jonathan Baines was now giving me shelter on my last night of freedom. Melissa and I slept with our arms around each other the entire night. The sense of loss I felt was overwhelming. In the morning, we made love for the last time.

I dressed in my suit for court. Then I took off my watch and signet ring and gave them to Melissa for safe-keeping. I looked at my little finger and realised that this was the first time I had removed the ring for twenty-four years. I felt strange without it. It had become part of me but perhaps that was what I had to do – leave a part of me on the outside to survive what I had to face inside.

I wasn't afraid of prison. I had served enough time in the army to be able to muck in with any of the people I'd meet inside. Spyway and Eton had prepared me for most conditions. I just wanted to get on with it, get it over and start a new life. I wanted to give the children the life that we should have had in the first place. They had lived through far too much hurt.

At 8.30 that morning Steven Barker and Desmond da Silva came to pick me up. In Steven's hand was the indictment, giving the full description of my crimes.

Melissa clung to me like a koala bear. She promised to visit me in prison. We had talked this through many times. Steven said that I should be in an open prison after four weeks or so. Once I was there, visits would be very relaxed. After a third of my sentence I would be allowed out for a day every other weekend. It wasn't too terrible a prospect.

An hour and a half later we parked our car in a scruffy Luton hotel car park and took a taxi to the court. The pavement was crowded with paparazzi and TV cameras. We declined to comment and forced our way into the court.

Poor Michael was there, to answer a charge that didn't exist. Rick was there, looking his normal confident self, and the two mechanics were huddled in a corner. I was not allowed to talk to any of them but I was going to prison anyway, so what difference did it make? I talked briefly to all of them.

One of the officers in the case approached my solicitor, Steven. 'Has your client decided what to do about the second charge? The SWB Ferrari?'

'How can he when you have not yet given us any evidence?' Steven retorted. 'You seriously expect me to tell any client of mine that he should plead guilty to something like this? You must be kidding!' That was the end of that conversation.

I wandered over to Steve Gwyther, the mechanic, and told him, 'You'll never believe it. They have just tried to land that SWB Ferrari on me.'

Then I spotted Inspector Kerlin, the officer in charge of the main case. He was down a passage and looking rather sheepishly at me. We stared at each other, like two gunfighters on a dusty street. People around us began to notice and everyone fell silent. I marched down the long passage towards the end where he was huddled with all the other police. As I finally reached him, Kerlin ducked. He thought I was going to hit him. I extended my hand and shook his firmly.

'No hard feelings. I know you were just doing your job and that you did it well.' With that I about-turned, leaving Kerlin open-mouthed, and unable to say a word, and returned to Steven to be summoned into court.

Michael Campbell-Bowling, Rick Furtado, the two mechanics and I sat behind a glass screen in a box. We were all asked to stand and confirm our names. The charges were read out. The mechanics and I confirmed that we were pleading guilty but Rick and Michael pleaded not guilty. Rick then produced a medical report, saying he was not fit to stand trial and obtained an adjournment in his case.

Michael was dealt with first. The crown offered no evidence – because there wasn't any – the charges were dropped and he was awarded full costs. But the crown, ever economical with the truth, claimed that the charges were dropped due to lack of 'sufficient evidence', thereby leaving the impression that Michael had somehow been guilty but got away with it, rather than being a completely innocent man who had been falsely and unjustly accused.

Then counsel for the crown turned his attention to me. And now I learned one of the huge drawbacks of pleading guilty. In the event of a not guilty plea, both sides put forward their best possible case, and each side challenges evidence and allegations presented by the other. But when a defendant pleads guilty, the only case heard is the prosecution's. None of it is challenged, and it all enters the record as fact, no matter how outrageous.

The prosecutor announced, in his most theatrical style, that I had 'coerced' the mechanics into helping me. He made Steve and Mark sound more like characters from a nineteenth-century novel than participants in a twentieth-century crime. They were portrayed as innocent working men, forced into wrongdoing by their evil, unscrupulous, aristocratic master. The truth, as I have described, was rather different . . .

The judge was clearly moved by the crown's tale of feudal oppression. He said that it was disgraceful that I had coerced the mechanics by threatening them with eviction and loss of their jobs. The public and media were given the unmistakable impression that I was a thoroughly bad man, who deserved everything he was just about to get. To a hushed court, the judge delivered his sentence.

Inside

ALL I HEARD WAS 'TAKE HIM DOWN.' THE GUARD TO my right took me by the elbow and opened the door behind the dock. As I began the descent into the bowels of the court I turned to him. 'What did the judge say? I didn't hear what the sentence was.'

'Five years,' said the guard, matter-of-factly, and carried on ahead of me.

'Five years?'

'You're lucky,' he replied. 'You got the discount for pleading guilty. The gross sentence was seven and a half.'

I carried on walking alongside him, almost in a trance. I'd prepared myself mentally for a short stretch: a few months of extreme discomfort, a bit like a tough army posting. I was expecting to see light at the end of the tunnel. Five years was just unreal.

I was led to a room at the end of the passage. There was not a window in sight, nothing except the glare of

fluorescent lights off the grey gloss walls. Two female
officers took all my possessions from my pockets.

I thought about my children and wondered when I
would see them again. A wave of sheer panic gripped
me as I thought of their fate for the next few years,
parted from their father and left with a mother who had
long since abandoned them for the nearest bottle of
pills. Then I thought of Melissa. She'd been worried
enough by the prospect of me being inside for a few
months. How would she cope with a five-year sentence?

I was put in a freezing cell and waited to discover
what would happen next. Each time I heard keys
jangle down the passageway I got up, thinking that the
door was about to be opened, but the jangling passed
and receded into the distance. Here was my first lesson
in prison life: you spend most of your time just waiting.

It seemed ages before my door was finally opened. I
was led to a loading bay where a large white truck was
parked. This, I'd later learn, was known as a sweatbox,
for reasons that would soon become obvious.

I mounted the steps and inside found a central passageway with individual cells on either side, twelve in
total. Inside each of these boxes, there was just enough
room to sit down on the plastic seat with my knees
against the bulkhead in front. The window was opaque
and smoked. Within a few minutes the truck was full
with the day's collection of society's debris.

The sweatbox moved out into the traffic, to be
met with an explosion of camera flashes. Then we left

the press pack behind and drove off to Bedford Prison, a typical Victorian jail, sitting behind massive gates and high stone walls. We were herded up some stairs to the reception area and processed one at a time.

When it was my turn, I stood at the desk as a prison officer – or 'screw' – poured my pathetic bag of belongings on the table.

'One watch. You can keep that. Tobacco, can't have that. Shaver, can't have. Nothing electrical unless it runs off batteries.' My scruffy jeans and T-shirts were thrown to one side. 'No personal clothes.'

When he had finished he listed the items and said, 'Sign here.' I did and was sent into the next room . . .

'In 'ere,' said another blank-faced man in uniform. I was taken into a booth.

'Strip off. Put your clothes in that box.'

I took everything off and stood naked. The officer went through my clothes, presumably to check for anything suspicious.

'Put what you want to keep in that bag and then sign for them. They will be stored for when you're released.'

An inmate who was acting as reception orderly came up to me. ''Ere, mate, grab these.' He tossed me a pile of clothes, wrapped in a sheet. I put them on: blue jeans, blue and white striped shirt, prison nylon socks and a sweatshirt to keep warm. The shoes appeared to be the same design as army officers' brogues. On closer inspection, I saw that they were made of plastic.

Now all dressed alike, we were led through a maze of gates to the main body of the prison. The first thing that struck me was the noise. It was sheer bedlam. There were several pool tables along the ground floor and several arguments were raging. At the end a TV was perched on top of a high bar stool and two inmates were fighting over which programme to watch while others stood nearby and jeered them on. Around the walls were little groups of prisoners, all talking animatedly while the inmates on the phones at the end were shouting to be heard above the din.

The cells lined the walls four storeys high with walkways around each level. The centre of the building was a massive well that had a steel mesh net strung across the first-floor level to prevent anyone jumping from the top floor . . . or being pushed.

A prison officer shouted out our names and then a cell number. 'Brocket, B 12.' The ground floor was 'A'. That meant I was the next landing up. I climbed the metal stairs, pushed open the steel door and ducked to enter my cell. From now on, this would be my 'pad', as everyone in nick always called it.

It was some six feet by ten, with a bunk bed. The bottom bunk was made up, so I plonked my stuff on the top. Opposite the bunks there was a single small table with a chair at either end. Next to the doorway was a combination stainless-steel basin and loo. The sole natural light was from a barred window, two feet by eighteen inches, high up below the brick-vaulted ceiling of the cell.

I had just made up my bed when an inmate came in.

'Hi, mate,' he said in a strong Scottish accent. 'I'm Eddie, yer pad-mate. Would ye like a brew?'

'Sure. I'm Charlie.' We shook hands. Eddie grabbed a plastic jug, disappeared for a minute and then returned with the hot water.

'The hot water's on the ground floor. Before lock-up you must fill it, as that's the last time until the morning.'

'What's the timetable?' I asked.

'We go downstairs to get our breakfast at 8 a.m. We must be at work by 8.30. We work until 11.45 a.m. and collect our lunch and take it to our pads, where we're locked up until 1.30 when we go back to work. Stop work at 4.30 p.m. and collect tea at 5 and take it to our pads. Locked up until 6 and then let out until 8 for association.'

'Association?' I asked.

'Yep. Means we can watch TV, play pool, use the phone and chat to others. If you want the phone you have to book your time at the wing office. Ten minutes only and the phone cards are special prison cards that you have to buy at the canteen once a week and they're fuckin' expensive.' Then, with a wink, he added, 'If you want extra cards they can be bought, but at a 50 per cent mark-up. Very fuckin' expensive! Oh yeah, and if you have your own money you're allowed to spend £10 a week. If you work you get £6 a week.'

'What sort of things do we have to buy?' I asked.

'You get fuck all inside,' he replied. 'You get cheap shaver blades that cut the fuck out of you, you get toothpaste that tastes of fuck-all and makes your teeth yellow, and you get horrible soap. Once a week you get a wee bag with some tea bags, milk-powder sachets and sugar. That's your lot. Anything else you have to buy.'

'What about laundry?'

'Every week at the CES – clothing exchange store. You take your stuff there and they change it but I don't advise it. The prison laundries operate on cold water and the soap they use gives you a rash, so most of us wash our own clothes in the basins.'

We sat down at either end of our little table while he filled me in on prison culture. He was rather surprised that I was taking it all in so easily but it didn't seem that different from the regime at my prep school.

We had arrived during the association period and Eddie wangled a space in the phone queue for me to ring Melissa. I had trouble making myself heard above the din. We were both very emotional. 'I'm going to get some photos and make a collage of the two of us so that you can put it on your wall,' she said. 'I love you.' She was trying to be brave but I knew that she was only hanging on by a thread.

I thought of ringing the children but I would have choked on my words. Anyway, I was forbidden by court order to ring Isa's house. And one thing you do not do in prison is defy a court order: it's a guaranteed extension to your sentence.

At 7.55 there was a lot of shouting by the officers: time to get back to our cells. For the next few minutes the slamming of steel doors resounded around the prison, explaining why it is called 'bang-up'. Eddie was wonderful, providing a permanent room service with his tea. I must have been on my tenth cup when he stripped off for a wash and I saw the horrifying state of his torso. 'Christ, Eddie. What the hell is that? You look more like a road map of England.' He was covered with angry pink and blue scars that criss-crossed his body.

'Och, just a wee bit o' trouble. I won £3,000 on a card game. I can't help gambling. I'll gamble anything. After my win I got drunk and collapsed on my bed at home. While I was out cold the two blokes that I had won the money off came into my room. They cut my face and throat and then my back. My back was just strips of flesh hanging off. I was found in the morning by a mate who came to get a beer off me. He got me to hospital. I had only two pints of blood left in my body.'

Eddie was twenty-eight. Later, he told me what he was in for. 'This fella owed me but wouldn't pay. I went to see him but he went for me. I'm no idiot, I was ready. I put my knife in him, cut out his guts and pulled them out all over the carpet. He should have died, the bastard, but they came and stuffed it all back in and he lived. Anyway, they nicked me and here I am. Got five years.'

This was the same sentence I had been given. 'You got the discount for pleading guilty,' said Eddie, 'but I didn't because I told them they could fuck themselves. Pity, I would have got less.'

So spilling a man's guts around a room was considered less serious than planning a fraud that you then decided not to commit. Nothing made any sense to me, but I soon learned that was par for the course.

Over the next few years, I would suffer from the system's apparently limitless desire to make my life hell.

When I talk to people about my prison experiences, they always ask, 'But why did the establishment go so far out of their way to make life difficult for you?' I wish I could supply a decent answer.

I don't know why I was given such an extraordinary sentence, let alone why my treatment in jail reached the point where the authorities started acting in ways that they knew would put my life in danger. Sometimes I think it was a political issue: I was just the scapegoat for years of so-called Tory sleaze. Other times I wonder whether my real crime was to be posh: David Rocker isn't the only person who longs to screw the aristocracy.

One chap in an open prison said to me that I should have joined the Freemasons, as he had done. I'd often been asked, but had always refused and had then been quite outspoken about my distaste for secret societies. If I'd been a Mason, he suggested, my crime would have been brushed under the carpet. By defying them, I was asking for trouble.

Any or all of these reasons might explain why I was hounded before, during and after my time in jail. But there could be another reason. As the old joke says, 'Why does a dog lick its balls? Because it can.' Perhaps the criminal justice system is like that. Why does it screw people over? Because it can. It's nothing personal. It's just the way things are. And I saw plenty of people suffer worse than I ever did.

As I lay on the top bunk, my first night in Bedford Jail, wisps of snow floated into the room through a cell window devoid of glass. I looked above my head at the perfect Victorian brickwork, marvelling at the craftsmanship. Then I gave a quiet laugh to myself: lying in my cramped bed, with the roof arching above me, I felt just like a bottle of wine racked in the cellars at Brocket Hall.

Of course, we made the wine a bit more comfortable. The beds were steel slats that dug into my sides and the mattress was just a thin sheet of foam rubber that had long ago worn to almost nothing. I was so cold I could barely sleep. 'You should have kept your clothes on, like me,' Eddie said.

The next day Melissa came to visit me. The contrast between us was surreal: me in my prison uniform, while she stood there in her Chanel blouse and skirt, looking absolutely gorgeous, as if she had just left a cocktail party. We hugged, then she rummaged in her bag and pulled out a white flannel. 'Darling, I've soaked this in my perfume,' she said. 'Put it under your pillow and think of me. I will always be there for you. It doesn't matter how long you're here. I love you and I always will.'

Big tears rolled down her cheeks, as they did mine. I think I knew that she would not be able to keep her promise, but I could only hope. When it was time for us to part, I felt ghastly: just total emptiness.

Then I was led back to life in the nick.

Most of the inmates at Bedford were curious to see what sort of person I was, but they were polite enough. The mickey-taking was no worse than I had encountered in the regimental corporals' bar. And I certainly learned a thing or two about life on the other side of the law.

Reg was a good example of a career criminal. He was a fifty-eight-year-old Londoner with the weather-beaten look of an old boxer.

'Bin doin' armed robberies all me life, since I was a teenager,' he said. 'Average take is about £40,000 a month and with that I've 'ad a great life. Holidays abroad, and I can always be good to me woman.'

'What sort of robberies?' I asked.

'Money transfers, wages and weekly takes. Private security vans like Securicor,' he replied, with more than a hint of professional pride.

'But if you were doing on average one job a month, and there are loads of others doing the same thing, how is it that we only see a few robberies a year on the news?' I asked.

Reg laughed. 'You fuckin' stupid? If these firms revealed all their heists they wouldn't get any business from their customers. An' they probably don't claim on their insurance, neither – not unless it's a fuckin' big haul that they can't keep quiet.

'I got eight years for armed robbery,' he went on philosophically. 'I was caught bang to rights with a shooter in me 'and. But I bear no grudges. After this I retire and if eight years is the price of a life of good living, then that's a small price to pay, innit?'

Another old boy, called John, had been 'manager' to the infamous Kray twins. He was almost seventy now and was one of the kindest, gentlest people in the prison, but it hadn't always been like that.

'I were a right hoodlum, I were,' John said, in his Yorkshire accent. 'When I were a lad I were fighting all the time. I would fight anyone. A billiard cue in my hand always spelled trouble, it did! I were sort of accountant to the brothers, and I collected debts for them.'

'What was most of your business, then?' I asked.

'Take-overs and loans,' he said, like a respectable City gent. 'Take-overs were the most fun. Reggie would fancy a business, a club for example. "Right, lads," 'e would say, and off we'd go in the car. Right funny, it were. We'd march right into the place and say to the boss, "Right. This is ours now. Sign this, now bugger off." And that would be that. If there were any allegations, we'd show the signed sale agreement and anyway the bloke wouldn't be so daft as to do that – not if he wanted to keep his legs.'

Slowly I got into the prison routine. I spent an hour a day exercising – walking round the perimeter of a yard, about sixty feet square, with a duffel coat wrapped around me to protect me from the icy chill. My children were constantly on my mind. What must they be thinking now? I wondered what Isa was thinking, too. Was this how she'd really intended things to pan out?

One night I managed to call Melissa again. Before I rang off she said, 'Darling, I want to marry you. I've thought about it. It really is what I want.' I went to bed on cloud nine. I thought of her next to me as her perfumed flannel permeated its scent through my pillow.

My birthday was two days later and I got a huge quantity of cards from friends, family, staff at the Hall and the public, but nothing from Melissa. With a sense of foreboding I rang her but there was no answer.

St Valentine's Day came and still no card from Melissa. I knew in my gut that something was wrong.

On 20 February I was told that I was to be moved. I gathered up all my bits and pieces in my pathetic plastic bag and realised that this was what my life had been reduced to. Many of the inmates came to my cell to shake my hand and wish me good luck.

– 23 –

Plastic Gangsters

I WAS HEADING FOR A 'C' CATEGORY PRISON, Wellingborough, which enjoyed a more relaxed regime. My solicitor, Steven Barker, anticipated that I would only spend some four weeks there before moving to an open prison, where life would be completely different. After a year or so, I'd be allowed out for two days every month. It was the visits and days out that offered the only real chance of keeping alive the relationship between the children, Melissa and myself.

Wellingborough was scruffy and claustrophobic. The only blessings were that the cells had a separate toilet cubicle and, best of all, an actual view from the window. I could see over the mesh fence right across some water meadows to the town of Wellingborough. For the first few days I often sat at the window for hours and dreamed of the children.

The jail had until recently been a young offenders' institution, or 'YO'. These places are full of youths who couldn't care less about rules or authority. There is constant fighting and they all think they are top 'Daddies'. The common prison slang for them is 'plastic gangsters', because – in the view of serious, grown-up, professional criminals – the young whippersnappers aren't the real item.

Much of the YO air remained in Wellingborough's claustrophobic atmosphere and the strong sense that a plastic gangster mentality survived among some of the younger, more psychopathic inmates.

· My reveries were interrupted by constant attempts by the local heavies to try to get money out of me one way or another. They were convinced that if I had a title I must be rich, no matter what anyone said. Nothing would convince them otherwise and so Sean, my new pad-mate, fended them off with a detached chair leg kept constantly by his side.

'First thing,' he said, 'is not to trust anyone. They'll all try and get information off you to sell to the press or they'll try and get money out of you. Take my word for it.'

Sean didn't want anything. He was not looking to ingratiate himself in any way. He was just surviving, like all of us.

After two weeks Sean moved to another wing and a twenty-three-year-old chap moved in. John was there for lifting videos from a warehouse. He had a three-year sentence and immediately became fiercely protective of me. The chair leg had some nails added to it and a table leg was on permanent duty by the door.

John was a cheerful fellow but there was sadness not

far below the surface. All cells have a small notice-board where the inmates can pin up pictures. Usually they get covered in naked birds cut out of porno mags but John's board had very little except several pictures of a girl with a small baby boy.

'Family?' I asked.

'Yeah. My woman and my baby.' He sighed. Then he added, 'My baby's gone. My woman cleaned out the house, took everything and buggered off with our little boy. He's only three.' Tears were in his eyes. 'It happened two months ago and I've been trying everything I know to find out where he is. I love him so much and I miss hearing him giggle on the phone.'

'There must be ways you can find out,' I said. 'Perhaps social services will help you. A father has a right to know at least where his child is, even if there's a problem about access. If you want I can make some enquiries.'

'I've tried all that. Bloody useless they are and they don't care anyway, because I'm inside.'

He was clearly hurting very much. But my own situation wasn't much better. Something odd was happening with Melissa. Before I'd gone inside, I had left some things for safe-keeping with my solicitor Steven Barker. These included some photos of Melissa and me together, and also recent pictures of the children, which were particularly precious to me. Now Steven came to see me on a legal visit.

'Melissa appeared at the office saying that you wanted her to get your things,' he said. 'You hadn't told me, so I was a bit cautious and I had someone stay with her so we knew what was removed. Basically, she just took the photos and her letters to you. Then she sat down and had a coffee with me. She was very positive and supportive. She said she loves you very much.'

I told Steven not to worry. Melissa had promised that she was going to make a collage of pictures of the two of us. It didn't occur to me that she might actually be destroying any evidence that we had been together for the last year. I had other, more important things on my mind.

My final divorce hearing was on 1 March. And the system was doing its best to make sure it went badly. My costs for the earlier hearings in the divorce court had been funded by legal aid, because I had no income and my debts far exceeded my assets. But just before the final hearing, the legal aid office stopped the aid. They decided that I did have an asset after all; to wit, a pair of cufflinks.

This attempt to scuttle me was, as my divorce lawyer (now a judge) remarked, 'criminally transparent'. Unable to afford a barrister, I would be forced to defend myself in court. Naturally, I was expected to lose.

The legal aid people failed to realise, however, that I had given many speeches in the House of Lords, as well as making literally thousands of appearances at dinners, charity functions and business meetings. The prospect of having to get up and speak on my own behalf was far less intimidating to me than it would have been to most people – including, I dare say, the mean-spirited little shits who'd forced me into this situation.

Besides which, I had the law on my side. When Isa

and I first split, I had made her a generous settlement offer, based on the income I was then earning from the conference business at the Hall. My lawyer signed the agreement on my behalf. Isa's lawyer, however, said that she could obtain an even better deal.

A year-and-a-half and £37,000 of legal costs later, Isa's bank account had been cleared out. Yet the court awarded her a settlement that was worth less than my original offer. To make matters worse, because the lawyers had dragged out the case for so long, by the time it was finally heard I no longer had any personal assets with which to pay her.

The entire action had achieved nothing except to render Isa penniless and line the pockets of her lawyers. Unable to support herself, and with me in prison, she would be forced to move in with her parents in Puerto Rico, taking the children with her, removing them from their home, their schools and their friends.

When the judgement was announced, Isa sat in court staring blankly, as if unable to grasp the reality of what had happened. The realisation that she would have to uproot herself and children, coupled with the fact that she had not been paid one penny, must have been too much for her. But if Isa had been defeated, I hardly felt like a victor. I faced the total loss of my children. I'd never see them at all once they were in Puerto Rico.

Even now, Isa could have requested another meeting with my trustees. They were willing to provide a home on the estate and income to live on until the whole business with Brocket had been resolved. At that point, there might be enough capital to give her something extra (and indeed, since my release from prison, I have been able to pay Isa substantially more than the court ordered). But Isa was either too worn down to think straight or was advised by her lawyers not to speak to us. So we all left the chamber empty-handed in our different ways.

My mother and stepfather were at the court and we were allowed to meet in a conference-room for a tearful few minutes. I feared for the children. Why should they be taken away from everything and everyone they knew? What had they done to deserve this?

At least the terms of my divorce allowed me to speak to them again, however briefly. William, my youngest, was his normal boisterous self, but in the forthright way that only children exhibit, he asked, 'Daddy, Mummy says you are in jail. Is that right?' He then told me that they were all going to live in Puerto Rico at the beginning of April.

Alex said very little. He idolised everything I did and had been plunged into confusion with me going to prison. Antalya was chatty but very sad. Her voice was strained and subdued and then she suddenly burst into tears, sobbing, 'You're the best daddy in the world.' I tried hard not to cry myself but the lump in my throat eventually got the better of me. The words just wouldn't come.

I talked to Melissa, too. She answered on the first ring. In tears, she told me that she wasn't strong enough to cope with the media following her all the time, and writing awful articles about me. She ended by saying that she would visit me on Sunday.

Isa, meanwhile, interrupted her packing for Puerto Rico to stick the knife in a little deeper by giving an interview to a tabloid. All the bills that she had run up on the lawyer's forecast of a massive divorce settlement now had to be paid and she had nothing to pay with. So when she was offered money to 'tell all', she erupted with every conceivable accusation and expletive against me.

I dare say that much of what she said was unprintable. But, between them, she and the journalist managed to concoct quite a story, even so. The paper stated, as a matter of fact, that I was, among other things, a habitual fraudster, shoplifter, wife-beater, adulterer, pervert and blackmailer. It claimed that I had committed criminal assault and shot my own dogs. With the exception of the offence to which I had pleaded guilty, the entire four-page article was completely untrue.

My stomach was churning like a cement mixer when Melissa arrived, three days after our last call. She looked absolutely terrible. Her face was colourless and her eyes were bloodshot. 'I've gone back to my ex,' she said, before bursting into tears and falling into my arms. We hugged each other and she clung fiercely to me, digging her fingers into my back. 'I love you and always will,' she said.

Then she sobbed, 'I've had the press outside my house for a week. They follow me wherever I go. You can cope with this but I'm so scared. Now your ex-wife has said all those horrible things in the papers. It's so hard for me. Some of my friends say you must be a horrible person.'

At the end of the visiting period, we said our good-byes. That was the last time I ever saw her.

And then things turned really nasty.

I'd got myself a job serving tea and buns in the prison officers' mess. One evening, I got back to the wing and was accosted by an aggressive Pakistani lad called Ali, flanked by two of his lieutenants.

Ali was a shade under six feet tall, with a close-cropped head. He spoke in an Asian, Brummie accent. At the top of his voice, Ali shouted, 'I'm the daddy now, so you'll do as I say.'

This was typical brash, plastic-gangster talk, nothing to worry about. Then one of Ali's men, a white guy, covered in tattoos, pushed me and said, 'Remember me, do you? Your place? Broke the antenna to your phone, didn't I?'

I looked at him. Then it came back to me. I remembered an incident in the eighties when a Mini came on to the estate with about eight youths in it. They got out and confronted the mechanic, Mark Caswell, and me.

I called the police and one of them grabbed the antenna on my brick-sized mobile phone in an attempt to stop the call. They left when a local police-woman came into the park. She pulled over to let them pass, came up to us and said, 'What seems to be the trouble, then?' I remember saying to her, 'You just let the trouble go!'

The lad with the tattoos said, 'Boot's on the other foot now, innit?'

There was no point in dodging the issue, so I

replied, 'Maybe, but so what? You still playing the tough guy?' He just grunted and wandered off.

That night, Ali came down to my cell. One of the men I got on with very well at Bedford was a real character called Clive, who'd lived close to Brocket on the outskirts of Luton. He was serving three years for criminal damage to a police car and resisting arrest. Seeing Ali approach my cell, he came bounding down the passage and piled in. 'You lay one finger on Charlie and I'll kill you.' Clive was a big, fit chap and Ali just looked at him.

Before he could move, a crazed Irishman called Liam came rushing in, brandishing a home-made knife. This was enough to make Ali back out and he sloped off to his lair. My pad-mate John was shaking.

'Those bastards'll get us,' he said. Then he described how Ali's gang went round people's cells, extorting protection money and 'pad-thieving': stealing prisoners' possessions, then demanding cash to give them back. This is one of the lowest of all jail crimes and the traditional inmates' punishment comes straight out of the Saudi handbook: you get your hand smashed in a cell door until all your fingers are crippled and you can't go thieving again.

One evening my old pad-mate Sean came to see me from the other wing. He had heard that Ali and his gang were planning to hit the cells on my wing to demand protection money. Sure enough, the next night Ali and his gang were round our wing, pinching radios from people's cells. Then they turned up at my pad.

'You need protection,' said Ali. It wasn't a question,

it was a statement. 'We'll give it to you, and you'll pay us £2,000 for it.'

'I don't need any protection and you can fuck off,' was my reply.

They looked at me and the tattooed one said, 'You'll fuckin' change your mind.' And with that they left.

I went back to Clive's cell to report events. When I returned I found that my diary had been stolen. Before I could say anything, Ali stood in the doorway. He said, 'Give us £2,000 and we'll return your diary.'

I thought about what was in my diary. Most of it was in army shorthand, so it didn't really matter. But what did matter were the addresses of my parents, brother and Melissa.

I bluffed it out. 'Go to hell. You can keep the diary. I couldn't care less.'

As if reading my thoughts Ali said, 'Okay, then we'll get our mates to see your family and your girl. We'll ransack their homes and slash 'em up. All right?'

Surely he was bluffing? But if he wasn't . . .

'Okay,' I said, 'just give me tonight to think about it.'

Ali and his henchmen walked off. John and I went to confer with Clive and his pad–mate Craig, a short, tough, heavily muscled Londoner, who was in for armed robbery and feared absolutely no one. We used to work out together in the gym. He was the kind of guy who doesn't mess about. He told it just like it is. I liked him a lot.

'One thing you have to understand about Ali and his likes,' said Craig, 'is that they don't operate by the rules. Most of 'em are smackheads. They don't know

what they're doing and certainly don't care. You ever
seen a face that's been slashed up?'

'No, don't think I have,' I replied.

'Well, they use a razor because no amount of surgery
can repair the scar. There's always a line down your
face and the more lines they cut the worse you look. It's
not a pretty sight. So you have two choices. Get some
muscle and take 'em all on. Or ask for a move to
another prison.'

We went to another wing and met up with another
gym regular, Spiderman – so called because his giant
body was covered in spider's-web tattoos – and two
more of the heavies from the London scene. The
general feeling was that we should sort out Ali's mob in
a fairly major way.

'What if that results in them hitting my family or
girlfriend?' I asked.

'Nah, they won't,' said Spiderman. 'We'll make sure
they know it'll permanently damage their fuckin' health
if they do.'

When I returned to my cell, I found Ali and his tattooed sidekick there. Before I could take in the situation,
Ali pinned me against the wall. In his right hand he was
brandishing a plastic lavatory brush that had had its bris-
tles removed and some thin razor blades welded into the
head. They glinted in the cold light of the cell.

'See this?' he yelled at me. 'Any funny business and
we'll fuckin' 'old you down and shove this up your
fuckin' arse. You'll never shit properly again.'

John just stared. But then I saw his hand slowly
moving towards the chair leg that he kept propped up

by his bunk. All my concentration was on the gleaming blades. The moment John waded in with his club I would have to grab the handle of the brush or God knows what damage that infernal thing would do. Just as John was picking up his makeshift club, big Craig's voice blasted down the passage.

'What the fuck's going on? Stop behaving like children and fuck off back to your pads.' The tattooed lieutenant instantly raced out towards Craig and took a swing at him. Ali lowered the brush and followed him out.

Craig ducked but slipped on some spilled water, cracking his head on the concrete floor. Quick to react, the tattooed one stamped on Craig's head and knocked him out.

Ali lost interest in us and, before anyone could take in what had happened, he and his other hoodlums grabbed the dazed Craig, held his head against the steel door-frame of the cell and repeatedly slammed the steel door against his head. It was like watching a walnut in a nut-cracker. There was blood everywhere and Craig's forehead had a long groove where his skull had been broken.

At that moment a screw came on to the landing and Ali's lot dissolved into the background. Craig was carried out and taken to hospital.

In the silence of our rooms we reflected on poor Craig's fate. Ali's spies must have got wind of our discussions with Spiderman and his crew. War was about to be declared. It was just a question of who whacked whom first.

24

Nonces

THE NEXT MORNING, THE CELL DOORS WERE unlocked at eight as usual. We had just collected our porridge from the counter and taken it back to our cells when the alarm went off and there was a 'lock down': all prisoners were confined to their cells. An hour passed and we heard keys jangling down the passage. Our cell door was swung open. 'Brocket, come with me please.'

I followed and was taken to the governor's office, where I was confronted by three plain-clothes policemen, a senior screw and the governor.

'Last night,' he said, 'Craig was severely beaten and is in hospital with a fractured skull. This morning, as soon as the doors were unlocked, someone entered Murphy's cell, poured boiling water mixed with sugar over his face and ran him through fifteen times with the sharpened shaft of a badminton racquet. His lung and his kidney were punctured. Do you know anything about all this?'

I looked blankly at him, trying to digest his information and decide what to do next. Murphy was Wellingborough's biggest phone-card dealer, which made him a major player. If Ali and his gang had hit him, they'd go for anyone.

I knew that there were strict rules about not 'grassing' on other inmates, but would they apply in this situation? I had no idea. I needed time.

'Do you mind if I have a moment back on the wing to think about this?' I asked. They looked at their watches.

'All right. Tell the officer when you want to came back.'

I was led back to the wing. Passing Clive's cell door, I whispered from the outside, 'What do I do?'

'You fuckin' joking, mate?' he hissed through the door. 'No fuckin' question. You do the nasty little slimeball. You fuck him big-time.'

I asked John and he expressed exactly the same views, as did Liam and the others. So I made up my mind. It was what I felt, anyway. I went to see the screw to take me to the governor's office.

On the way I asked him, 'Do they really use the bog-brush and blades?'

'Yeah, seen the effects myself,' the screw replied. 'Rips the hell out of your rear end. Makes a mess of you for life. A shit's so painful that you'd almost rather starve.'

'And why did the water have sugar in it?'

'You're an army man, you should know. It's like napalm. Makes the boiling water stick to the skin so it continues to burn right in. By the time you've wiped it off your flesh just falls off.'

Back in the governor's office I was told that they had found my diary. The inmate in the cell next to Ali had handed it in.

'He's terrified of getting involved now that word has gone round the prison that Murphy has died,' said the governor.

'Has he?' I asked.

'No, but they don't know that. In fact, by some miracle the badminton shaft missed all his vital organs. Now, will you give a statement? This sort of scum is worthless. You would not be grassing and we would be very grateful if you helped us on this.'

I hesitated. 'Okay,' I said, and I recounted what had happened.

At the end of the interview I was taken back to my cell. The prison was unlocked now and inmates were milling about the passages. Everyone stared at me, doubtless trying to sort out all the rumours in their heads. We were locked up again at lunchtime but I had only been in the cell for an hour or so when a screw unlocked the door.

'Okay, mate, we've got a problem. Word has got out that you were talking to the police and we've been tipped off that the gang have been told to kill you. Ten minutes. Get your stuff together and we'll take you down the block while we get our act together to ship you out to another nick.'

He shut the door.

John looked sad. 'I'll miss you, mate. You're all right,

for a nob.' I looked at him and wondered what his future would be and I thought of his little boy, who was God knows where. I would be beside myself if William had been taken away in similar circumstances.

'John, you've been a good mate,' I said. 'You've kept me steady when I was at my lowest. I won't forget that.'

Later, I arranged to send him some cash to pay for help to locate his little boy. I knew the money meant much more to him than me. I had the hope of a decent living on my release, but he had a much slimmer chance of getting a straight job. He would need all the luck he could get.

I gathered up my belongings in the prison plastic bags. The keys rattled but I was surprised to find that a screw stood either side of me, with another in front.

'Christ, what's this?' I asked. 'A guard of honour?'

'No, Charlie, they're serious.'

I noticed that we were suddenly on first name terms.

The screw continued: 'The way they do it is they hang about in the passages with concealed knives. When the thrust comes, it's a quick in and out to the side of the body. There's virtually no blood and the geezer's gone before the bloke that's been stabbed even knows what's happened. Quick and efficient.'

The 'block' or 'Rule 43 wing' is where prisoners who are in danger from other inmates are kept in solitary confinement. It's also a dumping-ground for the most disturbed inmates – the real loonies and smackheads. As I walked into the block, I heard howling from one of the cells and several men kicking the hell out of their doors. The place sounded like a madhouse.

The screw in charge was very polite and sympathetic. 'Charlie, just to warn you, Ali and his mate have been put in the block to be shipped out, too. They'll probably try to intimidate you to stop you from testifying. Just ignore them, but if you have any trouble, ring the bell.'

It didn't take long. Ali started screaming, 'Charlie, we know you're down here. You didn't say nothing to the Bill, did you?'

I lied. 'No, mate, I said nothing.'

'Good man, Charlie. Don't you say nothing, okay?'

A while later a hand appeared at the cell window, clutching a piece of paper. It read: 'Charlie, this is from Ali. Pay the money [the £2,000] to the address on the paper, okay?'

I let the paper fall to the floor. A few minutes later Ali shouted, 'You got that, Charlie? Make sure you do it, man.'

As I bent down to pick it up, the cell door opened. 'All right, I'll have that. We were waiting for this.'

A screw scooped the piece of paper up in a gym shoe to preserve the prints. 'We've been watching him. Saw him give it to the bloke to put it through your window. It will have his prints on it and the address where you're supposed to send the money will tell the police a lot.'

He turned to leave but paused at the door. 'You may be interested to know that Craig is okay. He's a tough guy. Also, he's agreed to give a statement about the incident. Looks like Ali and his crew will go down.' He shut the door.

The next morning the jangling of the keys preceded the opening of the cell door and I was told, 'Okay, Charlie. Time to go.' I picked up my bags and was escorted to the sweatbox truck. I wasn't sorry to be going.

My next stop was Littlehey Prison. It was a category 'C' jail, like Wellingborough, in Prime Minister John Major's Huntingdon constituency. It had been built in the last ten years and was clean, but the atmosphere was oppressive.

The prison consisted of four wings, connected by caged-in walkways, with a central education block and gym complex. To one side, in the reasonably attractive grounds, was a modern factory complex with workshops where all inmates had to work for the first three months.

I was stripped, processed through reception and led to my new cell. I met some of my neighbours, many of whom seemed to be elderly and a few on Zimmer frames. In no time a group of inmates came to see me at the iron bars that isolated the wing.

'Charlie, wot the fuck are you doin' in there?' one asked.

'In where?'

'In there, you idiot! It's a fuckin' nonces' wing. Every one, except you, is a bleedin' nonce. Child molesters and perverts. Jesus, there ain't no way I could live wiv 'em. No way, man. You must fuckin' insist on a transfer. Any other wing, but not the weirdos' wing.'

I went to the senior officer on the wing. 'I gather I'm banged up with a bunch of nonces. Any chance of a move to another wing?' I asked.

'No way I'd want to live with them, either, but the order came from high up that you were to be put in with them,' he said.

'What the hell for?'

'Their official reason is that it's for your own safety. Those are the exact words.'

'But what's the difference between this wing and the other wings?' I asked.

'None. Except that this is a sex offenders' wing and you're the only one who isn't a nonce. I think you pissed somebody off. Big-time. This prison has a strict rule that no inmate can be considered for a move until he's been here for at least three months, so this is where you'll have to stay.'

I suppose my attitude towards sex offenders was the same as most people's: total revulsion. I had always thought that if anyone ever laid a finger on one of my children, I would cheerfully castrate them and then personally deliver the bits to the local police station. Now I was surrounded by nonces, and the first thing that struck me was that few of them looked normal. If it wasn't their mannerisms, then many had odd-shaped heads or their bodies were out of proportion in some way. Their arms were too short, their neck was almost non-existent or their forehead sloped back at a strange angle.

The chap opposite me was a Greek. He and his brother had received life sentences for killing a girl and then keeping her in a chest freezer to be taken out whenever they wanted to have intercourse with her corpse. Their mother had been a prostitute and I shudder to think how their impressionable minds came to regard the intimate act of sex. I don't expect that the expression 'making love' meant anything to them.

A man at the end of my passage tried to kill himself not long after my arrival. He was only thirty-three, and had a wife and three children, whose pictures were on his wall. He had been convicted of assaulting a young girl and had got a five-year sentence. He was finding the whole thing too much to bear.

Early one morning he used a razor blade and cut both his wrists. He sank to his knees next to his bed, in a position of prayer. By the time the door was opened at eight in the morning, he was still alive but his legs had been deprived of blood for so long that they were virtually useless. The walls were splattered in blood. He survived, but now he could only drag himself around with a Zimmer.

Many of the nonces had themselves been victims of abuse. They told me how their fathers had forcibly sodomised them from an early age and that their sisters had received the same treatment. Often, all this was done with the full knowledge, and even participation, of the mother and was the only parental 'affection' they ever received. As time went on, committing the same vile acts on other children became the only way that they could express their emotions.

I am not trying to justify their actions, and this does not apply to all sex offenders, but the need to have forcible sex, often involving children, had its roots in the treatment that the sex offenders had suffered when they were young. So how could incarceration possibly change their personalities?

The more I got to know the inmates on the sex offenders' wing, the more I realised that many were mentally subnormal. You meet a man of sixty who has sexually assaulted two boys and then killed them, and your first thought is, Monster. Then you realise that he can hardly be thought of as evil, because he lacks the mental capacity to control his own actions or understand what he is doing.

Jack was about the same age. He was in for molesting children. He could only talk like a ten-year-old and his mental age was that of a child. So it was probably natural for him to play with children. It was just that his adult body turned play into unnatural sex.

I talked to the senior officer on the wing about this over a cup of tea.

'Many of these men should not be here, Charlie,' he said. 'They should be in hospital receiving treatment. But with all the cutbacks, there is no place for them in a psychiatric hospital. To go there they have to be registered as completely off their heads. Basically, someone who is mentally disturbed is allowed to roam the streets unless he either commits a crime, in which case he comes to prison, or is certified mad.'

Not long after this conversation, Jack was told that he was to be released in two weeks. Each day he looked more miserable. His skin became pale and he stopped eating. It was easy to see why. He was a paedophile. His family had deserted him. He had no friends.

'Where will you live?' I asked.

'They told me to go to a hostel,' Jack said. 'I'll hate it there. I feel safe here. I know everyone and I don't have to worry about my clothes or my food.'

He sat on the end of his bed and cried.

The day he left his face was completely colourless. Two weeks later there was an announcement over the Tannoy. 'For those who were friends of Jack Taylor, we are sorry to say that he died today of heart failure.' I wasn't surprised. There was nowhere for him in this world. There was no system to cater for him. I never thought I'd ever say this of a child molester, but I felt sorry for him.

So this was my home, and these were my new companions. There was nothing to be done except grin and bear it. At least the lads on the other wings knew I wasn't a nonce and would talk to me like any other prisoner. Most were very polite and, indeed, curious about me. Many offered their services, among them a wonderful chap called Jack, who was an enforcer with a London gang.

'Anyfink you want done, Charlie-boy, just tell me and me and the boys will sort it out for ya.' He meant it, too, and over my time at Littlehey he was always in the background to ensure fair play if he could.

Meanwhile, I was getting frantic about seeing the children before Isa spirited them out of the country to Puerto Rico. My mother and my brother Richard had arranged to pick them up and bring them to me. I missed them so much and was longing to see them but I knew that it would be an emotional meeting. I doubted very much that I would manage to keep my composure.

The visiting-hall at Littlehey looked like an airport lounge, with easy chairs and coffee tables. There was a small shop where refreshments, chocolates and toiletries could be bought. The day came and my stomach was in turmoil. I was called and my mother and Richard walked in, holding hands with Antalya and Alex – but no William.

I cuddled the kids and then asked about William. While Richard and I went to the canteen to get the drinks, he said, 'You won't believe it, but he was put on the first flight this morning.' Isa's mother, Brigitte, who had doted on William since his birth, had removed him to Puerto Rico, despite knowing full well that this visit was his last chance to see his father for years.

I sat round the table with the other two children and talked about the holidays we'd all taken together. I didn't know when, or if, we would ever have another one. Alex and Antalya both cried a lot and we hugged for a long time. I told them that they must help their mother in every way possible.

Then Antalya pulled out a letter that she had written to me. Her writing was neat and clear and there were little pink hearts painstakingly drawn around the edge of the paper. The last paragraph read:

Daddy, I'm going to miss you. I pray for you every night. I love you, Daddy. Just remember you will always be in my heart forever.

She had painted a picture for me that was a sky filled with big puffy clouds, behind which a huge sun was beginning to rise with long rays that pierced the sky.

Alex had also drawn a picture and they gave me one from William that was an owl, made out of little chips of coloured stone. As I held them in my hand, I realised how precious these little offerings were going to be to me over the coming months and even years.

After two hours we had to finish the visit. I stood by the door and hugged them both. As always, Alex struggled to fight back the tears but they rolled down his cheeks like the first few drops of a gathering storm.

Antalya cried openly and her face was blotchy with emotion. She clung to me and I felt her little body so full of pain against mine. No longer would I be there to laugh with them, to play with them, or to help them through their troubles.

We said goodbye for the umpteenth time and then their small figures faded into the darkness of the passageway. I wondered how long it would be before I would see them again. I had no idea that it was to be over four years.

Two weeks went by, then there was a commotion on the wing. 'Charlie, you've got a problem,' said one of my mates. 'There's a geezer just moved on to E wing says he's going to slash you up. Says 'e 'as a message from Ali in Wellingborough.'

It was Sellik, one of Ali's gang. I'd given evidence against him to the governor at Wellingborough. The very next day I was walking to the gym when a shout echoed down the long passage. 'Brocket, you're dead. We're going to slash you up if you testify. Message

from Ali.' The following morning the same thing happened.

I wasn't going to buckle under the threats, but on the
other hand I didn't particularly want my face to look
like a road map of England. I had an off-the-record
word with a screw who had been a sergeant in the
army. His advice was clear.

'Charlie, you won't get any help from the governor,
even though he's aware of the problem. So carry some
protection, and watch your back at all times. It could
happen in a crowd, so avoid groups of people. The
alternative is to stay on the wing.'

'There's no way I'm going to stay cooped up on the
wing,' I said. 'I'll keep my eyes peeled and I'll take some
precautions.'

A while later a couple of the inmates from another
wing came up to me. 'Charlie, we've asked around.
The threats are coming from Sellik and a headbanger
that he's teamed up with. The other bloke has never
met you before. He's just a smackhead who'd do anything.'

So I was up against two of them. I was thankful that
it wasn't more. Weeks of weight training in the gym
had made me fit and strong again and I could cope
with two, I hoped. This meant that the threat of being
'slashed up' was minimal, because to do this effectively
required several people to hold you down. What was
more likely was that they would try and 'stick' me
when I was least expecting it.

I went through my daily routine and I calculated
that I was at most risk in the gym showers and rounding

any of the numerous corners along the long passages. It was there that I might expect the quick thrust of a stiletto.

I thought about this. The moment a knife has been pushed in, the assailant is at his most vulnerable. His arm is out and his face and chest exposed. It is not natural to let go of the knife, especially in this case as it would have prints on it. I just needed something that the knife could go into without hurting me.

The answer was a prison laundry bag. These were small white bags the size of an eighteen-inch cube. I went down to the stores and talked the orderly into giving me some extra towels, which I stuffed into the bag.

If I carried the bag at all times at waist height and reacted quickly enough, I reckoned I would be able to absorb the knife blow into the bag and then try to deal with my attackers. For the next few months I was never without my bag.

But vengeful gang-members weren't my only problem. A Sunday paper had printed a massive 'exposé', claiming to prove that I had been dealing drugs, via Khun Sa. The story, a work of total fiction, centred around the trip Isa and I had made to Thailand, to help Rick Furtado.

For a rumoured fee of £25,000, Furtado had returned the favour by supplying the paper with a bogus yarn about my drug-running activities, lots of pictures of me in the Far East and a detailed list of precise payments into Far Eastern banks. None of which, I need hardly add, I had ever made.

Ironically, the reports that I was a major drug-pusher earned me hero status among the genuine dealers, who all came up and gave me extravagant high-fives, accompanied by cries of, 'Respect, man!' The prison authorities, however, responded rather differently.

I had been trying to see the governor to find out why it was that I had not been transferred to an open prison. I had been in a high-security prison for five months, having been told that I would probably be there for only a few weeks. Other inmates who had been convicted of similar offences at the same time had already been moved on. But no answer came. It took an appeal to the prison service area manager's office simply to get an answer from the governor, whose office was a few yards from my wing.

At last I was sent a written response, which stated: 'Brocket has very strong connections with Burma, and a well-known drugs warlord, Khun Sa.'

That newspaper article was keeping me on a sex offenders' wing. I went to see the deputy governor, who started blithering about what the papers had said about me. I couldn't restrain myself.

'Are you seriously trying to tell me that you base your decisions regarding the future of inmates on whatever the media say? Are you aware that the article was fabricated? I have never done any business with Khun Sa, nor did I ever put a penny in any bank account in the Far East. This is absurd.'

Finally the deputy governor said, 'We know that the media fabricate. The trouble is that the Home Office take note of the media. Perhaps your solicitor should write to the area manager, informing him that you had nothing to do with this drug warlord.'

Steven Barker did just that. But I was still in the Littlehey sex offenders' unit two months later when the prison authorities changed their tack and stated that the reason for my detention in closed conditions was because now there was a second charge against me that needed 'clearing up'.

Meanwhile, I was still hoping for an appeal against my sentence. Even the prison screws agreed that the gross sentence of seven and a half years was absurd. One chap had got five years for stealing £10 million of pensioners' funds and keeping it. Other inmates had got five years for attempted murder.

Yet, no matter what I did, the appeals office kept trying to prevent me getting a hearing. Steven sent an official application by registered letter, fax and telephone. But the appeals office wrote to me stating that they hadn't heard from me and I was now barred from appealing as I had run out of time.

'It can only be a deliberate conspiracy by the appeals office to prevent your appeal being heard,' said Steven. 'And I'm bloody cross.'

'Why don't they want the appeal heard?' I asked.

'Well, a strong reason would be that they would not want public examination of the rationale behind the ridiculously high sentence. There is no way that any appeal body could justify it. But the main reason would definitely be that the judiciary is a club. They move heaven and earth to avoid any criticism of fellow judges and any reduction of your sentence would receive considerable publicity. Add to that the fact that the judge is about to be promoted and I would say, Charles, that you have an uphill struggle. They really don't want this examined.'

It was Barbara Cartland who came to the rescue. She had been so supportive throughout all my troubles. I had written to her regularly to tell her my news, and one of my letters told her of the appeal situation.

Dear Barbara, who must have had some of Boadicea's blood running through her veins, wrote a personal letter to the Lord Chancellor. She flatly stated that there was a conspiracy to prevent my appealing and that unless he gave immediate leave to appeal, there would be all kinds of hell to pay.

The effect was instant. The Lord Chancellor sent a handwritten letter to Barbara, saying that clearly there had been some confusion and that in the special circumstances he was giving leave to appeal. Who'd have guessed that the Queen of Romance wielded so much power?

25

Fighting the System, Meeting a Kray

STEVEN BARKER WAS FIGHTING ANOTHER WAR, ON a second front. For there was another charge against me: the accusation that I had somehow defrauded the American, Peter Shirley, by selling him a fake Ferrari.

By now, it had been proved that the chassis plate I had bought from Jim Bosisto really was a fake after all. In late 1995 the real No. 3565 had been discovered gathering dust in a garage in rural France. It was this discovery that had sent Shirley running to the police, who then claimed that I had fraudulently conspired to sell a fake car as an original.

But I had sold the Ferrari as a replica. And I hadn't sold it to Shirley. What's more, I could (and still can) prove both those statements because Steven Barker had all the necessary invoices and bank statements. But no one wanted to see them.

'What I find hard to understand,' he said, 'is that I have written to the police and to the CPS, but they're not interested in any further evidence. They merely say that this can be produced at the trial.'

'That's absurd!' I protested. 'The current estimate for a trial date is May to June 1997. Next year! They're prepared to keep this matter hanging over me until then, and waste huge sums of money on legal costs for both sides, when the whole thing could be settled immediately if they just looked at your documentary evidence.'

For some reason, the establishment were determined to use any means they could to keep me in a prison where there was a known threat to my safety.

At least I now had a means of speaking to the children. Antalya's godmother Libby, one of my dearest friends, had given me a pin-number that would connect me to the American phone credit-card system. Now I could call Puerto Rico without decimating the prison phone cards. For the first time in five months I would be able to speak to the children.

I dialled the number and my father-in-law, Gus answered. After a chat, he put Alex on the phone. He bitterly missed his home and his friends but was trying to put a brave face on it. I tried to encourage him and told him that my time in prison would pass quickly. I so wished I could be there for him.

I then talked to William. He was now just five and my greatest fear was that he would forget his father. But he was as cheerful as ever and reeled off a list of his new adventures.

My conversation with Antalya was heartbreaking. 'Daddy, I love you. I pray for you. I miss you so much,' she sobbed. I gripped the receiver fiercely, trying to control my emotions. I had an awful feeling that, for some reason, she had been led to believe that our separation was permanent.

Antalya has always been a great romantic so I said to her, 'Darling, when you are far away on the other side of the world, I want you to look at the sun and remember that only a few hours before I was looking at the same sun. And at night always remember that Daddy was looking up at the same stars. That is how close we are. If you ever feel lonely, just look up in the sky and think of me and I will do the same and think of you.'

'What about the moon?'

'The moon, too. It's especially friendly. That's why it's always smiling.'

By the time I rang off I felt quite drained. I returned to my cell, sat on my bed and cried. I seemed to have lost everything. No matter how low I had sunk, however, I was still far more fortunate than many of my fellow inmates. At least I had had an education and this soon provided me with a way of making a living inside, and helping other prisoners as I did it.

Prisons, like Second World War prisoner-of-war camps, are full of people who use their trades to beat the system. Most inmates ran a scam of one kind or another. Those in the stores sold extra clothes for phone cards or 'burn' (tobacco). In winter they would get you the extra bedding that was needed to keep you warm. Kitchen orderlies ran regular supplies of fruit and other food to the cells, and laundry workers would run a personal service for items that were not allowed in the prison laundry.

There was a Chinese lad who was a brilliant artist. He could copy a photo expertly or draw an inmate's portrait. He had permanent commissions. Others made greetings cards for prisoners to send to their families, while some made toys and models. One particularly enterprising inmate relieved the stores on a regular basis of vast amounts of paint and then ran a cell-decorating service for two phone cards a cell. He was always busy.

I had years of experience in business, dealing with financial institutions, and these soon formed the basis of my prison trade. Prisoners often lack even basic education. Most had no idea of their rights. When a building society or bank wrote them an arrogant letter informing them that their home was not going to be theirs for much longer, most accepted it even if they issued a stream of profanities in doing so.

One day an inmate told me about the repossession proceedings on his home. 'My family's terrified. I'm only in for six months. We're only three months in arrears. They know that I can't earn until I get out and yet they say they're taking the house back. Can they do that?'

'The real problem,' I said, 'is that the mortgage officer dealing with your file is hoping to grab your home and sell it at a knockdown price to a friendly dealer. The dealer will get a cheap house, the mortgage officer gets a backhander, and the building society will get some funds back. You're just the jam in the sandwich.'

I wrote a letter on this man's behalf to the local court, asking them for an adjournment until he was free and could put his case to the court. Two weeks later he got his adjournment until after his release. He was over the moon.

All this time, the date was approaching for the crown's case against the gang at Wellingborough. I was getting almost hourly threats shouted at me: 'We'll get you. You're a dead man. You'll never make the court alive.'

The screws posted a full-time guard on the entrance to the sex offenders' wing, where I was still housed, to ensure no strangers entered. Finally, I was ferried to Wellingborough court, only to be told that the case would have to be adjourned: Ali had failed to turn up.

The prosecutor asked to see me. 'We understand that you have had some problems at Littlehey,' he said. 'I can assure you that the crown appreciates any inmate putting himself at risk to do what he knows is right.'

Yes, I thought, but not enough to reduce my sentence on appeal.

Back at Littlehey, I received a call from my friend Libby. She said that Melissa had telephoned her from France in floods of tears, saying that she loved and missed me so much. A week later I discovered that Melissa had married her ex-boyfriend. I received a letter from her new husband's solicitors, making it clear that if I, or any of my friends, were to contact Melissa, I would be reported to the police and to the governor. Charming.

I was determined to find out what was behind

Melissa's change of heart. Something didn't ring true. I had good contacts with the right people in the security and intelligence world. I placed a call from the prison phone.

My contact was the best in the business. Not long after our phone conversation, I received the first report. It arrived on plain sheets of paper so that the casual reader would not know its source or indeed its destination. The contents shattered me.

Copies of flight details showed Melissa's frequent flights abroad with the names of the passengers either side. Her travelling partner had been the same on most occasions. Six months of telephone bills, made on ex-directory lines, copies of all credit-card bills, bank statements and foreign bank accounts revealed even more. Christ! How had I been so gullible?

Worse still was the explanation for the car crash just two days before my sentencing. Melissa had said that she had skidded into a village pond while returning from the airport, having just got in from New York. The report confirmed that she had stayed at Cliveden Hotel all weekend and that she had crashed the car into the fountain outside. I felt sick.

For the entire time that we had been living together, she had been beetling off to see her 'ex', the man to whom she was now married.

He was a very powerful man, an oil industry Mr Fixit (today he is a close friend of the multi-billionaire Chelsea Football Club owner, Roman Abramovich). He was making $1 million a month as his royalty on just one of his deals. It wasn't hard to see why a girl like

Melissa, who appreciated the finer things in life, would want to be with a man who could provide them, rather than waiting for a disgraced convict like me.

Every day seemed to bring new media accusations to add to my long list of imaginary crimes. One day, one of the lads yelled, ''Ere, Charlie. Listen to this on Radio Five. It's a woman ringing in about you.' We gathered in his cell to hear:

'He's a terrible man,' she said. 'He actually shot a dog. Killed it, he did. I was there. What sort of a man would kill a dog because it wouldn't answer his call?'

The woman said she knew me well. She didn't know me from Adam. At the time of the interview, my two dogs, both still full of health, were sunning themselves in the Caribbean with Isa and the children.

I wanted to set the record straight, to make sense of my life and see where it had gone wrong. Soon I got the chance to do just that. I was given a job cleaning the education wing. This involved mopping the passages every morning, vacuuming classrooms, mopping out the kitchen used for cookery classes and then cleaning out the toilets. I used to leave the loos feeling strangely light-headed: it took me quite a while to realise that they were the nick's in-house drug-dealers' main drop-off point for 'brown' (as they called heroin) and crack. I was getting high just breathing the air in there.

I was also, unwittingly, helping the dealers make their products. I had been asked to get bicarbonate of soda from the kitchens. People would say, 'Can you get us some bicarb? I've got a gut-ache.' What I didn't know was that bicarbonate of soda is one of the main ingredients in manufacturing crack. As soon as I was told what was really happening, my supplies stopped, pronto.

If I was quick, my job took me only an hour and then I was allowed the free run of the classrooms and given the vital opportunity to use the computers.

Prison rules, however, ensured that all computers were strictly monitored. We had to save our work on to floppy disk and then hand in the disk at the end of every day. But I didn't want anyone to see what I was writing. I knew there were plenty of inmates who'd love to sell my innermost thoughts to the tabloids.

So I razored a straight line along the back of an ordinary manila folder. I would walk towards the computer with the folder in my left hand and the authorised disk in my right hand. By pressing the folder, the cut would open and I could switch the disks. At the end of every session I would return the correct disk, which was full of harmless copied information.

I didn't want the disk being found in my cell, either. There was no chance of the 'Gestapo', as the specialist search squad were called, missing it if the cell was 'spinned'. But if I kept it outside it would have to be retrievable and not spotted by external patrols.

Outside my window was a flowerbed. I made a little disk-sized waterproof wallet from a black plastic bin-liner that would not be noticed on the dark peat. Then I got a length of brown cotton from the stores, matching the colour of the brickwork. With one end of the cotton attached to the window and the other to the wallet, I cut the length so that when the wallet was on the ground the cotton would be tight. At the end of every day I sealed the disk in the wallet and perched it on the windowsill.

My precautions paid off. The Gestapo arrived one day for a search. Hearing the keys in the door, I knocked the wallet out of the window. After the Gestapo had gone I reeled the wallet back in. When I'd filled a disk, I smuggled it out via friends who came to visit me.

Several years later, those smuggled disks became the book you are reading today.

Through the summer of 1996 I spent every weekend outside. We were allowed to sit in a small garden area, where I could settle down for hours with a book. On the far side of the fence, I could hear the combine harvesters at work on a nearby farm. The fresh smell of hay and the drone of the bees in the lavender made me long for the freedom that had been taken away.

I wondered what the children were doing. At three in the afternoon, it was 10am in the Caribbean. The kids would have had their breakfast and would be in the pool in Puerto Rico.

It was soon time to appear in court again to face Ali and his lot. But once again, he seemed to be able to find an excuse for not turning up. I received the same hypocritical thanks from the prosecution. And now I began to see that Ali's ruthless desire to beat the system was paying serious dividends.

Back in the sweatbox, my old Wellingborough pal Craig was loaded into the cubicle opposite me. 'That's it, Charlie,' he said. 'I'm out. I'm sorry, mate, but you're on your own.'

'Why? These buggers deserve what they have coming to them. Murph was almost killed, they smashed your skull in and they're still running around doing the same thing,' I said.

Craig shook his head. 'These guys are headbangers. Last week they paid my missus a visit. They frightened the life out of her and said that if I didn't drop out as a witness they'd kill her. That's enough. I can't risk it. Sorry, mate.'

What could I say? I would have done the same thing if they had visited any of my family.

A few days later a new shout came down the passage at Littlehey: 'On your own now! You're the only one left! You'll be dead before you hit the court!'

Then I got a letter from John, my pad-mate at Wellingborough, who had been released. He described how members of Ali's gang had broken into his home, ripped out the phone line and tied up his mother as a hostage. They then took him down to their bank and ordered him to empty his bank account or his mother would be killed.

Terrified, John did what he was told. They then beat him up, making a real mess of him and putting him in hospital. He implored me not to give evidence, saying that the gang were capable of anything at all. I gave the letter to my solicitor but was even more determined to give the evidence that would send Ali and his cronies down for good.

The fluorescent lights that are omnipresent in prison

were giving me skull-splitting headaches. I needed some paracetamol, so I went to the sick queue, where prisoners lined up for sleeping pills and pain-killers, most of which were being taken just to relieve the boredom of prison or to feed their own addictions.

Next to me was a pensioner called Jock who was an ex-merchant seaman, a big-hearted, fearless man. After ten minutes in the queue one of the idiots who kept making the threats against me came up to us and shouted, 'Ha! That's the fuckin' grass! That shithead grassed on Ali and his mates! He's a fuckin' grass and what are you all going to do about it?'

Whack! Jock's walking-stick came down on his head.

'D'ya think we're all stupid?' Jock exploded. 'We know what happened and that's not grassing, ye miserable wee wop! Yer faggot deserves everything that he gets, and more. Now sod off!'

The bloke looked dumbfounded and turned to the rest of the queue, expecting general support, but he was met with blank stares, mostly because they were stoned. A look of total confusion came over him and then he ran, not wanting to face Jock's wrath again or suffer the blows from his walking-stick. Jock was highly amused and muttered something about the good old days.

I wish I could have used Jock's simple, straightforward approach to sort out all my problems. Libby wrote to say that she had received some more phone calls from Melissa, whose mood was swinging wildly between cheeriness and gloom. The poor woman was in a terrible state.

To add to her troubles, the police had decided to use her as a weapon against me. They wanted me to plead guilty to the second fraud charge, that I had mis-described the short-wheel-base Ferrari. I had always stated that I was on no account going to plead guilty to something that I had not done. So the police decided to try and make me change my mind.

Their first method was harassment. This, as I learned from fellow inmates, is standard practice. The police mount dawn raids on your family, your friends, your neighbours, looking for 'evidence'. Once they've hit enough people, telling them exactly why their property and privacy are being violated, you might as well be guilty. No one will ever believe you are innocent, or talk to you again.

My family were still well-enough connected that the police didn't dare attack them directly. Melissa, how-ever, was a different proposition. She was fair game.

Using the excuse of my 'drug-dealing', as revealed in the Sunday papers, the police raided her bank account in Jersey, went through all her phone records and searched her house. Of course, they found nothing because there wasn't anything to find. What they did do, though, was frighten the living daylights out of Melissa.

She must have thought that I was up to all sorts of no good. Why else would the police go to such trouble? Before I was imprisoned I had given her £3,000 to cover the cost of various meals that had been charged to her card. She was so terrified that this might have been drugs money that she returned it to my mother. Another great job by the lads in blue!

Far from making me want to change my plea, the crudeness of the police tactics just made me more determined to defy them. As part of the trial process, I was loaded into the sweatbox again and ferried off to Hatfield magistrates' court.

I was sitting behind the bars of the holding cell when I suddenly heard a familiar voice say, 'Fuck me! LB! Wot the 'ell are you doing 'ere?' It was Phil, a kitchen porter who had spent years working for me at the Hall, complete with his spectacular, multicoloured Mohican haircut. I'd hired him despite his criminal record and he'd never once given me reason to doubt my decision. But I thought he'd gone straight.

'More to the point, Phil, what are you doing?' I asked. 'I thought you'd kicked the habit?'

'Got into trouble with the wife,' Phil replied. 'Had an argument and got into debt. We're separated now. Shame, especially 'cos of the kids. I've only got five months to do.' We chatted a bit longer before I was called. Two weeks later, I received a letter from Phil:

Dear LB, It was great to see you again and I am sorry for everything that has happened . . . Those times at Brocket working with you were the best times of my life. You looked after us so well and you took me on when you knew that I had been inside. Looking back I can see what a mess I've made of things and that them days were so special. Good luck and don't worry about your kids. They will always love you.

Back at Littlehey I was told that the police wanted to see me. I went to the interview-room and was met by two officers investigating the accusation that I had mis-described the car.

'We hear that you are having a bit of a hard time,' one said.

'I suppose so, but I'm not complaining,' I said. 'I'd just like to stay in one piece and move to another prison.'

'You do realise,' the senior officer said, 'that you are only being held in a closed prison because there is a second charge outstanding? Why don't you plead guilty to this second charge?'

'Why should I? My solicitor has the bank accounts showing what really happened and I'm buggered if I'll plead on this, only to clear up your paperwork.'

'But we don't have that evidence, and we won't see it until the trial date.'

'But if you saw the bank documents, there wouldn't be a trial,' I replied, exasperated.

'Well, the courts are very busy at the moment and I understand that they won't be able to hear the matter at least until the middle of next year. You know how these things get delayed.'

So that was their game. 'What you are saying,' I protested, 'is that you won't examine the evidence until the trial, and that the trial won't be for another year, and I won't leave this sex offenders' unit until the trial. So I'll have to try to stay alive with these mad knifemen running around the passages for another twelve months!'

A week later my solicitor received a letter from the judge confirming that if I were to plead guilty, whatever sentence I was given would not be added to the one that I already had.

'There is no way that I'm going to plead guilty to something of which I'm innocent,' I told him, 'and they can sod off!'

Then I was called to the wing office.

'Charlie, you're moving tomorrow,' the screw said.

'Christ,' I said, 'I'd given that up as a lost cause. Why are they letting me move now?'

'Dunno, mate. All I can tell you is that you're off to Maidstone tomorrow. You have to go there first before being processed for another nick. Okay?'

But I didn't go to Maidstone that day. Instead, the sweatbox stopped off at three other prisons and then drew up in front of probably the most infamous set of prison gates in the country, Wandsworth, where I met my fourth jail receptionist. He was an ugly sod, with a neck the same width as his head, and he wore a large gold ring in his right ear. It struck me that it would be more at home in his nose.

'We don't give a fuck who the 'ell anyone is in this place!' he yelled. 'Titles mean fuck all 'ere! Think you're a fuckin' lord, do you? Well, we'll soon see about that!'

The screw grabbed my stuff, poured it out on the counter and swept it all into another identical bag saying, 'Can't have that . . . Can't have that . . . Can't have that . . .' until the counter was bare.

He screwed his face up, like a bulldog with severe

constipation, and growled, 'Strip off, and I mean strip off.'

I took everything off and stood there naked. He looked at me in disgust and laughed. Then one of the blokes chuckled. 'Can't hack it that Charlie's bigger than him,' and everyone started laughing. Bulldog got furious.

'Fuck off into the showers, then collect your prison gear,' he barked.

I showered and then, still dripping wet, went to a hatch to be handed prison clothes. Bulldog had got there first. With a huge grin on his face, he handed me a pair of size four socks full of holes, a tracksuit bottom that would not fit my younger son and a T-shirt that had been slashed. I pretended not to notice and walked away. I had learned long ago that a prisoner has no rights. In a prison like this, the screws could bury you if they wanted to.

As I sat down to dry myself, an inmate sat next to me and handed me another pile of clothes. ''Ere, mate, have these. Don't mind 'im, 'e's a fuckin' nuisance. We 'eard about you, good luck.' With that he was gone.

I walked over to the holding cell for new inmates who'd already been through the clearing process. It was a room about twelve feet square and contained some twenty-five inmates, most of whom were smoking. There was almost no ventilation and the temperature was stifling. It was now three in the afternoon and none of us had had anything to eat since six that morning.

A screw came in. 'Grub on the table,' he announced.

There were mashed spuds and spaghetti hoops but we all mechanically shovelled spoonfuls on to the plastic plates, if only because we didn't know when our next meal would be.

We were led through a maze of passages and then emerged into the central circular hub at ground level. The centre of the hub is a large metal grate, fifteen feet in diameter, and some made the mistake of walking on it.

'You fuckin' piece of shit!' screamed the same belligerent screw. 'You walk on that again and you get nicked and put in the block!'

I was shown to a cell on the top floor and the door was banged shut. It looked just like the cell at Bedford, only a bit bigger. The chap on the lower bunk jumped up and said in a public school accent, 'Hi, I'm James. Welcome aboard.'

He'd been in Wandsworth for four weeks but the regime was taking its toll on him. He had only been given one shower a week and, worse still, had only been allowed out of his cell for two hours a week. The minimum legal requirement was an hour a day, but this was not enforced in a determination to cut staff costs.

Ten minutes after the lights were out, James suddenly leaped out of his bunk. As he walked across the floor I heard a strange crunching sound. He switched the light back on. The floor was a carpet of cockroaches, a seething mass in search of anything that prisoners had overlooked.

I leaned over the edge on my top bunk to see that the clever buggers had scaled the metal legs of James's bunk and swarmed over his bedcover. 'You should grease the legs,' I said.

'Jesus,' James yelped, 'they were all over my face!' He spent the next hour slamming them with his slipper and flushing them down the loo. We slept the rest of the night with the light on to keep the marauding hordes at bay.

Before I had a chance to get any breakfast in the morning, I was told, 'Get your shit together and report to the office.' As I passed the cast-iron spiral staircase, an inmate was having the hell beaten out of him by some sadistic screws.

I gathered with a few other inmates and we were led back down to the bowels of the prison, where we were again strip-searched. I seemed to spend an inordinate amount of time standing in prison receptions with nothing on. We had our prison clothing taken off us, were told to dress in our own clothes and then were loaded into the sweatbox for Maidstone.

There we went through the normal reception procedure of checking belongings and being searched, but the atmosphere was completely different from that at Littlehey and certainly Wandsworth. The screws were all friendly and even brought us a meal while we were waiting in reception.

I was led into the Kent wing, which had a lower category of security than the other wings. The layout was the traditional four storeys of cells with a walkway round the walls and a large well in the centre. On each floor there were groups of inmates huddled round tables, laughing and joking while they were preparing vegetables or trimming joints of meat. It had the atmosphere of an oriental bazaar.

Unlike Littlehey, where you were not allowed any of your own food and the maximum spend permitted was £15 a week, here you could buy and cook your own food, and spend as much as you liked.

After a night in a cell that was like the one at Bedford, only twice as large, breakfast came as quite a culture shock. I could either select a ready-cooked breakfast or carry my choice of uncooked food to one of the many gas rings, cook it the way I liked it, toast my own bread and then sit in front of the TV!

It was at least eighty degrees outside and there was not a cloud in the sky. We were let out into the central area of the prison to exercise, use the gym and play football. I found a bit of grass next to the swimming pool, which was a converted fire-tank.

Maidstone is the main prison for London gangsters. There were lots of chaps with bull necks, flat noses and strong Cockney accents. While I sat reading, a steady stream of hoods came up to me. Then one said, 'Reggie Kray is sorta busy at the moment but would like to see ya later. All right?'

A while later, I was returning along the high walkway to my cell with hot water for a cup of tea, when I looked over the railings to see two large middle-aged men with Reggie Kray just behind them. Inmates, mostly younger and in awe of his reputation, scattered like dinghies before a large oil tanker. I watched the trio climb the steps to my level and come towards me.

'Reggie, my pad's down the end on the left. Come with me,' I said.

He put his hand out to shake mine. 'Good ta meet you, Charlie. Glad to have a bit of class in the place! Eh, lads?' The other two laughed and then introduced themselves.

I made tea for us all and, perching on what little furniture there was, Reggie asked, 'Now, Charlie, wot the fuck really happened wiv you? Getting fuckin' seven an' 'arf years for an insurance claim what you didn't even 'ave the balls to go through wiv is fuckin' daft! So what gives, Charlie? You shaft the judge's missus or summink?'

'No, Reggie, not quite. And if you saw the judge's missus, you—'

'Well, you pissed somebody off big-time to get that much time,' he said.

'Well, Reggie, what about you?' I asked.

'Governor here is a blinder, real good bloke, but 'e knows they ain't never gonna let me out. Them fuckers up top think I represent the unacceptable face of crime, big-time gangsters 'an that. Bad example to them plastic gangsters you met at Wellingborough, them fuckers that shoved blades in your face. Nah, they'll never let me out. They want their pound of flesh. I'm here till I die. I'm not in great nick meself, anyway. Got cancer, so they might just let me out the week before I die, to spend a few nights with me woman. Nah, my life's gone . . .'

The bell rang for inmates to return to their own wings and the gates to be locked. The delegation got up and we shook hands.

'If you want any help on the outside, Charlie, just tell me blokes. All right? Look after yourself, Charlie. Remember, those that fuck you always get fucked in the end. Always, Charlie!'

And so Reggie Kray, one of Britain's most legendary gangsters, said goodbye to me with almost the same words as an Irish padre had used to comfort me at Wellingborough. That was the last I saw of him. Two years later his cancer became terminal and he was, as he predicted, released in a blaze of publicity to stay in a hotel with his wife. He died shortly after, and the East End of London turned out for his funeral to say farewell to the last of the traditional gangland bosses.

The main gate had been locked for only a few minutes before the Tannoy announced, 'Brocket to the wing office.' I came down from the top landing and was met by the deputy governor. He was extremely polite.

'I'm afraid that I've some bad news. You have to return to Littlehey.'

'But why?' I asked.

'We've just discovered that you've an outstanding appearance at court. It costs the prison in which you are resident £400 in escort and transport costs every time you're produced in court. Because of the pressure on costs, we have a rule that we don't accept anyone who has an outstanding appearance. I really am very sorry.'

'But surely you must have known this when you accepted me?'

'No. Littlehey missed it out on the transfer form and we've only now been informed of it.'

'This makes no sense,' I complained. 'I have moved

here specially to stay in one bit so that I can testify for the crown at that hearing. If I return to Littlehey I'll be going back to the smackheads who want to finish me off. That makes no sense at all. If I'm dead, I won't be much use as a witness, will I?'

'I'm very sorry, but those are our rules and those are my instructions.'

Within the hour I was packed up again and dumped in a taxi with a screw either side of me to return to Littlehey, at goodness knows what expense. So much for saving £400.

26

Left for Dead

BACK AT LITTLEHEY I WENT THROUGH THE reception procedure yet again: the sixth time in almost as many months. My possessions were checked as if the screws had never seen them before and I was stripped naked. I was returned to a cell next door to my old one, which at least meant that I could see the sunset and had the flowerbed outside my window for the computer disk scam.

My return must have delighted the two thugs who were hell-bent on preventing me from testifying. The next morning they were ready for me. 'Thought you'd escaped us, did ya? We'll get you, you fucker. We'll cut your throat, then we'll see how much you talk!'

The screws on the wing were getting distinctly edgy. Again they mounted a guard at the entrance to the wing during association hours, but the real threat lay in the passages. All I could do was carry my stuffed laundry bag wherever I went and hope it would absorb a blade.

Then one morning, as I left the upper passage and descended the stairs by the gym, Sellik and his pal finally got me.

I went to open a door. I'd just put my hand out to the handle, when the door exploded inwards. I had no time to react. The edge of the door hit me squarely above my right eye. Dazed, barely conscious, I felt blood gushing down my face and somehow, almost subconsciously, sensed rather than saw the flash of a knife-blade coming towards me.

It was only some basic, animal survival instinct that made me put up my hand to protect my face. I felt the swish as the blade cut my fingers to the bone in a neat, oddly painless line. On reflection, I suppose it was the fact that I was falling backwards from the opened door that must have saved worse damage but I felt the knife go into my left side and then I blacked out as the back of my head hit the wall behind me.

I awoke to find myself sitting in a pool of blood, with long, scarlet smears on the wall behind me. I was getting to my feet when one of the senior officers came through the door. 'What are you doing?' he asked.

I wanted to laugh. What did he think I was doing? Meditating? Knitting? Redecorating the place?

He took me to the hospital, where I was photographed and patched up. Then the screw who'd found me told me what had happened. He'd used the lavatory next to the gym. As he came out, he locked the door. The jangle of his keys alerted the men who'd attacked me and they ran away before they could finish the job of killing me.

'You're lucky,' he said. 'If I hadn't needed a piss, you probably wouldn't be with us now.'

I didn't feel particularly lucky.

I spent the night in the hospital for observation because of the concussion. The officer in charge of security came to see me. He was genuinely concerned. 'There's no question that you'll be moved,' he said. 'They know who did this. They'll be moved too. Standard procedure, that is. You shouldn't be in a bloody closed prison, anyway. Bloody madness. You'll go in the morning. Okay otherwise?'

'Yes, thanks. Nothing that won't mend.'

I returned to my cell the next day, patched up and with my right arm in a sling, as my shoulder had been dislocated when I'd slammed against the wall, but the threats continued. The wing screws were now getting very restless. They were used to the occasional body being carried out of the place but they didn't want mine to be one of them. The deputy governor came to discuss the matter with the screws and me. He assured me that I would be moved in a matter of days.

A few days later, however, I was told formally that I would not be moved. The official reason was that the second charge against me had still not been resolved. 'For Christ's sake,' I protested, 'the police say that the second charge won't be heard for another year. They won't look at the evidence until then. This is quite wrong!'

I talked to my mother.

'Just get out of there, Charles,' she begged me. 'Plead to whatever you have to plead – anything to get away from those madmen and to get to an open prison. Don't worry if they've got you over a barrel. That is life and life is unfair. Just bite the bullet.'

Richard gave the same advice. 'Your sentence won't be affected and if the real perpetrators get away with it, so what? It doesn't affect you personally. Draw a line and get out, please.'

I thought about it all that night. It seemed so wrong to plead guilty when I was innocent. But what was the point of getting myself killed? It was perfectly obvious that the police and prison service were happy to see me die. They'd gone against every established procedure and kept me in a jail where I was not just facing the threat of death, but had already suffered an attack on my life. The best revenge I could have on the system was to survive. By the morning I had made up my mind to plead guilty.

Two days after the ambush I was standing in front of the same judge who had sentenced me at the beginning of the year, but this time with my arm in a sling, my hand bandaged, one eye with a big plaster on it and the other a real shiner. 'How do you plead?'

'Guilty, my lord.' It sounded ridiculous, like some password that I was supposed to recite to get to the next base.

The judge looked suitably solemn. 'I can see that you have been experiencing a difficult time and the court is not without mercy.' I realised that I must have looked quite a sight. 'I have decided to impose a two-year concurrent sentence.'

Bang! The hammer came down and that was that. Two years for something that I had nothing to do with.

We descended back into the bowels of the court to a meeting-room where I met my solicitor and my counsel. They were angry that the prison had done nothing to avoid the attack, but it was made crystal clear to me by the screws that it would not be in my interest to take legal action. As we talked, the clerk of the court popped his head round the door.

'Sir, there is a gentleman to see you,' he told us. 'He's been here since nine this morning.'

We looked at our watches. It was two-thirty.

The man was shown in. He was none other than the detective running the case related to the second charge. He apologised for the intrusion and said, 'We would very much appreciate it if you would give us the evidence that you have on the person who you say sold the car to the American. We understand that you have his bank accounts and transfer documents.'

There was a stunned silence. Until a few weeks ago they were refusing to look at the evidence until the trial. Now, just after I had pleaded, they wanted the real culprit, courtesy of me. In other words, they'd known all along that I was innocent.

They were confident that I would shop Furtado. Well, I had reason to do so. He'd got me into this mess. He'd sold lies about me to the press. Both before and during my imprisonment, he'd been working with Rocker to force me out of Brocket, and they'd clearly been planning some sort of scam with all the stock they'd been trying to shift from the car showroom. So yes, there would be a certain satisfaction in seeing him suffer.

But not if it meant doing the police a favour.

I had been brought up to believe in British justice. I had served my country under fire. I'd presided over police passing-out parades. But now I'd seen the other side of the system, and I felt the way men do when they've been on the receiving end. In other words: fuck you.

I spoke briefly to my lawyer. Then he told the detective, in language that was more formal and polite than I would have used, 'Under the circumstances, we are not prepared to hand over the documents. That is all.'

The detective turned on his heel with a look of utter astonishment and stalked out of the room.

I returned to the prison and was granted an interview with the deputy governor the next morning. He said I'd be sent to an open prison within the next few days. My new nick would be Spring Hill, in Buckinghamshire, which I'd requested because it was next door to my parents' home, and prisoners are supposed to be housed within easy reach of their families, if at all possible.

A week passed and nothing happened. The death-threats against me continued and reached such a pitch that the screws themselves met the governor, but still nothing was done. The chances of my remaining in one piece were dwindling rapidly. I was not actually afraid but I was beginning to despair of ever leaving this sex offenders' unit.

Then something unexpected happened. At nine o'clock one evening, there was a knock on my cell door. 'Come in,' I said by force of habit, instantly realising how silly this sounded in a nick.

There was a jangling of keys and the head of prison security came in.

'I hope you don't mind me dropping in like this but I am so angry about the whole situation that I wanted to talk to you about it,' he said. 'I've been a prison officer for most of my life and I've never seen anything like this. When an inmate receives threats it is standard procedure to resolve the problem by shipping out the inmate causing the problem. In your case nothing was done.

'When they eventually did let you move to another prison, they allowed you to be returned here in the full knowledge that you might be knifed. You were knifed, and you were lucky to survive.

'When an inmate is attacked it is unheard of for neither party to be shipped out. If the attacker isn't known, then the victim is shipped out. In this case the governor and all the staff know who's responsible and yet they've done nothing. Not only that, the threats have continued and still the governor does nothing. It's unbelievable!'

'But what can be done about it?' I asked.

'Simple. The first excuse for keeping you here was that you were a drug-dealer. When that was shown to be untrue, they said there was a second charge pending. Now that has been resolved, there's no reason to keep you here. Under current law you can hold the governor personally responsible should anything happen to you. Why don't you get your solicitor to ring the governor first thing in the morning and tell him this? If that doesn't have an immediate result, I'll tip off the press myself and tell them what's happening. I am so bloody cross about this.'

I thanked him and he left. He was truly one of the many decent people you meet in Her Majesty's prisons. The next morning I phoned my solicitor.

Ten minutes later the governor summoned me to his office in the presence of the deputy governor. 'I will not be threatened by solicitors! And I will not have an inmate manipulate the system!'

The deputy governor rolled his eyes, clearly demonstrating his disapproval of his boss's line. I was dismissed and as I walked back to my cell, I was stopped by one of the screws.

'Look, mate,' he said, 'we know about the call to the governor. Everyone knows. It's really got him going but if you want to force his hand, just demand to go down the block. He'll have to move you some time.'

'That's all very well but he could leave me there indefinitely in solitary confinement,' I said.

'Not really. There's a rule that an inmate must be moved within two weeks if his occupation of the block is for his own safety and not a punishment. And if the media was to learn that you were in the block over Christmas when you've done nothing wrong . . . See my point?'

Yes, I most certainly did. I went to the office and demanded to go down the block. I gathered up my bags. Word soon got about. The chaps I had got to know came to say goodbye. They knew that this time I would not be returning.

My farewell committee was like a multicultural gangsters' convention. First up was Sam. He was the head of a major Chinese Triad who operated out of offices in Jermyn Street, central London. 'Remember, Charlie,' Sam said, 'if you need us, we're there for you. Any trouble at all and I'll get men there, whatever time it is or wherever you are. Okay?' He gave me a hug and left. So I'd never get any grief in Chinatown.

Then Dave appeared. He ran a gang of Yardies in Brixton. 'You mind yourself, mon. Don't take no shit from no one, you see, Charlie? Any problems, mon, an' I'll kick those motherfuckers' asses. Okay?' Excellent. That was the inner cities sorted.

Two screws had been detailed to take me to the block. The only furniture in my cell was a cardboard table and chair. Both were in pieces. They had been broken so many times by junkies doing cold turkey that the screws had given up repairing them. The lavatory was blocked and was full of excrement. The basin was filled with teabags and lumps of gob where previous occupants had spat. The window was covered with a fine steel mesh and dripping with long strands of green phlegm. The floor was littered with stained bits of loo paper and rotting food, across which outsized cockroaches scampered.

Nine months ago I'd have been sickened by my surroundings and driven mad by the tedium of being locked up alone for twenty-four hours a day. Now I didn't give it a second thought. Every time Steve McQueen went into the 'cooler' in *The Great Escape*, he took his trusty baseball. Me, I had three good books, and I settled down to read them.

The following morning, keys jangled outside the cell door. It opened and the governor appeared. He wouldn't come in but was clearly angry. 'Brocket, get your stuff together. You're off to Ford.'

Ford was in West Sussex, more than two hours' drive from my mother.

'But I was told I was going to Spring Hill,' I said.

The governor just walked off: his way of saying, 'You won but I had the last laugh.'

I packed up my stuff and checked out of reception for what I hoped was the last time. This time I was sent with one of the screws in his own car and we set off for Ford.

Open prison, at last!

27

Meanwhile, Back in Hertfordshire . . .

AND NOW, A BRIEF INTERLUDE FROM LIFE AT HER Majesty's pleasure, as I make a short detour to the Hertfordshire countryside, and the fate of Brocket Hall.

When I went inside, the situation was as follows . . .

I owned the company that owned the car collection. But that was in debt to the banks for many millions of pounds. To pay off the debt, the bank had appointed Rick Furtado to sell all the cars (which he eventually did, at remarkably knock-down prices). Yet he had already sold cars on to new owners for far higher prices than he had declared to us, pocketing the difference, and he had been charged with the same offence of conspiring to commit a fraud for which I had already been jailed.

On the house and conference front, I was the majority shareholder in the company that owned Brocket Hall and the conference business. But I had been fired as an executive in the company, and now it was going down the pan, thanks to appalling mismanagement. This company, too, was in debt to the bank, which also owned 25 per cent of its shares, acquired at the time of the £15 million interest-free loan.

Meanwhile, my family home, my business and my rapidly diminishing car collection were left in the care of that paragon of decency, honesty and personal hygiene, Mr David Rocker, presided over by Sir Ian McLaurin.

Within days of arriving at Bedford Jail I was getting furious messages from the staff at Brocket and my brothers about the way Rocker was treating them. His standard tactic, as I had discovered when he tried to lock me out of my own showroom, while its contents were being prepared for removal, was to do something outrageous or unlawful, pretend that it was actually above-board and then dare anyone who complained to sue him.

Rocker's main aim in life continued to be to part my evil, aristocratic family from our house, by whatever means possible. He prepared a glossy brochure offering Brocket for sale to the highest bidder. As he boasted to Richard: 'I will sell Brocket to whoever I want to, and neither the trustees of your family trust nor Brocket can do a damn thing about it.'

Before the house was sold, however, Rocker seemed determined to reduce it to the worst possible condition. He felt that one good way to save money would be to stop carrying out various essential maintenance works on the fabric of the building. For example, he told the staff to stop the vital, regular cleaning of the roof gutters. As anyone could have told him, the gutters then overflowed and water poured through the building, causing thousands of pounds' worth of damage. Rocker didn't care: he knew the insurers would pay out.

Alan, the head butler, wrote to me and said that 'The house has lost its soul . . . It is almost as if the building is in such pain that it is weeping and its tears have run from its roof to the ground floor.'

He was heartbroken, as were the rest of the staff, who cared very deeply about the house to which they'd dedicated so much time and effort. They got their revenge on Rocker by passing on vital information to me behind his back. Desperate to maintain total secrecy about his actions, Rocker had the fax machine moved into his personal office. So the staff got a friendly telephone engineer to set up an intercept on the line. As one of their letters said:

LB, we thought it might be a good idea to see what the horrible man is up to so we plugged in another fax machine. Every time he got one so did we and here are the ones that arrived this week. You can see what he's up to. Hope it helps. God bless. The Girls

Given the treatment I had received from the legal system and the pounding I was getting from the media, the loyalty and friendship of the people who perhaps knew me best was more touching and more important to me than I can ever express. Before I had gone inside,

Rocker had tried to have me arrested for 'stealing' one of my own pictures from the hall. The staff had put a photograph of the picture on a mug and sent it to me as a reminder of the occasion with a note that read:

> Every time you drink out of this you can take comfort from the fact that whilst you may be in prison, at least you are loved and that people like Rocker will never have the good qualities that you have shown to us.

Over the next few months, various suitors came forward to purchase Brocket. The press would announce that Brocket had been sold to one group one week, only to decide a few days later that it had been sold to someone else. At one point, Rocker even announced to one and all that the place was sold, 'bar the shouting'. One by one, however, the would-be buyers drifted away once they had realised the effect of the 'poison pills' that my trustees had attached to the deal. These made it impossible for anyone of whom we disapproved to occupy or do business at the Hall.

Brocket suffered from another classic handicap for any property sale: a sitting tenant. And that tenant was me. Although I was in jail, I was still the legal tenant of Palmerston House, where I'd been living, and of an office in the Hall's stable-block. Both these properties had been made available to me, and renovated for me by the company, in exchange for me moving out of my previous home, Watershipps, which was now the golf clubhouse.

As long as I was a tenant, no one would want to buy Brocket Hall. So the obvious, sane solution was to make me a reasonable offer and come to a negotiated settlement. But that wasn't Rocker's style. He wanted to kick me out and he pursued the Palmerston action with manic determination.

He hoped to evict me on the grounds that I was an illegal squatter, despite the fact that I was a tenant in a property owned by a company whose majority shareholder was . . . yes . . . me. And how can you squat on your own property?

To establish that I had no right to Palmerston or my office, Rocker and the company secretary, Mr Ransley, signed sworn affidavits denying that the company had agreed to renovate my offices, or given me permission to move into Palmerston. Then he refused to let Jeff Clague, the estate manager, collect files from my office that contained evidence – correspondence, invoices and so forth that proved that what they said was not true.

I had already been transferred to Wellingborough by the time we ended up in Luton County Court to debate the matter in front of a patient and sympathetic female judge. She listened intently as Rocker's counsel claimed that I was occupying my property illegally. Then she simply stated, 'You seem not to have done any research on this at all. You have brought this case to me under the squatters' law and it is quite obvious that this is not the appropriate vehicle. I suggest that you do your homework and then appear again in front of me.'

Being a prison inmate, with no income, I was legally entitled to receive legal aid to fight an eviction order. As with my divorce hearing, however, the legal aid board were doing everything they could to delay giving me any help. And so, once again, I was representing myself in court.

'Your Honour,' I implored, 'there is a matter that I would like to bring to your attention. The sworn affidavits of both the company secretary Mr Ransley and Mr Rocker state that the company did not renovate the office complex and that I moved into the building without their knowledge or permission. Your Honour, I maintain that both Mr Rocker and Mr Ransley are deliberately withholding the truth, that there is evidence to prove this, and that they know where the evidence is.'

The judge looked at Rocker, gave a formal warning of the seriousness of withholding evidence and then – after I had described how Jeff Clague had been denied access to my files – added, 'As of this moment, you, Lord Brocket, are the tenant of the office complex. Mr Clague has your permission to enter and so Mr Rocker has no authority to deny this. Mr Rocker, I presume that you will not obstruct Mr Clague in this way?'

His lawyer stated that Rocker had no such intention. A date was agreed when Jeff could collect the files, and the case was adjourned. We rose and as I looked at Rocker, I really wondered if he would risk breaking the law after such an obvious warning. Outside the court Jeff said to me, 'What do you think, boss? Will he give two fingers to the judge? Personally I think he will.'

Jeff turned out to be absolutely right. Two days before he was due to collect the files, someone smashed their way into my office, ransacked the place, ripping open the filing cabinets and taking the files I needed that were the subject of the court order. Luckily, my brother Richard had been alerted to what was happening. He went into the office and took photographs of the devastation. He then rang the police to report the burglary but was told they were not proceeding, at Mr Rocker's request. Rocker later admitted in court that he had been in the office, but denied personally breaking down the door.

At the same hearing, I was able to show the judge company board-minutes, obtained by my brother Richard, which proved that the board had authorised my occupation of the office. There were even invoices for the refurbishment of the office, marked 'For Lord Brocket,' and signed by Ransley. I then told the judge about the break-in and produced the pictures as evidence.

Furious at such blatant disregard of her instructions, she agreed to adjourn the case until such time as I had been granted sufficient legal aid to hire my own barrister. In the meantime, she suggested that Rocker should give careful thought to the evidence he proposed to put forward at the next hearing. As Richard pointed out to me, there were only so many times when Rocker could mock the legal process before he got into serious trouble.

It seemed as though we were winning. But Rocker was not so easily dissuaded. I had been touched to the heart by the loyalty and friendship shown to me by my former staff. Rocker, however, was determined to make them pay for choosing my side, rather than his.

Jeff had already had his pay suspended for six months. Now, on Rocker's orders, the electronic gates to the estate were barred to his visitors, wrecking his social life and his business. Having failed to evict Shane Willis and his Prestige bodyshop from the car show-room building, Rocker simply cut off their power, making it impossible for the company to do any work. When the court deemed his actions unlawful and ordered him to reconnect, Rocker sneered at Shane Willis, 'You can fuck off. You haven't a pot to piss in so you can't take me back to court.'

Meanwhile, a summons had arrived for me to appear at Maidstone court to answer a claim from American Express for amounts owing on the company card. Rocker was trying to make me personally liable for the company's bills, even though I could prove that the lia-bility was theirs. And, of course, I could hardly have run up the bills from a prison cell.

At least it meant another day-trip from jail. I got back in the sweatbox again and went down to Maidstone. Once again the judge was very sympathetic and the company was duly joined as co-defendants. So Rocker had effectively forced himself into court. Yet again, the bank was on line to foot the bill for another foray into the legal world.

None of this stopped the ongoing battle at Brocket. The stream of interested parties circling above the estate seemed like vultures. Rocker kept telling people that the trust would agree to whatever was necessary to let the deal proceed, and we kept using every tactic we could to scupper the kind of cut-price sale that he was trying to arrange. Finally, after a story I had planted in the papers revealing the existence of the 'poison-pills' forced yet another would-be purchaser to pull out at the last moment, the bank got the message that there would be no deal without the agreement of the trustees and me. From now on they started speaking directly to us.

Rocker was now being sidelined. But it is only when a dictator falls from power that you learn the true extent of his crimes. I'd often wondered why I'd not had a single letter – not one – forwarded to me from Brocket Hall. Surely someone must have written to me there, if only to send bills or hate-mail? Then one day, about six months into my sentence, a big batch of letters arrived.

I looked at them and realised that this constituted one day's delivery. Jeff Clague had gone into the office and, on seeing them, simply took them and posted them on. The girls told him that Rocker had been going through my letters over the last six months and then not passed them on to me. So anyone who had written to me, including close friends, politicians and important clients, would now just assume I was too bad-mannered or ungrateful to reply.

Steven Barker, my solicitor, reminded me that 'tampering with Her Majesty's mail' was a criminal offence under British law. The girls were clear about what Rocker had done with the post. We made notes of the evidence and stored them away. As Steven commented, 'Your mail was not only tampered with, and read, but it was destroyed. That is most definitely an imprisonable offence.'

By now Club Corp of Asia, one of the companies that I had shown around the estate in the months before I was jailed, hoping to make a deal of my own, had returned to the table. The original deal with CCA would buy 49 per cent of the company, while I would retain my position in the company, my salary, my cars and my house. But with me in jail and the business in meltdown, they weren't inclined to be so generous. Unlike previous purchasers, however, they were prepared to talk to the trust, so an unusual negotiating process began.

My uncle David led the trustees negotiating with CCA, even flying back and forth to Hong Kong to negotiate direct with the company's owner, Dieter Klosterman. Notes from meetings would be posted to me at Littlehey. I would then blag every phone card I could to enable me to make almost daily calls to the trustees. Richard would come to see me with bundles of paper and we would thrash out various sticking points.

We weren't prepared to hand over the freehold to Brocket Hall. CCA weren't interested in a partnership. So we compromised. The bank needed £9 million to pay off the capital they had loaned to us (the outstanding interest could all be written off against tax, effectively leaving the great British tax-payer to pick up the tab). CCA agreed to pay £5.5 million of this sum, leaving the trust to find £3.5 million. In exchange, CCA would receive a sixty-year lease on Brocket Hall, free of poison pills. They would then pay an additional rent of up to £700,000 per annum.

So they'd get a long-term business opportunity, free of aggravation. And we would get help with our debts, regular income and the prospect of getting Brocket back, if not for me, or even my children, for my grandchildren at least.

Then, out of the blue, one of the trustees asked me to ring him. He told me that the trust had been contacted by an extremely respectable firm of solicitors. They had a client, who insisted on remaining anonymous. He wanted to buy Brocket Hall and had offered £35 million for the entire 1,500-acre estate. The trust had calmly informed the lawyers that this amazing bid was not quite high enough. 'We'll see what happens and we will come back to you,' my trustee said. He was clearly excited.

A week later, the trustee came to see me at Littlehey and revealed that the mystery buyer was now willing to pay £42 million. This was far in excess of anything anyone had ever offered for Brocket, roughly five times as much as the last offer Rocker had received. It would enable us to pay off the bank, buy another estate and have plenty over to provide income for the family. I could give Isa a final settlement and get the children back to this country. This time, we could not afford to say no.

We agreed to accept the offer and a full meeting was set up at Brocket. It was an absolute, non-negotiable condition of the deal that the buyer should remain secret until the purchase had been concluded. If his name was made public in advance, the whole thing would be off.

And so the interested parties assembled round the conference table in the library at Brocket. There were representatives from the two estate agents who had been charged with selling the estate; three bank officials; four of my trustees; David Rocker and Sir Ian McLaurin. I, meanwhile, was moping round Littlehey, wondering what on earth was going on.

I soon found out. Next morning, one of the chaps came running up to me.

'You are one stinking rich fucker!' he yelped. 'You've got more money than a pools winner! Look at this!'

Somehow he had got hold of a copy of that day's *Daily Telegraph*. There was a prominent article saying that the Sultan of Brunei was buying Brocket Hall for around £40 million. So he was the mystery buyer! But how did the paper know his identity? It was supposed to be top secret.

'Thanks, mate!' I yelled as I ran off to get permission to ring one of the trustees out of hours.

'What's going on?' I asked when the extension was picked up.

'Charles, we thought this might happen. There was a bit of a scene at the meeting yesterday.'

And then he told me what had happened. As the meeting began, almost all the people around the table were thrilled by the prospect of the large purchase-price. The bankers were delighted to be getting their money back. The trustees knew that all the family's money worries would now be solved. The estate agents were getting a massive commission. Even Rocker was on our side. He stood to pick up a fat bonus. The only people who stood to lose anything were the golfers, whose club would be closed once Brocket was sold.

As chairman of the company that owned Brocket Hall, McLaurin was legally bound to act in the best interests of its shareholders, who were the trust, the bank and myself. We all wanted the deal to go ahead.

Now, however, McLaurin insisted on being told the identity of the mystery buyer. The only people who knew were the estate agents. They tried to explain that they were not at liberty to divulge the name and that the whole deal might be jeopardised if they did so.

McLaurin was adamant that he would not carry on with the meeting unless he was told the name of the buyer.

With great reluctance, the agents divulged that it was the Sultan of Brunei.

Then the subject turned to the golf club. What would happen to the members, who had paid joining fees and subscriptions?

One of the bank executives said, 'We do not want to see the interests of the golf club members harmed. The bank will undertake to pay them all back.'

This did not satisfy McLaurin. He made it clear that he was extremely unhappy about the prospect of the golf club being closed. He left the meeting early with the golf club issue still unresolved.

The next day, the details of the deal appeared in the *Daily Telegraph*. They must have been leaked by someone who had attended the meeting. Someone, presumably, who did not wish the sale to go ahead. Within days, the Sultan had confirmed that he was no

longer interested in continuing with his purchase. A
£42 million deal had been fatally sabotaged. The deal
fell through and the golfers kept their club.

Funnily enough I wasn't too sad about it. Perhaps I
was simply not meant to sell Brocket. We went back to
CCA and concluded the deal. They paid the £5.5 million they had promised. The trust raised the remaining
£3.5 million by selling the Reynolds portrait of the
Prince Regent that had hung in the Saloon to Andrew
Lloyd Webber. So the bank got their £9 million.

CCA took possession of Brocket Hall on a sixty-
year lease. They agreed to build a second golf course,
which they have since done, and a £25 million leisure
centre, for which plans are currently well advanced.
They also began paying the rent that would guarantee
me, and my descendants, an income for the next six
decades. And they promised to retain all the staff who
had served me so loyally over so many years.

As for Rocker, well, he was forced to pay the outstanding debt on Brocket's corporate American Express
card that he had tried to foist on to me. The court
ordered him to return all my personal effects, which I
had stored in a barn on the estate and which he had
seized when I went inside. The girls in the office said
that Rocker was consumed with rage. A full twelve
months boasting that he'd got me by the balls had
resulted in defeat on every single count.

He had, as part of his assault on the aristocracy,
attempted to strip various members of my family of
their Brocket golf club memberships. These, too, had to
be restored. Still, it wasn't all bad news for Rocker.

As one of his final executive acts, he awarded himself a lifetime golf club membership and still plays there to this day.

And now back to nick, and the car that was taking me to Ford Open Prison.

28

Ali Brocket and the (Rather More than Forty) Thieves

IT WAS STRANGE SITTING IN THE FRONT SEAT LIKE a civilised human being, not trussed up like an oven-ready turkey, flanked by a screw on either side. We had a jovial journey down to the Sussex countryside. Finally we got to Ford, which sits on the site of an old Battle of Britain air-base, about three miles from the sea at Littlehampton.

I was dropped off at the gate and I hauled my prison bags on to the counter for everything to be examined. The officer clacked away at his computer, paused and then calmly announced that I was not registered and would have to go back.

No . . . it wasn't possible. After everything that had happened, they couldn't be sending me back to the sex offenders' wing again.

'Perhaps you should ring someone,' I suggested rather weakly. 'I think it has been arranged between governors.'

I waited nervously while phone calls went buzzing back and forth. At last they let me in. I couldn't believe it – it was easier getting a suite at Claridges during Fashion Week than a bed at Ford Prison.

Speaking of which, Ford had its own special menswear look. 'Today, Charlie is wearing fluorescent green Ford trousers, teamed with a simple T-shirt. The boys aren't allowed to wear proper shirts, with buttons or pockets, in case they try to impersonate an officer. Mmm . . . lovely!'

The huts where we all lived had been put up during the war as short-term barracks for the RAF. More than fifty years later, they were still there, and were expected by the present management to last well into the next millennium. Inside there was a central aisle with nine bedspaces down each side, divided by six-foot-high partitions. I settled into the only spare one and introduced myself to the others, who were grabbing their plates, knives and forks for the evening meal, which, as in all prisons, is served at five in the afternoon.

Standing in the meal queue, I was scrutinised by the inmates like some rare species that had escaped from a zoo. By now I was used to this. Then a chap in a suit came up to me. He was a governor.

'Hello. The last time we met you were presenting me with an award on behalf of the Minister of Trade and Industry at Brocket Hall.' Of course, I remembered the occasion well. He had introduced a new energy system for the prison that had gained him the award.

'I've got the picture of the presentation in my office.'

Well, now he'd got me in person, in his nick.

I sat down to eat with some lads from the hut. You meet a higher class of bad guy in an open prison. There was an American banker who had fallen foul of some investment rules, a softly spoken chap from Zimbabwe who had been rather over-ambitious in his statements on his mortgage application form, a delightful Asian chap who'd under-declared the value of a computer shipment into the UK to the value of £40,000, and a Moroccan jeweller, an ex-public schoolboy, who'd been driving while disqualified.

Another chap had stolen £148 million. One Friday, I found him sitting by himself, almost helpless with laughter. I asked him what was so funny.

'You fuckin' toffs don't know nuffink,' he said cheerfully. 'I just made two million quid.'

'How?'

'Where do you think I stashed it all? I didn't put it in a fuckin' box. It's all earning interest. So every Friday, I sit back and smile 'cos I just made anuvver two million quid.'

And they say crime doesn't pay!

Ford had a pretty standard jail routine: work from 8.30 until 12.45, a greasy fried lunch, then more work till 4.45. After the 5 p.m. meal, the evening pastimes were snooker, cinema, TV, gym, badminton and the library. In the summer months we could play tennis, cricket and football. Compared to most nicks, this was almost civilised.

To add to its delights, I discovered a useful tip, which I pass on to anyone who may have need of it. In common with all state institutions, the prison service is obsessed with political correctness and terrified of accusations of racism. So it doesn't just ensure that religious beliefs are respected – which is only right – it bends over backwards to accommodate anyone who claims to deserve special treatment, whether they deserve it or not. If you say you're a Muslim, they have to treat you as one, whether you actually are or not.

Muslims get their own food in prison, made from halal meat, which is often far better than standard nick grub. And they are given time off to pray, several times a day. So when I got to Ford, I announced that I was a Muslim. One of the huts had been converted into a mini-mosque, where we could go to pray and talk – bunking off work to do so – and where we could eat our halal food.

To make it even better, my fellow-prisoners included a chap who'd made millions smuggling contraband alcohol into the country. He persuaded the governor, who did not dare argue, that the official halal food was not up to standard. Instead, he insisted on having specially prepared meals brought in on a daily basis from outside caterers. And so, every day, a van would arrive, and waiters would emerge carrying delicious, spicy dishes, covered in silver foil, which my Muslim friends (none of whom seemed offended by my bogus conversion) and I would consume in a small room adjacent to the 'mosque'.

With my diet sorted out, I toured the camp to find a job that would enable me to get on with my writing. A bit of gym-time during the day, when it wasn't so crowded, would come in handy, too. I signed up as a chapel orderly, with two other lads, Gerry and Stewart.

Opposite our office was a small kitchen to cater for the endless cups of tea that we had to make for visitors. There was a fridge on top of a worksurface, where we kept the milk. One morning, as I opened the fridge door, I suddenly thought of the scene in one of the Pink Panther films where Inspector Clouseau, alias Peter Sellers, comes home to fend off the expected martial-arts attack from his Japanese manservant, Kato. Having destroyed most of the apartment looking for Kato, Clouseau opens the fridge to get a beer, only to be confronted by Kato leaping out, complete with frozen eyebrows.

I held the fridge door open and looked inside. It was small, very small, but if I took everything out, I would just be able to curl up inside it. Quickly emptying the fridge into the cupboards below, I clambered on to the worktop, squeezed into the cold space and pulled the door shut. In the dark of the fridge I was tittering like a five-year-old at the thought of Stewart's face when he opened the door to get some milk. Then I remembered something: I'd forgotten to switch the damn thing off. And I was only wearing a T-shirt.

After five minutes I was freezing. More minutes went by and my body began to go numb with cold. Frostbite could not be far away. Then I heard footsteps in the kitchen, followed by the clatter of a tea cup on its saucer. I knew what was coming next. The fridge door opened and a hand reached in for the milk.

'Ayyeeeeeeeeee!!!'

I let out a bloodcurdling Kato-like war cry and moved to pounce on a terrified Stewart, who had become rooted to the spot.

He emitted a strangled 'Ahaaaaaaaaaarrrrrrg . . .'

Only then did I realise that I wasn't moving. Far from leaping across the room, I was jammed between the top and bottom of the fridge. But my burst of energy had set the fridge moving. It began to rock back and forth, teetering on the worksurface edge.

Stewart was still rooted to the spot as both he and I realised that I was about to take the fridge crashing over the edge . . . right on top of him. Coming to his senses, he lunged forward and rugby-tackled the wobbling fridge, holding me and it in a frantic embrace.

At that moment, the chaplain rounded the corner into the kitchen.

'Just looking for the milk, vicar,' muttered Stewart.

'I see,' murmured the chaplain doubtfully. He retreated to the safety of the vestry and Stewart began to prise me out of the fridge, both of us helpless with laughter.

The media had their own thoughts about me being a chapel orderly. Cutting a hole in the perimeter fence, a journalist took a photo of me and printed a bogus story that the officers and inmates were up in arms that I had received preferential treatment by getting this 'cushy' job. The governor, not normally one to be directed by the media, took fright and moved me to the gardens department. I spent the next three months looking after 8,000 trees in the tree nursery, only to discover that once the trees had grown to a certain point, they all had to be shredded.

Even by prison standards, this was a black joke. Apparently, the trees could not be sold on the open market, because they would undercut the produce of local nurseries that had to use regular labour. No one ever seemed to consider that the trees could simply be donated to charities like hospitals or old people's homes. Madness.

After six weeks at Ford, I was moved into a single room, measuring about six by ten feet. There was only room for a bed, table and small cupboard, but at least there was a normal window that you could open. The showers and loos were down the end of the hut.

The first morning when I woke up, I heard the slamming of car doors and the excited cries of children attending the local pre-school. Then, one night, there was a very different kind of commotion – a loud, high-pitched sound that sounded like . . . well, it sounded just like a woman having sex. It died down when the screw came round for the 10 p.m. check, then started up again after he'd gone.

The next morning I asked the bloke in the next-door room what had happened.

'Me mates on the outside paid for a woman to come in over the fence,' he said. 'I had to hide her under the bed on the hourly checks, but she was game.'

So a woman scaled the fence, avoiding the surveillance, just to pleasure one of the inmates. That was one plucky – or exceptionally desperate – lady.

By now I had decided to join the rubbish collection team. No one else wanted to be a bin-man, but I thought it was perfect. Apart from the physical exercise, it only took an hour a day and I could go wherever I wanted in the camp. Then I'd have the rest of the day to myself.

Meanwhile, as I was carting rubbish, fortune had smiled on Ian McLaurin. It was announced that he had received a life peerage. Forgetting past events, I wrote to him to congratulate him and received a polite reply on new notepaper that was emblazoned with a multi-coloured coat of arms. What was it I said about being 'nouveau-posh'?

Yet another trial date for Ali's gang was fast approaching but I had no appetite for it. What the hell was I doing fighting the crown's battles for them, anyway? I had received absolutely no thanks for it and I'd almost lost my life. Well, the hell with that. I wrote a letter to the judge listing the threats and beatings that had been dished out to me and to anyone who had tried to help me, and the total failure of the prison authorities to do anything to stop them.

I concluded: 'I very much regret that I do not feel able to testify against any of the accused. Having withstood the threats for almost nine months, this decision is not taken lightly. I apologise for not supporting the crown and for any time wasted but the safety of my family and friends must come first.'

When we all assembled for the court case in Northampton, the judge read my letter and simply said that there was no point in proceeding with the trial. Ali had got away with theft, extortion, GBH and attempted murder. But frankly, and sadly, I did not think that was my problem.

Back at Ford, I found over 100 birthday cards, which really cheered me up. Some of the lads had got their hands on a tiny birthday cake and a bottle of cognac, which we drank out of yoghurt cartons, toasting the world outside and the passing of another year.

The time came for Furtado's trial. He had managed to delay it for so long by claiming that he was mentally unfit to stand trial, but he eventually found himself in the dock. He had contributed to our scheme by pretending the deal with the Japanese was still live and producing a signed affidavit from Warren Liu, the intended purchaser of the ten-car package of Ferraris and Maseratis, which was given to the insurers as evidence of the cars' value. In return, we had paid him thousands of pounds to settle his claim for lost commission on the 'stolen' cars, and allowed him to make additional profits on the cars he sold for the Brocket collection. I had always thought that the stamped, notarised document was genuine. But the prosecution revealed that it had in fact been forged. Furtado was sent to prison for eighteen months.

I was glad when the trial was over, especially since it attracted unfair and unwelcome publicity for the family and me. I realised how damaging this could be when I applied for my first day out. At the one-third mark of a sentence, inmates are allowed out for a six-hour period at a weekend, twice a month. Now this date was approaching for me.

My family were longing to see me. My friend Libby had arranged a slap-up lunch. But three days before the magic date, the prison was instructed not to allow me out. The official reason was that I was 'high-profile'. When other inmates went out to see their families I was confined to camp.

The Ombudsman later ruled, as the authorities must have known he would, that the denial of my rights was unlawful and I was then allowed out. But I had still spent seven extra months locked up on days when I should have been getting a brief taste of freedom. And it hurt.

Then, in May 1997, I got an urgent message to ring Gus Lorenzo.

'It's Isa,' he said. 'She's in hospital. She's bad. She has acute septicaemia and a lung has collapsed. She's in an oxygen tent in a coma. Her heart stopped for a minute and a half last night but they brought her back.'

Isa had suffered from kidney problems, which had caused a blood infection and set up a chain reaction.

'Do the children know?' I asked.

'Yes. They know their mother might not make it.'

That was all the poor mites needed. Father was in prison, and now their mother was dying.

Over the next few days there was no change in her condition. Time stood still. She was confined to the oxygen tent around her and I to my prison. We all prayed. By the end of the week our prayers were answered. The doctors had the infection under control and Isa spoke again for the first time. She had survived another crisis. But how many more could she stand?

A few weeks later, yet another highly prejudicial newspaper feature about me was published – this time in a supposed 'quality' broadsheet paper. The constant untruths, inventions and downright lies were really getting to me, and they were seriously affecting the way I was treated by the prison authorities. So why didn't I sue for libel?

For one thing, I couldn't afford to. For another, the basis of a libel claim is the harm that has been done to the plaintiff's reputation. A convicted prisoner has no reputation to harm. So a newspaper or TV programme can say whatever they like without fear of being sued.

Carlton TV produced a hatchet job on me, called *Lord Fraud*. It was supposed to be a documentary, which implied that it was based on fact. But its producer told Flick, my former marketing director at Brocket Hall: 'I don't want to hear the good things about Lord Brocket. The public are not interested in hearing that sort of stuff.'

I complained to the Broadcasting Standards Commission. The programme-makers had claimed that I was a blackmailer, despite being given evidence that I was not. It took nearly three years before there was an adjudication on the programme. At the hearing, the authority's chairperson, Lady Howe, got the producer to stand up in public and admit that he broadcast allegations he knew to be untrue. But to what avail? Under UK law, I received no damages, not even a postcard to say sorry.

The constant untrue publicity almost certainly scuppered my appeal against the length of my sentence.

The appeal was finally heard in November 1997, after I had served 21 months. Steven Barker was confident that my sentence would be reduced. As I walked to the sweatbox, hopefully for the last time, dressed again in my suit, inmates and screws came up to shake my hand. Most of them said, 'Don't expect to see you back.' I set off for London in genuine excitement, cramped up in the tiny plastic box.

At the Court of Appeal, my counsel got to his feet before the three judges and told them that my sentence was far in excess of the guidelines and actual practice. He then referred to the treatment I had received: being hounded for eight months, then stabbed, then returned from Maidstone to Littlehey, despite the authorities' knowledge that my life was being put in danger.

Looking back, I don't know why we bothered. I should have known what would happen. The judges decided that the sentence was not extraordinary. They said that my treatment in jail had nothing whatsoever to do with the sentencing. Worse still, in narrating the events at Wellingborough, the senior judge stated that I had 'grassed' on another inmate and that the knifing problem arose from this. He must have been aware that his words would put me in danger. As any judge would certainly know, being officially labelled a 'grass' in prison is a recipe for disaster.

The appeal was dismissed and I was led back down to the cell.

I spent another two months in Ford and then, in January 1998, I was transferred to Spring Hill – a mere two years after I should have arrived there.

Everyone said that this place was different, and they were right. It had a much more relaxed regime than Ford; the screws were keen to help and they treated everyone as people. Rules were important but decisions were based on common sense and inmates with genuine problems usually had them resolved quickly.

Under normal circumstances as an inmate of an open prison, I would now have started working in the outside world. But that was impossible for me because I was bound to be hounded by the media, as was anywhere I worked. So I got a job in the prison vegetable garden instead. There was a mini-heatwave in February and I discovered a wheelbarrow that made an excellent deckchair. I'd close my eyes and dream of waves lapping on a white sandy tropical beach, a dream spoiled only by the manure heap nearby.

There was a well-known guitarist at Spring Hill called Dave Mumford, who'd started out in the sixties playing with P. J. Proby and the Walker Brothers and had kept working with countless big names until the Customs and Excise happened to find a ton and a half of cannabis on his yacht. Dave got a six-and-a-half-year sentence, but swore that he'd been fitted up. He had never smoked dope, and the bust was made while he was in England and his boat, which then 'disappeared', was moored in the Med.

Dave was starting up a band to play a prison concert and he asked if I'd be interested in playing keyboards. I'd been vaguely trying to learn the piano as a way to pass the time. Now I had five weeks to master a complete set of rock classics, ranging from 'All Shook Up' to 'Crocodile Rock'. Luckily, my fellow band-members were almost all professional musicians, so I crammed a year's worth of lessons into a single month. In return, I came up with the band's name, the Time Lords, because we were all doing time. And at least one of us was a lord.

The performance was planned as a proper stage spectacular. It would open with the James Bond theme tune, with me pacing across the stage wearing a white DJ, mask, snorkel and flippers, mimicking the James Bond silhouette. As I filed away at a piece of wood in the carpentry workshops, and then painted it matt black it did occur to me that sauntering around a nick with an imitation gun was not the brightest idea but this was Spring Hill, not Wandsworth, and no one seemed to mind.

For Bob Marley's 'Buffalo Soldier' we all had Rasta dreadlock wigs made of prison mops, coloured with black dye illegally smuggled into the joint because prisoners were not allowed to own anything that could help disguise their identity.

Our debut show went down so well we thought we ought to do another. And this time we'd record it. I rang Andy, a well-respected sound engineer I dealt with at Brocket.

'I'd like an eight-track digital set-up, with a twenty-four-track mixing desk,' I said, without revealing my identity or location. 'Trouble is I don't have much money available at the moment.'

'Well, the equipment's no problem,' said Andy. 'But it's not cheap, I'm afraid.'

Now for the really tricky bit. 'Er . . . before we go any further, I think I'd better tell you that we need this in, ah . . . a . . . prison. Spring Hill Prison to be exact.'

No reaction. I could see our chances of getting a recording of our music were dwindling. Oh well, in for a penny, in for a pound: 'Suppose you'd better know my name, too,' I said. 'It's Charles Brocket.'

Suddenly Andy's mood seemed to change. 'Ah! Then don't worry about the money. How long do you want it for?'

'Er . . . two weeks,' I said, and not sensing any resistance added, 'to a month?'

'No problem. I'll bring the stuff over on Saturday with my fiancée and we'll just give you a bell when we need it again.'

Of course, prisons were not particularly keen on allowing large objects to be smuggled in and out. Luckily, I had a plan. I called up Andy and asked if he had a plain white shirt and black trousers.

'When you come to deliver the gear, wear those clothes with the shirt collar open. Drive right up to the barrier and honk your horn. The guard-room TV monitors aren't clear enough to show small details. All they'll see is what looks like a screw reporting for duty. Are you on?'

There was silence.

'Andy?'

'Okay, Charlie. Jesus, the things that I do for the love of music. It had better be good.'

So there was another helpless innocent I'd 'coerced' into a life of crime. The next day the gear was driven right up to the dining-hall store, then hidden under our makeshift stage. The band couldn't hide their excitement. Now we really were rockin'!

* * *

By our second show, we were a seriously tight band. Dave had written a theme for us – a chain-gang song called 'Crackin' Rocks', accompanied by the clanking of a massive tractor-chain I'd borrowed from the prison farm department. As the chains crunched and inmates joined in the chorus, the watching screws applauded. Little did they know that Stewart – an ex-policeman acting as sound-recording engineer – was lying under the stage, recording the whole event, using £30,000 worth of recording equipment smuggled in and maintained by someone impersonating a screw.

A few days later Andy arrived under the pretext of servicing the prison's official tape-recorder, while we sneaked round to his car and loaded up all the equipment that he had lent us, plus a tape of our show. Once home he transferred the whole thing to CD and sent the finished article in to us. It was remarkably good, if I do say so myself.

By now I was close to serving the two-and-a-half-year minimum sentence before I was eligible for parole. Amazingly, no one could find any reasons, no matter how spurious, for denying me that basic right. But as August, the month of my release approached, every day seemed like an eternity.

On the eve of my release I looked at the ceiling and listened to the silence of the night. I thought of freedom: no more prison beds; no more queuing for meals. I longed to walk in a field, to smell the new grass under my feet and the wild flowers about me. How long had it been since I had heard the sound of the sea or had a swim? How wonderful to wake up again in the arms of someone I loved and to have my privacy restored. Best of all, I would be able to hold my children again.

A journalist friend had tipped me off that a tabloid newspaper had organised a high-performance sports car to chase me on the day of my release. I rang my old friend Jonathan Palmer, an ex-Formula One driver.

'Charlie, no problem,' he volunteered. 'We'll sort the shits out. I'll fly in my chopper and land next to the sports field. Quick in and out!'

But then I could see the headlines: 'Lord Fraud's Freedom Flight'. So I changed my mind, turned down Jonathan's kind offer and looked for a different way out.

Another friend, Tony, agreed to provide me with a Harley Davidson motorbike and protective leathers. That was just the ticket. He just made one condition: 'Press the button in the left pocket of the jacket once you're on your way.'

There was another minor detail: the leathers had Hell's Angel colours, complete with winged death-head, emblazoned on the back. I grinned at the discovery that I'd just joined the New Forest Chapter.

As I walked towards the prison gate, looking like a cross between Mad Max and Easy Rider, half of Fleet Street seemed to have gathered outside, all jostling one another to get a better view. I was touched to see that the other inmates had come out in force to see me off, shouting, 'Good luck, Charlie!' as I walked by.

The screws had also gathered at the gate to shake my hand and wish me luck. They were a good bunch of blokes. One of them shook his head and sighed, 'Jesus, the governor's doing his nut. Nick discipline's gone clean out the window.'

As we approached the barrier, the cameras started going off. I stood in front of the salivating press-pack and made a short statement, saying how much I regretted the hurt and pain that I had caused my family and friends. Then I got on the bike, parked ready for me outside the guard-hut, and kicked the engine into life.

Parked at the main entrance gate on the main road was a bright yellow beach-buggy, with a camera-laden passenger. I saw the driver mouth, 'Oh shit,' as he thrust the machine into gear and smoked the tyres. Two other cars tried to follow me, but once I hit the open road, I opened up the Harley and left them for dead.

Then I remembered Tony's instruction about the button in the left breast pocket of the jacket. With the speedo showing just over the ton, I punched the button. The sixties rock band Steppenwolf came blasting through the helmet headphones with '*Born to be wi-i-ild . . . Born to be wild!*'

I felt the wind rush across my face, heard the sound of the exhaust almost harmonising with the pounding music and gave a huge, delighted grin. Then I opened the throttle even wider and rode into the free world.

– 29 –

A Changed Man

I LEFT PRISON IN AUGUST 1998. BUT MY SENTENCE did not truly end for more than four years after that.

The Home Office didn't see any reason to stop the private war that the criminal justice system had been waging against me, just because I was out on the streets. And the next target they chose was my children.

All the time I was inside, I'd dreamed of the moment when I could get out of nick, get on a plane and fly to Puerto Rico. I hadn't seen Alex and Antalya since April 1996, when they came to visit me at Littlehey. William had not come with them: he'd already been put on a plane to the Caribbean. So we'd been apart for even longer.

In the meantime, Isa's continuing problems had made it very difficult for her to take a full part in the children's upbringing. They had mostly been raised by their grandparents, Gus and Brigitte Lorenzo, which made me want to be with them even more. I knew how much I had missed a father's guidance through my childhood and I didn't want my children to miss out, too.

This should not have been a problem. The Home Office rules state very, very clearly that when you are out of prison, you're out on licence until you've served the three-quarter stage of the sentence. I had another fifteen months to go before that was up. A prisoner on licence is not allowed to travel abroad, except in particular circumstances. But one of them is to see your family.

Common sense and compassion both suggest that it is a good idea to reunite ex-prisoners with their children as quickly as possible after their release from jail. It is extremely difficult, and even unusual for a family unit to survive the trauma of a prison sentence and the poverty and stress that follow once the major breadwinner has been locked up. There is no point in making matters worse by denying a father and his children the chance to re-establish some kind of relationship.

My probation officer therefore recommended to his superiors that I should be allowed to fly to Puerto Rico to see my children. There was no legitimate reason whatever why the request should be refused. I wasn't a threat to my wife or children. I certainly wasn't going to do a runner. So my probation officer confidently said, 'You'll get this.' But then the reply came back from Whitehall. They wouldn't let me go, and they wouldn't say why not.

My probation officer was doing his nut. He'd never known a case like it. For me, it was just one more blow to the gut. And why should the children suffer, just because someone up there wanted to get at me?

Once again, I wondered what the motivation was behind this unrelenting hostility. I thought of a screw I'd met at Littlehey. He'd been a military policeman in Hong Kong when I'd been serving there with the regiment. He came up to me and said, 'Charlie, I gotta tell you, they're 'avin' a fuckin' laugh with you, mate. They're gonna keep movin' you around. But don't let the bastards get you down. Don't let them see they're getting to you. Hold your head up and stick with it.'

I'd tried to do that when I was inside, and I stuck to the same principle on the outside, too. There's no point in turning a drama into a crisis, when you can just as easily see the funny side.

Not long after I got out, I was a guest at the twentieth-anniversary celebration of the Audi Quattro, sitting next to the racing driver Derek Bell. A birthday cake in the shape of an Audi Quattro was wheeled on-stage. As a champion rally driver cut the cake I muttered, 'The last time I sliced a car up, I got seven and a half years.' The room erupted in laughter and raucous cheers, and it took some while for order to be restored.

At the 1998 Motor Show I couldn't resist visiting the classic car stands. A smart, enthusiastic young salesman, not recognising me, told me about a 1951 Ferrari roadster, priced at over £1 million.

'Why are you smiling, Charlie?' asked the friend accompanying me.

'That was one of the cars that we dismantled for the insurance claim!'

'So?' she asked.

'Nothing, except that it's been rebuilt as a completely different car.'

'But wasn't that what some expert accused you of doing?'

'Yes, but now it's true.'

A few months later chassis No. 0138A was auctioned in America where its provenance stated that having been dismantled by Lord Brocket, in a well-known incident, it had now been totally restored to its former glory. Well, I suppose that's one way of putting it.

But for all my jokes and wry remarks, it wasn't easy re-entering the outside world. I don't think it ever is for anyone who's been inside. The old lags all told me that prison would affect me, and they were right.

My back was not what it was: too many nights in prison beds had taken their toll. The fluorescent lighting had left me needing glasses to read. Driving in London, I found that I had to check an *A–Z* a few times, something I'd never had to do before. I handed back a coin to a shop assistant, saying it was foreign currency, only to be told that it was a £2 coin and had been out for two years.

I was lucky that I had money to spend at all. Most prisoners are penniless when they re-enter the world. But thanks to the deal on Brocket Hall, I had a pretty substantial income. Even so, as an ex-con, obtaining a bank account was well nigh impossible. Coutts said that even if I deposited £100,000 with them and had no overdraft facility, they would not give me an account. It took six months to get an account and a further year to get a credit card.

Some of the marks prison had left on me disappeared remarkably fast. There's no trace of the knife that stabbed me in the guts. The only scar I still carry is a very faint line across my hand where I was slashed when I tried to protect my face.

The single biggest piece of long-term damage that prison did to me had nothing to do with attempted murder, but owed everything to official spite. Ever since my rowing days at Eton, I've had weak knees. By the time I got to Ford, the cartilage of my right knee was shredding and I was in constant pain. Simple keyhole surgery would have solved the problem, and prisoners are entitled to the same healthcare as anyone else. Moreover, prisoners at open jails are allowed to travel to and from hospital appointments unaccompanied, by taxi.

The Home Office, however, refused to allow me to be treated. For months, I hobbled round Ford in agony, with only a bandage and pain-killers to help me. Finally, I was allowed to see a surgeon, but I was forced to travel in a prison van, guarded by two screws, like a violent criminal. When the surgeon saw me, he said it was too late. The knee had deteriorated to such a point that all he could do was remove the remaining scraps of cartilage completely. So now I have a knackered knee, courtesy of the British government.

Other, more subtle changes stay with you for ever. At an outdoor event, one of my friends pointed out that I always made sure that I walked in direct sunlight. I'd go out of my way just to get out of the shade. I hadn't been aware that I did that. But as soon as he mentioned it, I realised that it was a reaction to spending so much time locked up. I'll never stop appreciating the sensation of fresh air in my lungs, sunlight on my face, the smell of wild flowers and freshly mown grass, and the simple but overwhelming privilege of being able to do what you want, when you want.

When my parole was served and I was free at last to travel I set about re-establishing contact with my children and becoming a father again. We'd written countless letters and spoken on the phone. But by the time I flew to Puerto Rico at the end of 1999, it was almost four years since I'd seen them, or they me, and of course they'd changed. Alex, for example, had been a little boy when I'd last seen him: now he was a strapping, six-foot-four teenager. The three of them spoke in American accents. They went to American-style schools. It was wonderful to be with them, to play on the beach with my children like any other dad, but it was painful, too.

Our time apart had left great gaps in our relationship. I hadn't seen my children grow. I didn't know their friends. We hadn't done all the little, apparently trivial, things that families do every day that build up into a life together. I couldn't help but feel that I'd been a terrible failure as a father: to this day, that is the one consequence of what I did that makes me feel truly guilty.

The hardest thing was getting to know William again. I had not seen him since he was four. He had no memory of England or Brocket. And Brigitte's influence upon him — for he was the apple of her eye: the son she had never had — was so strong that he now called (and still, to this day, calls) her Mamma. Not surprisingly, Isa was hurt by her mother's usurpation of her role, but in her condition there was little she could do.

Isa and I saw each other every day. I'd go to the Lorenzos' house, pick the children up, take them to a beach, or a water-park, or the movies. The children loved our expeditions. Gus was getting on a bit, and Isa was unwell, so they rarely got the chance to leave the house under normal circumstances. Sometimes, Isa would come with us. We got on very well, but I felt sorry for her: there seemed no way of jolting her out of her condition.

At least the children still wanted to be with me again, a fact that was soon proved in the most conclusive possible fashion. When I was in Puerto Rico, I left Antalya an open plane-ticket to England, for use in an emergency: I knew she was unhappy in Puerto Rico. A few months later, I came back to London from a trip to Italy and there was Antalya, aged twelve, waiting for me. She'd flown the Atlantic by herself to come and live with me, which she did for the next two and a half years.

Towards the end of her time in England, Antalya started having horrible nightmares. Before leaving Puerto Rico, she had saved her mother's life by calling an ambulance, after Isa had collapsed. Now Antalya was terrified Isa might be in distress again, and she would not be there to help her. In the end, she had no choice but to go back to Puerto Rico.

Alex came over to England in the summer of 2002 – his first time back here in more than six years. The very first thing he did was to ask me to take him to

Brocket, so that he could play a round of golf there. By the end of his stay, I almost had him talking like a proper Englishman.

Through all this, the thing that helped me most was the support I received from other people. One old army friend gave a party for me when I left jail. He was about to become the High Sheriff of Hertfordshire, carrying on a family tradition for the third generation. Just before the party the Lord Lieutenant of the county wrote to him along the lines of 'It has come to our attention that you are to give a party to an ex-convict. We are sure this is mistaken but if it is true we suggest you reconsider your forthcoming position as High Sheriff.'

My friend's reply was unhesitating. He simply wrote back, saying that if the establishment that he represented did not understand the concept of forgiveness, loyalty or penance, it was not an organisation worth joining. He asked that his nomination be withdrawn and his family not be considered again.

Another friend, the McLaren racing-car designer Adrian Newey, invited me to bring the Time Lords to be the entertainment at his fortieth birthday party. Adrian has a sizeable house near Ascot.

We got up and started playing and soon the whole place was heaving. And then a slender, dark-haired figure came up to the stage and asked if he could sit in with the band.

It was George Harrison.

I'd known George for quite a while, because, like a lot of rock stars, he was a car fanatic. He was also a gentle, charming man, who never used his status as an ex-Beatle to try and impose himself on people around him. Once he'd picked up a guitar, he was just another musician having a good time.

After a while, Damon Hill – who's also pretty handy on guitar – got up and joined in, too. So there we all were: a bunch of ex-cons, a Beatle and a Formula One World Champion. We must have played for another hour, ending with a mad blues jam-session.

Not long afterwards, George Harrison revealed that he was suffering from cancer. I was told that his night as a stand-in guitarist with the Time Lords was George's final live performance. I hope he enjoyed it as much as we all did.

Some of the most moving acts of kindness, however, came from people I barely knew, or had never met at all.

Throughout my time in jail, I received hundreds, even thousands, of letters from all over the world and only one was negative. After I got out, there were times when I'd be sitting in a pub, or walking down the street and total strangers would come up and wish me luck. Often they'd tell me of some connection to Brocket – one chap, I remember, had been a bricklayer on the golf clubhouse, another was a bus-driver who'd taken guests to the Hall – just to let me know that they trusted their own experience more than tabloid muck-spreading.

A lot of my clothes had not survived storage while I'd been inside, so I went to a clearance sale in London to buy some new ones cheap. I'd selected a handful of shirts when a man came towards me from behind the counter. 'Oi, remember me? I was at Ford with you.' Grabbing the clothes and stuffing them in a bag, he said, ''Ere, Charlie, I'm running this clearance sale. You can 'ave those. Good luck, mate.'

Moments like that are incredibly encouraging. But they were counterbalanced by the continuing fabrications, exaggerations and downright lies that were printed in the papers and broadcast on TV. It began on the morning after my release. I opened one tabloid to discover that I'd made a 'failed getaway'. Apparently I had dropped the bike keys on leaving. Really? Difficult to drive off without keys in the ignition, though, as even the dullest reader must have realised.

What I've learned over the years is that people don't remember the details of a story like that. They just remember the smell. They couldn't provide chapter and verse about my supposed sins. They just knew that I was a bad egg.

I found myself crossing names out of my address book: people who'd once been my friends, who'd happily accepted my hospitality at Brocket Hall, but who now no longer wished to know me. Well, the feeling was mutual.

The worst part was the uncertainty, the never quite knowing how people would react when they met you. Within the past year, I've had a friend invite me to a lunch party as her companion, only for her to call up a while later and say, 'I'm terribly sorry, Charlie, but the hostess says you can't come. She won't have a wife-beater in her house.'

I've learned what to do in situations like that. You go

anyway. You let people see who you are and what you're really like, and you trust that they will come to the right conclusion. In this case, as it happens, the hostess did. By the time the meal was over, we were firm friends.

But it's still not easy walking about feeling that you're always one step away from someone else's criticism. What made it particularly ironic was that I was a very different, and I hope rather nicer, person than I had been in my late-eighties pomp, when everyone wanted to be my friend.

I think I became pretty smug about my success. It's hard not to start believing your own myth when your business is turning over £25,000 a day, you fly everywhere first class, your house is known around the world and you travel to film premières with your supermodel wife in a custom-built Bentley. And, of course, you own forty-two Ferraris.

But when you've spent two years as a prisoner, with no rights, no status and no freedom, you readjust your attitudes sharpish. If you don't you're in trouble.

People in prison suss you out very quickly. If you put on airs and you talk down to them, you're going to have a bloody hard time for all of your stay. But if you talk with them as equals, you're accepted within five seconds.

It's a tough education, but I learned a thing or two about life in nick. I'd always thought I was reasonably aware of the pressures people lived under. I'd been responsible for a troop of Hussars when I was twenty years old. I'd spent a decade running a big house and a business, with staff whom I saw every day: people I cared about and who cared about me. But thirty months inside made me understand people's problems in a way I'd never done before.

In the cell, over a piece of toast and a cup of tea, they tell you, blow by blow, what their daily life is all about. And some of them lived my problems, too. I told my pad-mates about the girl who'd left me and what it was like not seeing my kids because my ex-wife had taken them to Puerto Rico. They realised that this guy Brocket is a regular bloke with just the same problems as us. Prison is the ultimate leveller.

It certainly made me reassess the preconceptions with which I'd grown up. I met some seriously decent people in prison. Some of them had done terrible things and deserved their punishment. But many were completely honest, loyal and true to their word, even if the rules they lived by were very different from the ones I'd always known.

I remember one geezer, an old enforcer for one of the London gangs. There wasn't one part of his body that hadn't had a sawn-off shotgun bullet through it. He'd been blown to bits, but somehow he still functioned. Anyway, he came to me one day and said, 'Charlie, I just wanna tell ya, we've 'ad a bit of bother, dahn the wing. Some of them plastic gangsters was planning to sort you aht in the showers.

'But we've sorted it aht. One of 'em's got a broken fuckin' leg and the other's got a broken arm, and 'is face is a bit of a mess. But don' worry, 'cos it won' 'appen again.'

I said, 'Thanks, but for Christ's sake, cool it. If this happens every time there's some gossip about doing me in the shower, this place is going to end up like a morgue!'

Another time – and this is funny looking back at it now, but it certainly wasn't at the time – one of the lads ordered a hit for me as a favour (an unwanted favour, I might add). It was in Wellingborough, just when things were really rough. I'd lost absolutely everything and then, as the final straw, Melissa walked out on me and went back to her boyfriend.

I was devastated and didn't bother to hide the fact. One day, one of the chaps came up to me and said, very cheerfully, 'I fink that bird of yours'll be coming back to ya, Charlie.'

'No,' I said morosely, 'she's gone for good.'

'Nah, mate,' he said. 'I fuckin' know she's gonna come back. That bloke of hers ain't gonna be around much longer.'

Alarm-bells went off in my brain. I grabbed the chap, slammed him up against the wall and said, 'What the fuck are you playing at?'

He looked horrified. He'd thought he was doing me a big favour and now he was getting stick. Eventually, he told me that he'd got his mates on the outside to put a contract out on Melissa's man. He was just about to be killed, on the pavement outside his Chelsea home; a silenced .22 bullet to the head – no mess, no evidence, the standard professional hit.

It was a seriously sphincter-loosening moment. I didn't want a man getting killed just because he'd taken my girlfriend. And I didn't want the consequences of that killing, either. If Melissa's boyfriend was lying dead on a Chelsea street, it wouldn't take long for the police to discover that she had a bitterly upset ex-boyfriend, who'd been mouthing off in jail about how unhappy he was that she'd gone off with another man. Suddenly I could see a murder charge being added to my ever-lengthening rap-sheet. I was in danger of spending the rest of my life in jail. And then I discovered something else. The hit was due to go down in roughly half an hour.

Luckily, we were in the middle of association time, when prisoners were free to leave their cells. I dashed to the phone queue, barged everyone out of the way and grabbed the receiver from the poor chap who was on it. Then I called a friend who runs one of London's top security firms and told him to get a team round to Melissa's boyfriend's house, immediately.

I knew that the hit crew were waiting to do the job, sitting by the kerb in a Volkswagen Passat. The security men had to approach the car, nice and easily so that no one started shooting, tap on the window and say, 'The job's off.'

And that, thank God, is just what they did. The villains drove off, there was no trouble whatsoever, and Melissa's man came home that evening and let himself into his house, blissfully unaware that he had been minutes away from a bullet in the brain.

Back at Wellingborough, there were no hard feelings on either side. But I tell the story to illustrate the lengths to which some people would go to help out a mate.

I'm not recommending the particular method they chose to express their support. In fact, I utterly condemn it. But on the other hand, I do have to wonder whether the criminal decision to carry out a hit was morally any worse than the callous bureaucracy of civil servants and policemen who deliberately put me and kept me in a situation where they knew I might get killed, purely to make me confess to a crime they knew I had not committed.

Prison really taught me that you can't judge people by their labels. The simple presumption that some people are on the side of the good guys, and some are automatic bad guys simply did not and does not apply.

It's a funny thing to say, given all that happened to me there, but I'm almost grateful for my time inside. There are some things about that part of my life that I really don't want to remember: the smell of the lino floors, the smell of Dettol everywhere, and bleach. But, by God, you learn about yourself when you're put in that situation.

It's a bit like going into the army and having to face live bullets being shot at you. You wouldn't want to do it. But if you go through it, you're glad you did.

In my case, prison stripped away all the irrelevant stuff that had defined me. Forget about Brocket of Brocket Hall, the man with the fancy house, the sexy wife and the collection of Ferraris. All that had gone. So either I could keep on play-acting, or I could be honest about myself and my life.

I've tried as best as I can to be honest. Ever since I stepped into Bedford Jail, I've been just Charlie Brocket. Take me or leave me, here I am.

When I came out, I found I had a different set of values. I'd spent years flying first class, but now I go everywhere economy.

When I'm in London, I ride almost everywhere on my scooter. If I'm going further afield or I need to take a passenger, I drive my ten-year-old Audi. It runs like a Rolls-Royce and I can't see any point in changing it. I've got the money. But why bother?

For years, though, no one knew that I had changed. They thought I was a toff who'd been done for fraud. Some of them thought reasonably well of me. Some thought I was a bad egg. So I spent years feeling slightly disconnected from the world around me, not quite normal or whole, trying to find a purpose to my post-prison life.

It was as if I were in limbo. I couldn't escape from my past. The press seemed determined not to let me escape, and I couldn't see a way forward to the future. I worked on this book. I set up a small business, using all my architectural and business experience to work as a designer. But I couldn't find a way out.

Actually, that was just one of my problems. The other was that in one vital respect I hadn't really changed at all. My dealings with the opposite sex were still as hopeless as ever.

I reached the ripe old age of fifty without understanding why I found it so hard to commit myself to a single person, why I was so scared of real intimacy, and why it was impossible for me to make a choice and stick to it. Or her, as the case may be.

Soon after I left jail, I was introduced to a neighbour in Chelsea, where I was living at the time, and over the next few months a friendly relationship became a loving one. A strawberry blonde of about my age, with a taut, almost tomboyish figure, she was vivacious, caring and generous. I absolutely adored her and still do. One day, a couple of years into our relationship, we were having lunch when a mutual friend joined us, bringing a slim, pretty blonde girl with him. Her name was Harriet, she was twenty-seven and she needed help.

She had recently been badly injured in a traffic accident, her boss was giving her a hard time at work and she was short of cash. In other words, she needed a big, strong man to come along, put an arm around her, and make all her troubles go away. Guess who volunteered for the job?

It flattered me to feel that I could help solve her problems. Harriet combined a kind, thoughtful nature with a highly intelligent, precise mind. I knew that my first attempt to create a family had been a disaster and thought that perhaps I should try again. Maybe Harriet could give me that second chance and help me right that wrong.

Here were two wonderful women, both totally different, yet both of whom I loved, and I couldn't decide between them. By the middle of 2003, I had even proposed to both of them . . . and broken up with both of them, too. That's when I thought I should speak to a shrink, just to see if he could tell me why I was behaving like such a prize idiot.

And then, in December 2003, I got a call from

Granada TV and somebody said, 'We're doing another series of *I'm a Celebrity, Get Me Out of Here*. Do you want to be on it?'

And I think we all know what happened next.

– 30 –

I'm a Celebrity, Stick Me in There

MY IMMEDIATE REACTION WAS TO SAY NO. BUT then I discovered that a successful contestant could raise many thousands of pounds for charity, from money raised by the telephone votes. The more votes you attract, the more you make for your chosen charity: the winners have been known to raise up to £400,000 and even the first people to be eliminated can make around £50,000. I should be able to make a decent amount of cash for my charity, the Malcolm Sargent Cancer Fund for Children. That was a huge attraction.

I also began to think that it might be fun, which is always a good reason for doing something. And I suppose, if I'm being honest, I thought it might help give people a different image of me. With any luck they'd see someone with a decent sense of humour, who had at least one foot on the ground. That seemed like an awful lot to gain, just for handing over two weeks of one's life. So in the end, I said, 'Yes.'

Even then, I hadn't the slightest idea what I was letting myself in for, or who my fellow contestants were. There were other people on my mind. My love-life was as chaotic as ever: at this point it looked as though I'd managed to lose both of the women in my life. Soon afterwards, I joined our children in America for a two-week skiing holiday: we had a great time celebrating being together since my first visit to Puerto Rico.

I got back to England a few days before I was due to fly to Australia. By now, Harriet had gone back to her previous boyfriend. I went to see her on the night before I flew Down Under. The visit was strictly 'just good friends'. We sat and talked about what I was expecting to happen in the jungle.

I told her I wasn't nervous. One thing I learned in the army was that you prepare and train for all the circumstances you can control, and you don't waste time or energy worrying about the things that you can't. I'd chosen axle-grease as my luxury item to take with me to the jungle, because if you smear it all over your bed legs it stops bugs climbing up and biting you. Everything else was out of my hands, so no point fretting.

By the time I'd got to Australia, I still had not met any of my fellow contestants. We finally met up at a get-to-know-you party at the Versace Hotel on Australia's Gold Coast, a wildly ornate pile with gold taps, marble floors and loads of gilt everywhere, which looks like a remarkably gaudy bordello.

The first person I met was Razor Ruddock. We hit it off immediately and were cracking jokes within seconds. I felt I knew him right away.

Mike Read came across as a really nice, intelligent bloke and he was a walking encyclopedia of music. Diane Modahl was nice, sweet, and very softly spoken. Alex Best had the air of a woman who'd been through a very hard time and been quite badly wounded by the experience. Kerry was sweet, Jennie seemed perfectly nice. And then there was Jordan.

She was standing on a balcony looking out across the pool. I went to join her and when I saw the view from the balcony I thought I'd take a picture with the little digital camera I had on me. One small problem: I was carrying a glass of champagne and I couldn't get the camera out of its case with one hand. So I had to find somewhere convenient and safe to put the glass while I fiddled with the camera.

'Hold on to that, would you?' I said, and stood the glass between her boobs, where it nestled happily.

Now, there are plenty of women who'd have been offended, but Jordan is not one of them. She's pretty well unshockable, has an agreeably filthy sense of humour, and, in any case, she doesn't really think of her breasts as intimate parts of her body; they're simply tools of the trade.

But although she'll show anyone her boobs, she's much more reluctant to reveal Katie Price, the woman behind the Jordan mask. She protects her at all costs.

The final person to arrive was John Lydon. There'd been lots of rumours swirling around about how he was being really difficult and refusing to turn up. Everyone else had been trying to be friendly and make a good impression, as you'd expect when we were all about to be flung into a jungle camp together for the next two weeks. But when John finally graced us with his presence, he was quite offhand.

I remember saying, 'Mr Rotten, how frightfully good of you to turn up.'

He just scowled at me and stalked off.

Later, Johnny told me that his attitude had nothing to do with rock-star arrogance, or punk rebellion. He's just terribly shy and hates going into rooms where he doesn't know anyone and there are cameras everywhere.

By this point, we'd had some basic training in jungle lore: how to find our way in the woods; how to start a fire; what to do about all the bugs and beasties we were liable to find. And I'd come down with flu. By the time we were all lined up, early one morning, ready to climb on a chopper and be flown off into the jungle, I had a raging temperature, my voice was going, and I was feeling wretched.

They gave us each two changes of clothing, then flew us in by the scenic route, round rocky escarpments, over palm trees and waterfalls, really giving us the sense that we were going deep into the jungle.

We were dropped in a clearing and then had to follow signs through the rainforest, accompanied by the cameramen who'd follow every move we made for the next two weeks. It was obvious from the start that Kerry was really apprehensive about what she was about to encounter: the nerves and sheer terror that came across on TV were entirely genuine.

There were snakes and spiders everywhere. At night, particularly, the whole place was overrun with rats. There were crayfish and leeches in the river and the pond where we used to bathe. And the endless bugs and creepy-crawlies bit everything that moved: poor Kerry, in particular, was chewed to bits and needed special medical treatment.

Even the vegetation could be hazardous. There were poisonous plants we were told not to go near under any circumstances. Some of the trees could make you itch or even bleed if you so much as brushed against them.

The two toughest aspects of camp were the boredom – God, how I longed for a few good books! – and the hunger. The producers swear that the tiny ration of rice and beans that they give contestants is enough to survive on. But what they don't seem to allow for is the severe salt loss that occurs when the body is constantly sweating in extreme heat.

No jungle traveller would dream of setting out without salt tablets. But we weren't given nearly enough salt and the result was that we were drained of all strength and energy. Razor probably suffered the worst, but we all found that tasks we would normally have performed without thinking twice became incredibly difficult. Perhaps that's the idea, but I don't think it's a good one: sooner or later, someone's health is really going to suffer.

Now, I'm not going to give a day-by-day 'What I did on my holidays' account of *I'm a Celebrity*. If you saw it, you'll already have a pretty good idea of the general events. And if you didn't you obviously weren't interested, and won't appreciate me banging on and on.

Instead, here are the answers to the questions I've been asked most often over the past few months, starting with:

Go on, Charlie, be a sport. What do Jordan's boobs really feel like?

Not bad, actually. We were having a conversation about implants when Jordan, who doesn't mind them being looked at or prodded, any more than a grocer minds you looking at his fruit, asked me to check whether they felt real or not.

And they do. They feel good, not at all like the twin blocks of concrete some poor women have got attached to their chests.

Then I checked them again, just to make sure they still felt good. And they did. Next question . . .

What were you doing touching up Alex Best by pretending to 'wash' her, you dirty beggar?

I'd like to plead 'Not guilty' to this one, Your Honour. Or not terribly guilty, anyway.

You see, Alex had gone off to her bushtucker trial. When she came back into camp, I was actually fast asleep. But I was woken by the sound of her steps as she walked by me. I looked up and she was covered from head to toe in muck, slime, bugs and feathers. She really did look a terrible mess, and I know how women hate feeling dirty. A bloke that filthy has a pint and a fag and then he thinks maybe it would be a good idea to wash. A woman has to get clean, *now*!

I thought, 'The poor girl's going to need some help getting all that off.'

Then I noticed some bits of fake fur lying around, that we'd been given to make costumes for a fancy-dress party. It struck me that they'd make pretty good substitutes for flannels or sponges. I genuinely wasn't thinking about anything other than being a gent, and helping a damsel in distress.

I went up to Alex and said, 'Come on, my girl, I'll give you a good scrub down.'

Alex seemed glad of the assistance, so I worked up a good lather with the fake fur and some shampoo and started cleaning away. And then, as I got to her bottom, I thought, This is going to look a bit odd. And then I thought, But it does feel rather nice.

I probably scrubbed a wee bit longer than I really had to. And then I lifted up Alex's T-shirt (she wasn't wearing a bra) and worked away under that, too. Alex is a grown woman, and I'm sure she would have made her feelings known if she'd wanted me to desist, but she didn't seem to object.

Is the voting on I'm a Celebrity . . . *rigged?*
Tricky subject. I wouldn't dream of suggesting that Granada cheat in any way when it comes to counting votes, or reporting them accurately. But I certainly think that the producers can have a huge influence on

the way people vote, simply by the decisions they make as to what they're going to show or not show on TV.

The biggest victim of that process was Mike Read. The way the programme was edited made him look dull, as if he'd done nothing all the time he'd been in camp. In fact, that was a million miles from the truth.

Mike put on an amazing production of *Oliver*, with Razor in the title role (perfect casting, since the poor chap was desperate for more food), Peter André as the Artful Dodger and Johnny Lydon/Rotten as an absolutely brilliant Fagin.

It was a wonderful performance. But none of that came across on TV. The result was that Mike was the first person to get voted off the show. He was typically magnanimous about it, but he must have been dreadfully hurt, and I think he was robbed.

Why did Johnny storm out of the show?
For those who don't know, Johnny didn't wait around to be voted off by the viewers. He just walked out one day. And I think I know why.

Like me, Johnny has been inside. He did a short stretch when he was a kid. And if you've ever been in jail you know what it's like to have no control whatsoever of your own destiny, and to be completely subservient to other people's orders and decisions.

I think that experience has left him with an absolute hatred of being told what to do, by pretty much anyone. It wasn't that he was frightened of being voted off, or that he bottled it. He wasn't going to let anyone else tell him whether to stay or go. So he went on his own terms.

It's not the way I would have played it, but I understand why he made that decision. And the one thing I will say about Johnny is that what you see is what you get. In his own way, he's a very honest individual. I like him a lot.

Do you genuinely dislike Jennie Bond?
I've done some pretty stupid things in my time: this book is full of them. But however public my mistakes may have become, at least I actually committed most of them in private.

With one exception, that is. When I decided to call Jennie Bond 'a slag', I did it in front of the horrified gaze of 11 million people. So why did I make such a bitchy remark? And why did I do something so self-destructively mad? Within three minutes of my saying the word 'slag', Ladbroke's apparently switched my odds from being the favourite for King of the Jungle, to favourite for immediate eviction. And they were right. The moment the footage was shown, voting for me took a dive, and I was on my way out.

The irony was that 'slag' wasn't as much of an insult in the camp as it must have seemed to everyone on the outside. Razor and I regularly called each other 'you old slag' or 'you old slapper'. It was just a bit of banter. And that's why I used the word when I was talking about Jennie.

Still, I must admit that all of us except Kerry had been badmouthing Jennie in private. Late at night, she would tend to stay on her bunk, while the rest of us gathered round Razor's bunk, right in the middle of the camp, for a bitch about the day. And Jennie. But Razor warned us, 'Do you realise, whoever gets caught slagging her off is going to get chucked out?'

I replied, 'I don't care. With what I've been through, I'd rather say it like it is.'

Peter André agreed. Then Alex Best got up, stuck her hands out in front of her and said, 'If she isn't gone by tomorrow morning, I'll have a public strangulation.'

We were just being ourselves, for better or worse. I'd always known that if I tried to act a part people would see straight through it, because I'm not clever enough or talented enough to do that sort of thing. But Jennie was quite subdued for the first two or three days, and then – I think it was after she'd seen Mike put on *Oliver*, and realised she'd better match him – she totally switched gear, her whole character changed, and she started acting very much to camera.

Suddenly, she transformed herself into this outspoken radical socialist. According to Jennie, all private schools should be abolished and parents should be forced to send their children to comprehensives, whether they liked it or not. Razor, who really knew what inner-city schools were like, laughed at that. And when I dared to disagree, Jennie simply dismissed anything I said on the basis that I was too rich and privileged to understand about real life. She wasn't able to back up her arguments by anything other than insults. Next, she laid into Razor, saying that the money he earned as a footballer was inexcusable and she wouldn't have accepted it.

Another time, we were all talking about music,

which is a genuine passion of mine. Jennie had been silent for the entire conversation when she suddenly piped up and said, 'I like Eminem.'

So I said, ' Really? Name one track of his.'

Jennie couldn't name a single song. But she insisted there was one track she knew really well because she listened to it every morning, taking her daughter to school. Sadly, she was unable to remember a single word of the song. And then she made a point of saying that she did the school-run in her dressing-gown and pyjamas, as if that made her sound down-to-earth.

You could see everyone else thinking, How stupid. What if you need to get out of the car, or you have an accident, or you're stopped by the police?

With the sole exception of Kerry, we all thought Jennie was creating a phoney persona to look good in front of the camera. To me, the whole thing was summed up in one incident involving Jennie and Kerry. We'd been given some wine as a special treat and the drink had gone straight to Kerry's head. She was sitting in a big, inflatable-rubber chair, and I was sitting opposite her. I suddenly realised that she was falling, very slowly and very gracefully, out of the chair. She'd gone out like a light. So I walked across, caught her before she hit the ground, picked her up and lay her on her bed.

I'm sure Jennie saw what I was doing, putting Kerry to bed, and thought, I must get in on the act. Because the next thing I knew, she was practically shoving me aside and crouching down at the side of Kerry's bed.

By this point Kerry had fallen asleep. She was

completely out of it. But Jennie started cuddling her, stroking her hair and even singing a little lullaby, just like a mother comforting her child.

Now, there were three wide-angle cameras, mounted in a wall of fake rock, across the stream from the camp. When Jennie — the old TV pro — went to Kerry's bed, she angled her body so that she was facing the cameras. And to the cameras it looked as though she was humming Kerry to sleep.

I said, 'Come on, Jennie, she's out of it.'

Jennie just looked at me, gave one of her little smiles, and then carried on stroking and humming. I thought, I don't believe this. She's even going to kiss the girl good night. Sure enough, the next moment, Jennie kissed Kerry and murmured, 'Night-night.'

When I saw that, I thought, If that's what you have to do to win this thing, forget it. I haven't been bombed, shot at and jailed, to start pretending now. I'm going to say what I really think.' And that's the reason why the next question is . . .

What does it feel like, getting voted off the show?
Well, as you'll have gathered from the last bit, I wasn't surprised to be voted off. And I certainly wasn't upset — I'd already survived longer than I'd ever expected. I was curious to know who was voting for Jennie. And then I thought, Back to normality. A proper meal! A drink! A bath! Hooray!

Okay, then, what happened to the goldfish?
Ah, yes, the poor drunken fish . . .

I crossed the bridge that separates the camp from the outside world, and walked up towards the tree-house studio where Ant and Dec present the programme, assisted by a crew of about forty or fifty technicians and production staff.

There was a butler waiting for me, bearing a tray with a glass of champagne: pretty decent champagne, too, I might add. I was feeling demob-happy, as they say in the army. In other words, extremely cheerful and a tiny bit manic. It took me about half a second to down the champers, so I grabbed Ant's glass and downed that, and then I grabbed Dec's glass, too.

Then I looked at Ant and Dec and thought, What can I do to wrong-foot these guys?

They had a goldfish bowl on the table in front of them. My eyes lit on the fish, and I thought, Aha!

I reached into the bowl, picked up a goldfish and just dropped it into the champagne in front of me. It was, though I say so myself, a completely brilliant moment. Ant and Dec looked at each other in total amazement, mixed with a hefty dash of panic. Then they looked at me. They knew there was an RSPCA inspector on-set. They had no idea what to say. I was, if you'll excuse the vulgarity, absolutely pissing myself.

After no more than five seconds, I picked the poor fish out of the glass and dropped it back in the tank, where it swam around, looking distinctly woozy. Apparently, there was a bit of a public outcry about my cruelty to that little fish.

Excuse me, this is a programme in which bugs are

eaten alive — and you're worried about one drunken goldfish? Perhaps a sense of proportion should be called for.

And finally:

What happened after you got out of camp?
To put it simply: more camp, only of a rather different kind.

When the whole show was over, the production team held a final wrap-party. We were told it would be fancy dress and I decided to do the job properly. And for a proper, upper-class public schoolboy, proper fancy dress can only mean one thing: women's clothing — and lots of it!

Now, I always feel that if you're going to look stupid, you should look very stupid. Looking only slightly stupid is completely inexcusable. So I did the job properly. I went shopping and acquired a flamenco dancer's frilly dress, high heels, suspenders, a wig and a diamanté necklace. Alex Best did my make-up and gave me the full works: false eyelashes, painted cheeks and scarlet lipstick.

I teetered downstairs on my heels to find that Mike Read had been thinking along the same lines and come as a charlady. We looked at one another approvingly, made a grand entrance to the party and realised, to our horror, that we were getting some very odd looks indeed.

No one else had worn fancy dress.

No problem. I was determined to have a thoroughly good time, and I achieved that aim with the assistance of considerable alcoholic refreshment.

The next morning I awoke, somewhat groggily, and realised that I was due to get on a plane from Brisbane to Sydney and from there on to London, via Bangkok. So I packed my kit, staggered off to the chauffeur-driven limo that was waiting to take me to the airport, practically crawled on to the plane at Brisbane airport and flew off to Sydney.

Once I got there, I had to check in to the London flight. So I went up to the desk and the girl behind the counter looked at me and said, 'Mmm, you do look nice.'

I gave her a cool half-smile, like a smooth, handsome lady-killer. 'Thank you very much,' I said.

And then she replied, 'But your lipstick needs touching up.'

Unlike a proper lady, I'd forgotten to take my make-up off before I went to bed. And I hadn't even looked in a mirror since I'd woken up. So my mug was still plastered with rouge, mascara and smudged lipstick. And I'd looked like that walking through the hotel, sitting in the car and flying halfway down the east coast of Australia. The Aussies must have thought I was a right Pommie pooftah.

Perhaps my life would be simpler if I were.

Oi, Charlie!

WHILE WE WERE ALL IN THE JUNGLE, WE HAD NO idea at all about the impact the programme was having at home, or the wall-to-wall coverage it was getting in the media.

From the moment I got on the plane home, people had been coming up and saying hello. They all seemed to know about the programme, and they were all being incredibly nice. The same thing happened at the baggage carousel at Heathrow. It was only six in the morning, but people kept going, 'Hello, Charlie. Well done.'

I just smiled back at them and thought, This is odd. But that was nothing.

Later that morning I was walking past a building site when I heard a shout of, 'Oi! Charlie!'

Three lads were hanging off the scaffolding, waving and giving thumbs-up signs. Just then a post office van screeched to a halt beside me. The window was wound down and a black guy leaned out and shouted, 'Charlie! Respect!'

It was completely surreal. Everywhere we went, people were honking horns, waving, even stepping out of shops and offices to shake hands and say hello. Everyone seemed to recognise me. And every single person, without exception, seemed to be genuinely affectionate and kind to me.

I can't tell you how different and wonderful it was to be able to walk around and feel that people actually liked me. One man even offered to fund my campaign if I ran for Mayor of London. I'd had so much public humiliation and denigration that I'd never imagined my reputation could possibly recover. Yet suddenly the people of Britain seemed to be forgiving me and accepting me. I just didn't know what to say – still don't – except, 'Thank you. You don't know how much your kindness means to me.'

My newfound popularity took some surprising forms. *Closer* magazine offered me a fortune to pose for a nude centrefold. And a film company flashed a £100,000 contract in front of me as the star of a porno movie. I immediately thought of my family. It was one thing my girlfriend stripping – they'd go ballistic if I was putting the Brocket family assets on display as well!

Unfortunately, one or two people seemed unable to share in the general jubilation. I was informed by the gossip columnist of one best-selling tabloid that the reason why he'd written a particularly snide item about me was that his editor did not want to write good things about a former prisoner. And Cherie Blair successfully proved that her husband, Tony, was just as disapproving of me as a TV celebrity as he had been when I was just an upper-class fraudster.

The only difference was that he now did not dare make his disapproval public. I know, from sources close to Downing Street, that specific orders were issued to Cherie, who would otherwise have been happy to speak to me, that she was on no account to acknowledge my presence in any way, or even allow her daughter Kathryn to come near me.

At the time, of course, I just thought she was being rude . . .

It began on 4 March 2004, soon after I'd got back from Australia. I'd been asked to give a nice, light-hearted speech at a dinner for the Simon Weston Foundation, which raises money for inner-city kids. That lunchtime, Cherie Blair's office rang up the organisers and said that Cherie wanted to come to the dinner and give a speech . . . instead of me. Her people insisted that she would only speak if I were removed from the bill.

The organisers could not say, 'No,' to Downing Street, so I was axed from the bill and moved to a lesser table. Cherie turned up, dutifully ignored me for the entire evening and gave a speech, full of political spin, telling all the people from the Simon Weston Foundation what the Simon Weston Foundation actually did for young people. As if they didn't know.

I then had to explain to all the people who came up and asked me why I wasn't speaking that I hadn't chickened out, or gone off in a strop. I'd simply obeyed Downing Street's instructions.

Exactly a week later the same thing happened all over again. This time I was a guest of honour at a bash that the Malcolm Sargent Cancer Fund for Children were holding at the Café Royal. I'd given the Fund all the money made from my telephone votes, and it amounted to £160,000. That was one of the largest single donations in the charity's history.

At lunchtime on the day of the dinner, the Sargent people got a call from Downing Street. Cherie happens to be the Senior Patron of the Fund. She wished to attend the evening's festivities and give a speech. But, my Downing Street sources tell me, they insisted I had to be banned from the event.

This time, however, the organisers stayed firm. They said Cherie was welcome to come and even to speak. But there was no way that anyone was going to disinvite a major donor to the charity.

The Downing Street brains trust gave this some thought, then came back with their decision. Cherie would attend, but on no account could she be photographed with Lord Brocket.

Cherie waited until all 400 guests were in the dining-room before making a grand entrance, roughly fifteen minutes after everyone else. She then spent several more minutes making a sort of royal progress across the room, stopping to talk to people as she went.

By now, people were becoming pretty cross. You could actually hear people hissing in disapproval. Many of the guests were cancer patients, some of them children – one little fellow on my table had no hair, because he'd just had chemotherapy. And they were all having to stand and wait for Cherie.

She was just about to join us on the top table when she spotted her daughter Kathryn across the far side of the room. At once, Cherie bustled off to have a family chat. (I have since learned that Kathryn begged her mother for an introduction to me, only to be told that the family were all under orders to avoid me.)

Meanwhile, I said, 'Let's all sit down.' Cherie eventually returned and we all stood up again while she took her place. She didn't apologise for keeping us waiting. She didn't even say, 'Hello.' She plonked herself in her chair and started talking to the man on her right.

After half an hour, she got up and asked if she could swap places with the next woman round the table, so that she could talk to someone else. And so it went on, with Cherie shifting round the table until she reached a point where her next move would take her to the chair next to mine. So she simply got up and went to another table.

Cherie left soon after dinner. She didn't even stay to watch Mike Read, Razor and me perform our Top 30 charity record 'Jungle Rock'.

Not surprisingly with so many people present, press reports of the Sargent Cancer Fund dinner appeared in the following Sunday's papers, accurately describing the events of the evening, and the hours of negotiation that had preceded it. Yet Downing Street put extreme pressure on the Fund to deny the stories. Officials were asked to lie to save face at Number 10. I went to prison for telling a lie. I don't think it's a laughing matter.

Never mind. As the old prison padre said, 'What goes around, comes around.'

In the end, we all get what we deserve. Had my grandfather not raided the family trusts, and disinherited my father, I would have lived a life of amazing wealth and privilege. Today I'd be the master of Brocket Hall. My children would have attended England's finest private schools. And – who knows? – I might even have a collection of Ferraris, bought with my money, rather than the bank's.

But would I be a better, happier or more interesting person? Somehow, I rather doubt it.

People say, 'Do you regret committing a fraud?' Of course I do. Was it wrong? Without question it was illegal and it was wrong. But when they ask, 'What do you think you should have done instead of faking an insurance claim?' I turn the question back on them and say, 'Well, what would *you* have done?'

The answer's always the same: 'I dunno, but I wouldn't have done that.'

Actually, I know the proper answer. I should have ballsed it out with the bank and said, 'Go ahead. Bankrupt me. Let's just see you do it.' My guess is they wouldn't have dared. We'd have gone straight to the £15 million bail-out loan. I wouldn't have tried to fake an insurance claim. I would never have been disgraced. I would have been running the conference business at Brocket Hall, which would never have suffered the collapse that occurred after outside management were brought in.

Isa and I would still have divorced, but perhaps the

circumstances would have been less painful. I certainly would have been able to play a full part in my children's upbringing, here in England, where they belong. Of course, I'd still have had forty-odd Ferraris and Rick Furtado to worry about. But I dare say I'd have coped.

I definitely wouldn't have gone to prison if I'd followed Mark Caswell's advice and simply dumped the 'stolen' Ferraris in a crusher or dropped them in the Irish Sea. As Mark liked to say, 'No body, no crime.' Without any physical evidence of fraud, the police would only have had Isa's unsupported allegations and the whole case would have collapsed. So I'd have got away with it.

But would I really be better off? Even if I hadn't been jailed, I suspect I'd have paid for my crime in other ways.

As it is, I think I've emerged from the various dramas of the past fifty-two years in reasonably good shape. I wish I could have been a better father. The way my children have suffered because of my mistakes is by far my greatest regret. But I am trying my hardest to make it up to them in any way I can, and I'm amazed and humbled by the fact that they still seem to love me, for all my obvious failings.

Antalya has started at a new school in Phoenix, Arizona. Alex has begun his studies at Bristol University. Only William remains with Isa and his grandparents in Puerto Rico. The children seem highly amused by their aged father's new career as a pop star. Mike Read, Razor and I had a second chart hit with our follow-up single, 'In the Summertime', which gave me a thrill and — what really mattered — raised more money for our favourite charities.

My emotional life is, I admit, as hopeless as usual. Perhaps by the time this book is published I'll have learned how to make one woman happy.

I still have issues to resolve with my family, too. Most people go through a rebellious phase in their teens, then they establish their independence as adults and then, with any luck, they build a new relationship with their parents as something close to equals. I was never able to do that.

I hardly knew my father. He was sick. I was away at school. And then he was gone for ever.

When I inherited the title of Lord Brocket, I was still a boy, dependent on my elders. I suspect that my uncle, stepfather and mother — understandably, perhaps — continued to think of me as a foolish, irresponsible youth long after I'd proven myself as a man.

It was almost as if my adolescence went on for twenty years longer than it should have done. We never really communicated openly, as equals, so we were never able to understand one another properly, or help one another when things went wrong. Only now, in my fifties, have I become determined enough and strong enough to live life on my own terms, and make decisions based on what I believe is best for me and the people I love, rather than what's supposedly best for the family name.

A sense of duty is a noble thing. But doing some-thing because you feel you ought to, not because you want to, can sometimes do more harm than good: my marriage is the proof of that.

For all that, though, I have finally reached a point where I know about myself and about life, in a way that would never have been possible if I'd had an easier, more comfortable existence. The misfortunes that have befallen me turn out not to be so misfortunate after all. They've made me the man I am. That's what I mean when I say that there's a reason for everything in life. It may not be obvious at the time. But it's there.

I've done wrong. I've been punished. And I'm a better person for it. But my sentence only really ended when I came back from the Australian jungle and felt the incredible warmth that I received from the British public. It was as if the final door had been unlocked, the last bars around me removed.

I've done my time. I'm a free man at last.

Acknowledgements

MY RATHER CHAOTIC AND OFTEN UNPREDICTABLE
early life might have ended in some sort of normality
had it not been for inheriting Brocket Hall. But that
was my destiny, even if by unexpected means, and the
Hall's journey from obscurity to its current success
would not have been possible without staff whose loyalty would humble any man.

This book was written secretly during my years in
prison on computer disks that were smuggled out by
friends. The powers-that-be have gone out of their way,
by threatening and cajoling, to try and ensure that this
book would never appear. Finally it has.

There are many people who will have my eternal
gratitude for the support that they have given me but I
would like to mention a few besides my family to
whom I dedicate this book.

The indomitable Flick and Jean Lenderyou were
mainstays of the development of Brocket Hall and
helped turn it into the premier establishment in Europe.
It's no coincidence that this was the period when the
most laughs were had! I must thank my long-suffering

trustees who never expected to have to work so hard to put the ship back on course. My brother Richard dropped everything at a crucial time in his life to give invaluable advice that was way beyond his years, and protect and re-possess my assets and my home that Mr Rocker was determined to relieve me of. I must thank Steven Barker, my solicitor, who despite his vast experience, admits that he has never come across a case such as mine. He has become, and always will be, a firm friend. I must thank John and Tessa Robson who have been there for me during times of trouble since the day I inherited Brocket and whose advice, to my cost, I have not always taken.

Special thanks go to Helen Baines and Libby Hubbard whose selfless support sustained me through the darker years of imprisonment and whose continuing friendships are so special to me. Thanks to Adrian Hamilton who worked tirelessly to correct many of the myths that the media, and some 'experts' created regarding the car collection. I must thank Lord Colwyn who did so much on my behalf when the government was having fun playing musical chairs with me around the prisons of England, and who secured the Commission hearing into the Carlton documentary. Also, thanks to Nigel and Bumble Hadden-Paton for their support and the wonderful 'coming out' party that they held for me despite knowing it would deny them high office.

The list is endless and I apologise for not mentioning the people who wrote over five thousand letters of support, many of whom visited me and sent me essential rations, at a time when I had been scandalously labelled by the tabloids. Lastly I must thank Di for restoring my self-respect by her selfless generosity as well as reminding me that love could still be found.

That this book has seen the light of day is thanks to my dear and wonderfully indefatigable friend, Nancy Holmes, who, bolstered by her eighty years and some, doesn't have the word 'no' in her vocabulary. Also to my agent, Nicola Ibison, and the team at NCI Management, who refused to accept the obstacles put in our way; Ian Monk who has fended off some media attempts to sabotage the project; and David Thomas whose experience in editing has ensured that the reader has a fighting chance of understanding the whole story.

Index

Unattributed relationships are to Lord Brocket, who is referred to as 'Charles'.

Abramovich, Roman 361
Adamson, Mr and Mrs 29,
    39, 43
Agnelli, Gianni 203
Agnelli, Umberto 203
Aldergrove Barracks 65
Ali (prisoner) 334–8, 340,
    341, 343, 350–1, 360,
    365–6, 410
Allen, Col. Forte 86
Allied Breweries 10
American Express 121, 362,
    395, 401
André, Peter 446, 448
Angela, Lady Brocket (wife
    of 2nd Baron) 17–18,
    19, 22, 91–3, 99
    and 1921 Trust 93
Anglo-German Fellowship,
    the 13

Anne, Princess 75–7
Ant and Dec 451
Applegarth School 54, 56,
    107
Argyll, Margaret, Duchess
    of 147
Ascot 146
Aston Martin company 198
Australia 183, 440–53

Bad Harzburg 70–1, 76
Baines, Jonathan 273, 311
bankers 115, 116, 209, 232,
    280–1, 288, 388, 395,
    397–8, 461
    first (£1-million) loan
        200, 202–3, 234–5,
        296
    added £5 million 204,
        237, 296

bankers – *cont*
  refuse to finance
      insurance claim
      249
  refuse to increase
      borrowings 218–22,
      234
  refuse to write off car
      debt 293–4
  second (£15-million)
      interest-free rescue
      loan 237, 243, 248,
      280, 389, 461
  securities 218, 296
Barbados 184
Barker, Steven (solicitor)
      275–6, 278–9, 303,
      306–7, 312, 327,
      329–30, 354, 356, 396,
      413, 465
Bedford Prison 317–26,
      335–6, 372, 374
Bell, Derek 344
Bennett, Don (estate
      manager) 210
Bennett, Jack 242
Berlin 78, 245
Best, Alex 441, 444–5, 448,
      452
Blair, Cherie 455–8
Blair, Kathryn 456, 458
Blair, Tony 1, 4, 457
Bond, Jennie 441, 447–50
Bosisto, Jim 128–9, 196–7,

199–200, 202, 207,
      212, 216, 219, 235,
      240, 356
  dies 210
Bovington Camp 59–60
Bowes-Lyon, David
      'Bowsie' 62
Bradshaw, Adrian 298
Bramshill estate 19–20
Brenda (Ferrari's PA) 200,
      235
Brennan, Brian and Mary
      54, 107–8
Broadcasting Standards
      Commission 413
Brocket, Rt Hon. Sir
      Charles Nall-Cain, 1st
      Baron (great-
      grandfather) 1, 4–9
  ennobled 3, 9
  sets up 1921 Trust 7
  sets up 1925 Trust 19
  dies 9, 18
Brocket, Ann, Lady (second
      wife of 1st Baron) 9
Brocket, Rt Hon. Ronald
      Nall-Cain, 2nd Baron
      (grandfather) 9, 17,
      149, 460
  inherits 9
  farming 21
  marriage of 17, 36
  and Nazi sympathies 1,
      10–16, 78

relationships with son
and grandchildren
23, 41–2, 49–50,
52–3, 87, 112
and 1921 Trust 88, 93
strips 1925 Trust 19, 87,
309
dies 52, 87
will and litigation 20–22,
53, 83–8, 93
Brocket, Rt Hon. Charles
Nall-Cain, 3rd Baron
(author):
ancestry 1–23
army service 55–86, 94,
120, 182, 270, 423,
431, 435
birth of 23
Brocket Hall regained by
87–94
as architect 56, 119
given personal
ownership of it by
1921 Trust 166,
296
threatened with
eviction 299, 305,
382
classic car company and
collection of 129,
193–219, 230, 388,
411, 423, 431, 461
closed down by
Rocker 288

workshop and
storeroom
incident 290–1
see also Ferrari,
Maserati *and below*
education 29, 33, 37–9,
44–49, 52–4, 56, 90
inherits title 52, 89, 462
and insurance fraud
221–9, 237, 269–70
planned 221–7
arrested 264–72,
282–5, 299, 301
bail 258, 274–80,
290–1
accusation of violating
bail conditions
278
cars disposed of 222–7,
260–1
insurers void claim 228
insurance claim
withdrawn 233–4,
245, 249, 253,
254, 255, 256,
265, 271, 303
Isa informs on 243–7,
253, 265, 269
sentence 308, 314–15,
321, 375
appeal against sentence
354, 413–4
prison term 1, 303,
316–420

Brocket, Rt Hon. Charles
  Nall-Cain, 3rd Baron
  (author) – *cont*
  and insurance fraud – *cont*
    effects of 303, 421–38,
      424–6, 460, 463
    threats of violence and
      ambush 350–1,
      360, 365, 377–9,
      384, 410, 414,
      425, 432
    released from prison
      418–20
  and Ferrari
    misrepresentation
      197, 207, 235,
      239–40
    trial 307, 311–15, 357,
      381–2, 392–3
  in estate agency 96
  and House of Lords 96,
    231, 265, 330
  in *I'm a Celebrity* 439–54
  relationship with mother,
    father and family
    31–2, 40–1, 186–7,
    349–50, 357–8, 411,
    421, 426–7, 460,
    462–3
  relationship with Isa 131,
    176–92, 245–6,
    256–8, 277
    marries 160–3, 176
    divorce proceedings

    176–9, 252–4,
      259, 330
    assaults 246, 256, 259,
      262
    phone-tapping 259
  running Brocket Hall, *see*
    Brocket Hall
  skiing 263
  writes autobiography
    364
Brocket, John (*c.* 1550) 5
Brocket Hall 5–7, 8–9, 13,
  18, 21, 40, 52, 88, 90,
  91–3, 94–5, 96, 97–9,
  100–1, 112, 116–18,
  123–5, 142–3, 146,
  164, 170–2, 177, 197,
  201, 218, 220–1, 232,
  265, 296, 388–402,
  430, 460
  as conference venue 113,
    113–14, 116,
    115–28, 139–42,
    164–71, 180, 198,
    201, 219, 232–3,
    237, 240, 261–2,
    266, 280–301, 331,
    388, 461
  burgled 172–5, 205–6
  European Summit at 105,
    127, 139–42, 266
  Jewish wedding incident
    at 143–4
  Deed of Compromise 94

as film and photography
    site 93–101, 103,
    127–8, 196
golf course and club 219,
    240, 274–5, 282,
    297–8, 402, 429
raided by police 266–69,
    274
repairs and refurbishments
    115–25, 168
flushing sewers 120–1
Charles threatened with
    eviction from 289,
    382
sale proposals 116, 288,
    293–301, 389–95,
    398–9
leased 397–8, 401
see also Palmerston House
Brunei, Sultan of 399–400
Buccleuch, Duke of 11, 15
Budweiser 167
Burma 353
Busch, August 167
Bush, President George
    (Snr) 230
Buxton, Felicity ('Flick')
    (marketing director)
    126, 127–8, 143, 146,
    176, 189, 204, 232,
    413, 464
Byron, George, Lord 6

Cabassi, Carlo 108–9, 110,

    160, 181
Cain, Robert (né O'Cahan,
    great-great-
    grandfather) 2–3, 49,
    64
Cain's Brewery 2
California 113, 245, 254,
    255
Calvi, Roberto 181
Camfield Place estate 189
Campbell-Bowling,
    Michael and Rory
    241, 243–5, 274, 313
magistrate's court
    hearings 284
Carlton Television 413, 465
Carrington, Lord and Lady
    139, 140, 142
Cartland, Barbara 189, 355
Carton estate 20, 30, 134–6
Cashel Palace 20
Caswell, Mark 199, 221–2,
    221–7, 234, 237, 243,
    254, 257, 258, 314,
    334, 460
reveals where cars are 272
Chamberlain, Neville 11, 15
Charles, Prince of Wales
    159, 205, 251
Cheysson, Claude 139–40
China 63
Churchill, Winston 13
Cirencester Agricultural
    College 112

Clague, Jeff (estate manager) 305, 392, 393, 396

Clare, Brian 294–5

'Clive' (prisoner) 335, 336, 340

Closer magazine 455

Club Corp of Asia (CCA) 397, 401

Collins, Joan 99–100

Colombo, Massimo 207–8, 235

Colwyn, Lord Anthony 233, 465

Corfe Castle 37

Corfu 107

Cosmopolitan magazine 103

Craig (prisoner) 336–8, 339, 343, 364–5

Croft, Anne Page, see Brocket, Ann Lady

Crump, Richard 216, 217

Cyprus 79–86

da Silva, Desmond, QC 275, 307, 312

Daily Mirror 454

Daily Telegraph 307, 399, 400

Dale, Sarah 226–7, 263, 276–7, 278–80, 283–4
  statement to police 278–9

Dashwood, Sir Richard 98

Daub, Herr 211

Dave (prisoner) 386

Davidson-Lamb, Alan (head butler) 165, 169, 170, 172, 189, 240–1, 268, 390

Dawnay, Hugh 135

Diana, Princess of Wales 159, 164, 238, 251

Duncan, Graham 128–9

Dutch forces 80

Eddie (cell-mate) 318–21, 323

Edward VIII, King 13–14, 22

Elizabeth I, Queen 5

Ellis, George 38

Elton, John 116

English Drilling Equipment Company (EDECO) 23

Eton College 43–9, 52–4, 90, 311, 425

Fergal, Monarch of Ireland 2

Ferrari, Enzo 200–1, 208

Ferrari corporation 200, 203, 235

Ferraris 193–7
  Charles's collection of 129, 197–200, 203, 206–9, 215, 219–20, 230, 266, 281, 288, 411, 461

Ferrari 365 Boxer 198
Ferrari 250 Europa 199
Ferrari 250 SWB 3539
    197, 207, 255
Ferrari F40 203, 220
Ferrari 365GT 196
misrepresentation of
    Ferrari 250 SWB
    3565, *see under*
    Brocket, Rt Hon.
    Charles Nall-Cain,
    3rd Baron (author)
Niki Lauda's 254, 255
value changes in 199,
    203, 206–8, 212,
    269, 288
destruction of 223–8
Fiat 203
Finn, Joel 216–17
'Flick', *see* Buxton,
    Felicity
Flynn, Barry 230, 236, 256,
    268, 273
Ford Open Prison 387,
    403–10, 411, 414, 425,
    430
and women 409
Fran (housekeeper) 226,
    250, 251–2, 253,
    276–7, 280, 291
Fruiter's Gate 43, 48
Fuller, Major-General John
    15–16
Furtado, Pam 246

Furtado, Rick 212–15,
    216–17, 219, 227, 228,
    239, 246, 255, 268,
    269, 289, 313, 352,
    382, 388, 460
buys cars from Charles
    215, 236
charged 289
trial of 411

Gabor, Zsa-Zsa 146–50
Galloway, Earl of 11
Gauntlet, Victor 198
Genscher, Hans Dietrich
    140
George IV, King 5
George V, King 8
Germany 70–86
Gerry (prisoner) 407
Glanfield, Annie (boss of
    Locations Unlimited)
    98
Gloucester, Duke of 149
Granada Television 438,
    445
Great Depression 9
Greece 107–8
Griffith, Professor Richard
    15
Grimshaw, Corporal 75
Gwyther, Steve 209–10,
    221–6, 227, 234,
    254–5, 261, 290–1,
    313, 314

Halifax, Lord 11, 16

Harriet 437, 440, 454–5, 462
  Charles proposes to 455

Harrison, George 3, 428–9

Harry, Prince 238

Hatfield House 5

Heather 44–5, 104

Hepburn, Katharine 100–1

Hertfordshire Police 78, 256, 265, 306

Heseltine, Annabel 131, 132

Heseltine, Michael 131, 132, 266

Hess, Rudolf 16, 78–9

Hill, Damon 429

Historic Houses Association 133

Hitler, Adolf 10–14, 15–16

Hong Kong 63–4, 70, 76, 397, 423

House of Lords 1, 11, 96, 231, 265, 330

Howe, Lady 413

I'm a Celebrity, Get Me Out of Here! 438–54
  Charles voted off 450–2
  goldfish and 450–1

Inkpen Hall 20

insurance fraud, *see under* Brocket, Rt Hon. Charles Nall-Cain, 3rd Baron

IRA 55–6, 66–7, 182

Iraq 220, 230, 235
  see also Kuwait; Saddam Hussein

Isa, Lady Brocket (wife) 54, 103–11, 130–1, 161–4, 200–5, 212, 236, 239, 251, 252, 257–8, 273–4, 304, 308, 320, 348, 427
  marries Charles 160–3
  accuses Charles of assault 256
  and car insurance fraud 223–6, 234
  reports it 244–7, 253, 256, 264–7, 273–4, 461
  claim to Watershipps 297
  depression 188
  disappearances 181, 186, 188
  drug habit 180, 203, 205, 219, 226, 230, 234, 236, 239, 243, 245–6, 247, 249–50, 251–2, 253, 262, 274, 280, 289, 421
  arrested on drugs charge 253, 265
  treated 206, 241–2, 262, 276, 280, 412
  pregnancies 179, 190,

219, 226, 231
and sale of Brocket Hall
299
divorce proceedings 176,
252–3, 259, 302–3,
330–2, 461
settlement 252, 331
see also Lorenzo, Gus *and*
Lorenzo, Brigitte
Ives, Inspector 266

Jack (prisoner), *see* Taylor,
Jack 347–8
James (prisoner) 372
Japanese ten-car deal
212–20, 227
Jock (prisoner) 366
John (cell-mate at
Wellingborough)
328–9, 335, 337–8,
340, 365
John (prisoner at Bedford)
324
John (woodsman) 210,
227
Jones (schoolboy) 47, 53
Jordan 441, 444
Jordan, Arthur 121
Judy 133–4, 136–8, 142, 148,
150–7, 161–2, 163,
176–7, 178, 179–80
Charles proposes to 150
pictures revealed 153
marries 179

Kerlin, Inspector 169, 266,
313
Kerry 441, 443, 447,
449–50
Khun Sa 230–1, 236, 239,
268, 352, 352
14th/20th King's Hussars
55–86, 94, 431
Kinnersley estate 20
Klosterman, Dieter 397
Knave magazine 156
Knebworth House 126
Knoydart 13, 16–17, 19
'Seven Men of Knoydart'
17
Kray, Reggie 324, 374–6
Kuwait, invasion of 217

Lamb, Emily 6
Lamb, Lady Caroline 6,
101, 171
Lamb, Sir Matthew 5
Lamb, Sir Peniston 5–6
Laughing Waters plantation
184
Lawrence, Mr 52
Le Fevre, Dr Robert
241
legal aid 302, 306–7, 330,
392–3, 394
Lenderyou, Jean 126,
464
Lennon, John 3
Liam (prisoner) 335, 340

Libby (godmother to
    Antalya) 357, 360,
    366, 411
Littlehey Prison 344–70,
    376–81, 383–7, 397,
    398
  Charles released from
    387
  sex offenders in 344–48,
    369
Liu, Warren 229, 411
Liverpool 2–3, 7, 8, 64
Lloyd George, David 1, 4, 9
Lloyd Webber, Andrew 401
Locations Unlimited 98
London Philharmonic
    Orchestra 167
Londonderry, Marquess of
    11
Lorenzo, Brigitte (mother-
    in-law) 161, 187, 232,
    248, 251–2, 253, 276,
    280, 349, 421, 426
Lorenzo, Gus (father-in-
    law) 158, 186, 187,
    212, 250, 259, 262,
    263, 277–8, 279–80,
    357, 412, 421, 427
Lorenzo, Isa (wife), *see* Isa,
    Lady Brocket
Lothian, Lord 12
Ludgrove Preparatory
    School 238, 250, 303
Lui magazine 101–2

Luton County Court 310,
    392
Lydon, John 442, 446

MacDonald, Ramsay 9
MacDowell, Andie 104
Mafia 181, 183
Maidstone court 395
Maidstone Prison 370,
    373–6
Maisemore estate 23, 27,
    28–9, 30, 35, 196
Major, John 265, 344
Malcolm Sargent Cancer
    Fund for Children
    439, 457–8
Margaret, Princess 22
Martin (Isa's boyfriend) 263,
    276
Maseratis 128, 196, 197, 198,
    209–10, 214, 217, 230
  Maserati 5000 228
  Maserati 'Birdcage' 2456
    216, 223
McCartney, Paul 3
McLaurin, Sir Ian 282,
    286–7, 288, 292–3,
    295, 296, 389, 399,
    400, 410
media coverage 27, 289,
    265, 270, 273, 307,
    333, 352–3, 362, 367,
    408, 412–3, 419, 429,
    454, 456, 460

Meg (PA) 231
Melbourne, Lord, 1st
    Viscount 6, 152
Melbourne, Lord, 2nd
    Viscount 6
Melissa 301–2, 303, 310–11,
    312, 316, 320, 323–7,
    329–30, 332, 333, 336,
    360–1, 362, 366–7
  proposes marriage 325
  contract out on husband
    433
  marries 360
  during prison term 360,
    366–7
  walks out 433
Mells Park estate 50
Milan 109, 179, 184
Mimpriss, Peter (solicitor)
    151, 153
Mitford, Diana 12
Mitford, Unity 12
Modahl, Diana 441
Mons Officer Cadet School
    57–8
Monte Carlo 207
Monza 201
Mook 231, 236
Morris, David 300
Mosley, Oswald 12
Mount-Temple, Lord 12
Mumford, Dave 415, 418
Muslim food privileges 406
Murphy (prisoner) 340, 341

Nall-Cain, Alex (son) 187,
    188, 219, 231–2,
    238–9, 242–3, 250–1,
    263, 280, 303–4, 332,
    349–50, 357, 421,
    426–8
  birth of 187
Nall-Cain, Antalya
    (daughter) 190–1, 219,
    242, 280, 332, 349–50,
    357–8, 421, 427, 462
  birth of 190–1
Nall-Cain, Sir Charles
    (great-grandfather), *see*
    Brocket, Rt Hon Sir
    Charles Nall-Cain, 1st
    Baron
Nall-Cain, David (brother)
    36, 389
Nall-Cain, David (uncle)
    11, 20, 88, 94, 134,
    151–3, 247, 397
Nall-Cain, Elizabeth (aunt)
    20, 30
Nall-Cain, Elizabeth
    (mother) 22–3, 32,
    32–3, 36–7, 39–41,
    42, 43, 46, 48–9, 52,
    89, 111, 138, 163,
    178, 186, 238, 247,
    258, 303, 332, 348–9,
    367, 380–1, 462
  contests 2nd Baron's will
    89

Nall-Cain, Elizabeth
(mother) – *cont*
and Isa and Judy 138,
163, 178
remarries 50
Nall-Cain, Florence, Lady
(first wife of 1st Baron
Brocket) 3–4
Nall-Cain, Richard
(brother) 28, 39–40,
41–2, 49, 50, 51, 232,
282, 348, 349, 389,
394, 397, 465
Nall-Cain, Ronald (father)
9, 17, 20–3, 24,
29–33, 34–6, 38, 39,
40–3, 49, 52, 89, 138,
460, 462
marriage 23, 36, 138
relationship with father
36, 112
sues his father 23
final illness and death
30–3, 38
Nall-Cain, Ronald
(grandfather), *see*
Brocket, Ronald,
Second Baron
Nall-Cain, William (son)
251, 276, 280, 332,
349–50, 357, 421, 426,
462
born 231–2
National Trust 88, 89

Natural History Museum
262
New York 158, 216, 310,
361
Newey, Adrian 428
Newhold, Werner (chef)
125, 185
Nick (boyfriend of Isa) 188
Node, The 4, 5
Northern Ireland 55–69
Nuremberg 12, 15

O'Brien, Vincent 30
O'Cahan, Robert (great-
great-grandfather), *see*
Cain, Robert
O'Cahan's County 2

Paine, James 5
Palmer, Jonathan 419
Palmerston, Lord 5, 171
Palmerston House 254,
256, 258, 263, 277–8,
280, 295, 298, 299,
302, 305, 391, 392
transferred to Charles 296
Parker-Bowles, Camilla
159
Paton, Mr (gardener) 8
Pennyman, Rev. W.G. 17
Pennyman, Angela, *see*
Angela, 2nd Lady
Brocket
Phil (porter) 368

Philharmonic Dining Rooms 3
Philip, Prince, Duke of Edinburgh 146, 149
Phillips (auctioneers) 215, 223, 228, 270
Phillips, Captain Mark 75
Potter, Beatrix 190
Pound, William 232, 253, 287, 293
Pourret, Jess 207–8, 255
Powell, Sgt-Major 'Singe' 77
Prestige Coachworks 288–9, 290, 292
Price, Katie, *see* 'Jordan'
Promise drug clinic 241
Prunet, Antoine 235
Puerto Rico 237, 248, 259, 276, 280, 331, 332, 333, 348, 349, 364, 421, 426, 427, 432, 440, 462

Ransley, Mr 392, 393, 394
Rawlings, John 65
Read, Mike 441, 446, 452, 458, 460
Reagan, Nancy 171
Reagan, President Ronald 171
Redesdale, Lord 12
Reg (prisoner) 324
Roberts, Mr 119

Rocker, David 280–2, 287, 288–92, 293, 294, 298, 299, 300, 301, 305–6, 322, 382, 389–91, 392, 393–6, 398, 399, 401, 465
Roe, Marion 263
Roe, Philippa 263–4, 267, 270–1, 292, 298, 299
Roosevelt, President Franklin 14
Rotten, Johnny, *see* Lydon, John
Rowberry, Gilbert (solicitor) 18–19, 21, 89, 309
Rubin, Bob 216–17
Ruddock, Razor 441, 443, 446, 447–8, 458, 460
Russia 12

Sachs, Andrew 169
Saddam Hussein 217, 230 *see also* Iraq; Kuwait
Sally (receptionist) 258
Sam (prisoner) 385–6
San Francisco 245, 246
Sarch, David (solicitor) 249, 267–8, 269, 273, 275, 283, 290–1, 305
Savoy Hotel 150
Sean (prisoner) 328, 335
Sellik (prisoner) 350, 351, 379

Shan people 230–1
Sharon 160–2
Shirley, Peter 239–40, 306, 356
Sihanouk, Prince 236
Silverstone racetrack 217, 254
Simon Weston Foundation 456
Simpson, Wallis 14
Smith (schoolboy) 47, 53
Snagge, Carron 47
Snipe incident 24–6
Sobers (butler) 184
Soviet Union 12, 70
    see also Russia
Spandau Prison 68–9
'Spiderman' (prisoner) 337, 338
Spring Hill Open Prison 383, 387, 414–20
Spyway Preparatory School 37–40, 44, 238, 311
Stalin, Josef 12
Stallard, Elizabeth (mother), see Nall-Cain, Elizabeth
'Steak Supper' 223–5
Stewart (prisoner) 407–8, 418
Sugar Creek Country Club 114
Summers, Mrs (cleaner) 380

Swannell, Major and Mrs 95–6, 97, 100, 111, 126
Swedish forces 80
Switzerland 263

Taylor, Jack (prisoner) 347–8
Thailand 231, 236, 239, 352
Thatcher, Denis 167–8
Thatcher, Margaret 131, 167–8, 233
'Time Lords' band 416, 428–9
Tomlinson (maintenance man) 95
Tony 419
Trotter, Colin (stepfather) 48, 50, 332, 462
Trotter, Rupert (half-brother) 50, 268, 301
Trust (1921) 8, 18–19, 88, 93–4, 156, 297, 389–9
    set up 7, 18
    gives Charles personal ownership of Brocket Hall 166, 296
    and Judy 151–6
    Charles becomes beneficiary of 94

Trust (1925) 18–19, 309
trusts, nature of 7
Turkey 79–86, 190

Ulster 2
United Nations 79–80, 86
USA 70, 112–14, 146,
158–63, 171, 202, 220,
230, 264

Val (secretary) 264, 278
Victoria, Queen 6
von Ribbentrop, Joachim
13, 14

Walker–Cain brewery 4, 10
Wandsworth Prison 370–3
Wardby, PC 291–2
Warner, Eric 37, 39
Warner, Geoffrey 37, 38,
39–40, 44
Warren House 297

Waterloo, picture of 139–40
Watershipps estate 191, 215,
215, 221–2, 236, 237,
250, 254, 262, 297,
391
   bugged by police 275
'Watershypps' 5
Wellingborough Prison
327–43, 344, 350–1,
364, 365, 375, 376,
392, 414, 433, 434
Wellington, Duke of 11
Westminster, Duke of 11
White, 'Chalky' 75–6, 81,
84–5
William, Prince 238
Willis, Shane 289, 395
Wilton Crescent mansion
20
World War I 4, 8, 11, 12
World War II 11, 95, 358
World Wildlife Fund 146–9